Alchemy of Soul

The Art of Spiritual Transformation

Also by Lee Irwin

The Dream Seekers

Visionary Worlds

The Gnostic Tarot

Awakening to Spirit

Alchemy of Soul

The Art of Spiritual Transformation

Lee Irwin

Lorian Press
2204 E. Grand Ave., Everett, WA 98201
www.lorian.org

Alchemy of Soul
The Art of Spiritual Transformation

Copyright © 2007 by Lee Irwin

Cover Illustration by Deva Berg

Edited by Catherine Evans and Hiro Boga

Published by Lorian Press
2204 E. Grand Ave.
Everett, WA 98201

ISBN: 978-0-936878-14-0

Irwin, Lee
Alchemy of Soul/Lee Irwin

Library of Congress Control Number: 2007923816

First Edition: March 2007

Printed in the United States of America

0 9 8 7 6 5 4 3 2 1

www.lorian.org

Acknowledgements

This work is dedicated to David and Julie Spangler, the Star Shamans of the Lorian Association, and to all the spirit presences that surround and guide that loving group of spiritual seekers.

I also want to thank my lovely wife Catherine Evans for her editorial help on this work.

Table of Contents

Forward.. i

Prologue iv

One: Starting Where You Are .... pg 1

Becoming Your Own Teacher
Learning from Others
Discovering Your Idea-beliefs
Feelings from the Center
Trusting Your Unknown Self

Two: Revising Collective Groundwork .... pg 40

Old Order Thinking
Learning from the Past
Deconstructive Paradigms
The Courage Not To Be
Weaving New World Patterns

Three: Unbecoming, Then Rebecoming .... pg 71

The Why of the Not-yet
Reimagining the Future
Dreaming the End Of Time
Non-possessive Responsibility
Necessary Reciprocities

Four: Magical Universes Rediscovered .... pg 101

The Vital Source of Life
Body-soul-mind-spirit
Soul-being In Visionary Mode
Transcendental Dissolutionments
Bringing It All Back Home

Five: Pranic Self as Hidden Love .... pg 133

        At The Heart of the World
        Listening With Open Ears
        Seeing With Receptive Eyes
        Healing with Unmoving Touch.
        Sculpted Bodies of Light

Six: The Sophia-Christ Work .... pg 164

        From Wine into Water
        Manifest Miracles of Everyday
        Family, Children, Friends
        Work, Play, and Inner Discipline
        Mysteries of Initiation

Seven: Communal Will and Acts of Creation .... pg 195

        The Hallows As Right Relations
        Entering Ritual Space Unadorned
        Following a Path Less Known
        Blessings and Angelic Beings
        The Evolutionary Spirit of Change

Epilogue I

Glossary VIII

Bibliography XXXV

FOREWORD

In June of 1996, the Findhorn Foundation, an international spiritual center and community in the north of Scotland, hosted a major week-long conference on Magic and the Western Esoteric Tradition. It took place over the summer solstice which inspired the creation of a ritual to celebrate this moment of passage in the year's calendar when the longest day gives way to the progression that will lead to the longest night six months later. This celebration was no small undertaking. Given the presence of a host of trained ritualists and ceremonial magicians, it was certain that this event would be elaborate and well-staged.

The centerpiece of the celebration was a ritual combat between the God of Light and the God of Dark. The former was played by a friend of mine, William Bloom, who is one of Britain's most innovative and magical of spiritual teachers. The latter was played by a man who I didn't know but who could have been sent by some celestial Central Casting for the part. Dressed in black with black hair and beard and piercing dark brown eyes, this gentleman looked for all the world like some chthonic figure who had emerged from the depths. He seemed to emanate power as he moved gracefully through the dance of the ritual combat. I was impressed and wondered who he was. When I asked one of the organizers, I was told simply that he was Dr, Lee Irwin, a professor from Charleston, SC.

The next day, for reasons I no longer remember, there was a shuffling of accommodation among the conference speakers. To my delight, I found myself sharing one of the community's bungalows with the Lee and his lovely wife, Cathy. That evening, discovering that we had a number of interests in common, we talked late into the night, sharing stories of inner world contacts and adventures.

Out of that fortunate shift of accommodations has come a friendship I have treasured for many years now. We live on opposite sides of the continent, so we don't see each other very often. But my hard drive is filled with voluminous files of email correspondence between us exploring a host of topics including the image of self in Lakota religious cosmology, the possible emergence of a new subtle body within the inner constitution of the human being, new forms of ritual magic, and the nature of incarnation itself.

Our long acquaintance has only confirmed for me the sense of power and depth I felt with Lee when I first saw him draw the Dark God into our midst that Solstice night.   Not that there is anything "dark" or negative about him. He is unquestionably one of the most compassionate, loving, light-filled people I've had the privilege of meeting. But he is also someone deeply at home in the vastness of our many-cornered reality, a true shamanic visionary and adept, intimately familiar with many of the forces that go into creating the world we know—as well as the world we only suspect or see just out of the corner of our eyes.

Indeed, I think of Lee as an esoteric and shamanic Indiana Jones, lacking only a hat and whip, either of which I'm sure he could come up with if necessary. And like George Lucas's fabled character, Lee is also an outstanding scholar and popular teacher, in this case of religion and spirituality, particularly in the area of the comparative religions of the Native North Americans.   In that role, he is currently the chairman of the Department of Religious Studies at College of Charleston.

It's not that Lee goes around advertising himself as anyone special. Quite the contrary. His strength lies precisely in being integrated into the world around him. Having spent years as a professional carpenter and house builder before turning to the academic life, he has the confidence and skills of a man who has made his way with his hands as well as with his head and who knows the world of substance as well as the worlds of spirit. Further, he has the modesty and natural reticence of someone more interested in serving than in drawing attention to himself.

For this reason, I have found that he listens more than he speaks. But when he does get to talking, my gosh, what stories he can spin. My favorite concerns a time when he was working one night in his study, thinking and envisioning about the Pawnee tradition of putting sacred meteorites in their medicine bundles.   The next morning, he stepped out of his house and discovered that a small meteorite had landed during the night right in front of the steps leading up to the house.

Synchronicities and magical happenings like this seem to follow Lee the way cats follow fish.   It is the mark of a man deeply integrated with his world.

I have been privileged to know others like that as well, men and women who are outstanding shamans, mages, scholars, or mystics. What makes Lee so unusual and outstanding is that he brings so many different facets together: the erudition of the scholar, the practical skills of a craftsman, the inner world experience of a gifted shaman and healer, the ritual skills and knowledge of a mage deeply familiar through both study and practice with the Western Occult Tradition, and the grace and groundedness that comes from many years of practice of Tai Chi. And this convergence of traits is alchemized into a wise wholeness in the cauldron of a mystic's heart and vision, as you will see in this book.

It is impossible for me to fit Lee into a single category. To the extent that "adept" means someone who has developed and polished certain skills through discipline, hard work and practice, he is an adept. But an adept of what?

Here we come to the nub of Lee Irwin. I know him well enough by now to know that he has no interest in being associated with some rank or title associated with anyone's imagination of esoteric hierarchies and their work; he has no truck with glamour or images. If he is an adept, it is at the task that challenges and calls to us all, the human task of drawing on our visionary depths to participate in the ongoing calling of world-building.

For that is what we all are: world-builders. Whether scholars or shamans, mages or mystics, business people or homemakers, artists or construction workers, whatever our role and identity in life, we are all shaping the world we know and the worlds we will come to know. We do this for better or for worse, and these days it seems as if the worse may be overcoming the better.

It doesn't have to be that way. We can shape worlds of peace and healing, worlds of wonder and abundance, worlds of joy and accomplishment. To do so we need to look into the cauldron of self-discovery and there find how we can integrate more lovingly and knowingly with our own souls and the Soul of the world. It asks that we go beyond the narrow limits of a life lived only for ourselves and in our own way, give room for the richness of the world and the wonderment of spirit to fuse in an emergence of imaginative power and compassionate action.

This is, as Lee puts it, an alchemy of soul, an act of inner chemistry, transformation, and new formation that is at the heart of what it means to be human. It is the visionary life grounded in skillful actions that generate blessings.

Over the years, I have seen that this is the life that Lee lives. And it is the life he shares with us in this book, that whoever we are and whatever we do, we also may become alchemists of soul.

David Spangler

PROLOGUE

Alchemy is an inner art, one of transformation and spiritual maturity, based in soulful, deeply felt, heart-centered relationships to the world and to others. We are each a center of awareness whose full commitment to actualizing our potential requires us to answer the question of the importance and the value of embodied life. Our challenge is to engage life with depth and sincerity, to create a shared, open space within which creativity can flourish, and to discover the value of love as a resource for enhancing mutual discovery. We must learn to sink down, into the depths of our inmost being, to discover the deep wells of our full capacities, to transform embodied life into an overflowing actualization that enhances the very basis of our communal coexistence. This can happen if we each discover within the context of daily life, within existing forms and structures, the beauty, joy, power, and inspiration that leads to a true alchemy of soul.

Such beauty is an upwelling from within, an intensity and openness that recreates and sustains our image of the world. The power flows forth as a stream joining with others to absorb the energies of incarnate life and to give those energies new expressions. The overturning of older forms, their transformation into new creative expression, is the primary alchemical work within world-becoming. We are each a nexus, a center of creative potential and possibility that cannot be strictly determined by any tradition or teaching. We may choose to follow a teaching; we may find a particular spiritual worldview valuable and central to a specific way of being. We may follow a traditional religious path. However, the alchemy of this work is not based in any particular esoteric school or traditional religious teaching but attempts to articulate a spirituality that seeks embodied, soulful connections within a context of world-becoming. This book is an exploration of living an authentic spiritual life without dependency on dogmatic teachings; it is meant as a guide to those who seek a path of love and wisdom through responsible living. The deep inner power of our actual human capacities far exceeds those articulated in most religious, scientific, and aesthetic theories of what it means to be human. We hardly know our full potential as embodied beings; we barely recognize the capacities we carry for world-transformation.

Far deeper than the boundaries of normative, collective beliefs, there exists an inner capacity, an alchemical depth of Being that can flow into individual life as a transformative call to shape a new Being-With, to form new images of self-realization. This new Being-With is a participatory call, a call for engagement, a call to embody in the direct sense our inner capacities, to unfold hidden potentials through a wide range of possible relationships, through a full spectrum of interactions, both visible and invisible. It is an incarnational call, a resonance that seeks to embody in practice and perception, an awareness of a more subtle, transformative, and soulful world. This new relatedness is not limited to religious teachings; it is not a matter of scientific discovery; nor is it a consequence of rational analysis or detached observation. It is a spiritual call, a call to embody creative principles that enhance love and wisdom at the center of our being. When we sink down, into dreams, into visionary horizons, into the imaginal making and unmaking of worlds, we discover that this power is fully incarnational, that is, fully capable of embodiment in many subtle forms. The challenge is to become resonant with those powers, those manifestations, those embodiments of love, insight, and far-seeing that makes the world a worthy place for our heirs.

The guidelines for this kind of discovery cannot be formulated as laws or fixed doctrines for simple assimilation. This transformation must be earned through responsible living, opened through genuine loving concern, and actualized through committed, life-long efforts. Alchemies of soul are created on earth, through incarnational processes. Such alchemies are part of a Great Work that flows up from the depths of Sacred Beingness and attains expression in the qualitative life and fine, exemplary actions and thoughts of real persons who have grown beyond the norms and boundaries of alienated, isolated, and fearful living.[1] Alchemies of soul unfold from a simplicity that is not afraid to love, to give, to reveal itself as incomplete, unfinished, but in process. The goal is self-realization; the ideal is a continuous development, a gradual incorporation of world possibility into spiritually mature relationships. The alchemical process is one of refinement through many stages, a forming that crystallizes a way of life which is then subject to further sublimation and further refinement. This process has no predetermined end, only ongoing stages and cycles of becoming whose goal is not perfection but a realization of fully mature embodiment.

All too often, perfection is a static ideal rooted in didactic beliefs and limited by historical precedents, codified doctrines, and institutional authority. We are not perfect in any ultimate sense but only relatively perfect in reflecting inner spiritual potential. In reflecting that potential, we give embodiment to relative truth, while the absolute ideal remains primarily an intellectual and dogmatic construct. When Christ spoke of perfection, as "be perfect even as the Father is perfect," he spoke of loving those who do not love you; thus teaching not a prescriptive behavior, but a general principle.[2] The actualization of this principle of loving kindness toward others results not in perfection but in a practice that reflects our own limits and inner boundaries, where it is difficult to know how to express such love. The "perfect gift," coming down from the Father of Lights,[3] is an inner capacity to open to the creative possibilities of loving kindness without denying our immaturity, fears, or prejudices. The enactment of such kindness is relative, the principle an ideal, the reality an embodiment in genuine loving relations.

What we seek through embodiment of soul is an authentic, expressive life that recognizes limits and boundaries but nevertheless strives to surpass those boundaries, to open to a fullness that is an intrinsic feature of world-becoming. The world does not change unless we change; this change is not merely external, nor a function of reflecting the known and recognized. Change comes through exploration, discovery, new modes of thought, greater subtlety of perception, opening to a less visible world of inner capacity and outward spiritual expression. The ordinary world is a form of containment, a kind of protective barrier that screens us from realizing our inmost capacities. It is also a refuge from the challenges of opening to new possibility. We easily become dependent on common, collective norms that sanction rudimentary ideas regarding the value and significance of human (or other) life. Many of these norms are perpetuated by individuals whose status and social position are dependent on maintaining those norms. But a creative spiritual life is not about conformity to social norms, nor is it about simply accepting normative views based in religious or scientific thought. Those views can contribute to a creative spiritual life, but they are not the basis for the necessary inner transformation.

The alchemy of soul, as a spiritual paradigm, concerns individual commitment to self-discovery, loving human relationships, and to a search for place within an expanding cosmology of infinite scope and possibility. The heart of the alchemical paradigm requires us to honor the soul as a true basis for inner transformation and for outer world change. It also requires us to realize that in an infinite universe, one no longer bound by local cosmological perceptions, such a path leads to many branching ways and possibilities. Thus, there are many alchemies of soul, not only reflecting alternative spiritual teachings but an emergent universe of vast and unfathomed potential, interdimensionality, and multiple visionary horizons. Our search for place has hardly begun. Our local cosmology, now overturned and reducible to a single local heliocosm (the sun and its planets), opens into an immensity of potential worlds, stars, galaxies, planes, hidden dimensions, mirror universes, vacuum energies, and a diversity that defies comprehension and facile spiritual summary. Yet, this is the place of our spiritual emergence; this is the foreground within which world-becoming will increasingly reflect our expanding cosmological horizons beyond known historical, local, and planetary construction. In this expanding universe, we can each be a significant center of manifestation and a genuine source of co-creative realization.

The language and processes of alchemy are highly symbolic, metaphorical, imagistic, visionary, and psychic. The alchemy of soul requires opening the whole person to the whole cosmos, or to the wholeness within which cosmos and soul find resonance and inner harmonization. It is an unpredictable track whose course cannot be laid out in a prescriptive sense, nor can its end be predetermined nor theorized in an exact, reproducible sense. It is a process whose manifestations are present-centered and future-oriented, a process of integration that does not deny the past but learns from it and cherishes the good that is in it. The alchemies of soul follow three principles: a sustained commitment to individual growth, a cultivation of loving kindness in all relationships, and a willingness to open to an expanding cosmos of subtle energies, beings, and worlds. These subtle worlds and beings are not well-understood, but they are accessible through an inner opening that moves beyond the analytic and into the visionary, imaginative, and symbolic languages of myth, dream, and the surreal possibilities of soul.

The human capacity for visionary knowledge is immense, as is expressed in the rich pluralisms of world spiritual traditions. The full spectrum of consciousness is hardly recognized in a world preoccupied with material gain, economic and political dominance, technological excess, and a failed imagination in the realm of spiritual growth and development. Science can offer no substitute for the spiritual needs of humanity, nor can it offer a moral basis for carrying out its actions and instrumentalizations. We, as conscious beings, must take in the whole of our experience, the whole of our capacities, and the whole of the complexities of manifest existence, resisting the temptation to reduce life to collective norms and social paradigms of "correct behavior." The truly correct behavior is to honor the gift of our creativity, to honor creativity in others, and to co-discover a richer, vaster, and more layered world of possible Being-With. We must open to the full spectrum of our inner capacities and explore that spectrum through direct experience; without such commitment we will only contribute to the failed imagination that takes life to be nothing more than the obvious, known, and definable.

The spiritual needs of humanity are many; they proceed out of a very deep well of times past and times yet-to-be and cannot be reduced to one particular system of ideas, practices, or beliefs. For this reason, alchemies of soul must be multiple, diverse, and as creative and imaginative as human spiritual potential allows. What the alchemist discovers is that he or she is not alone, not simply functioning within a closed horizon of only human potentials. Alchemies of soul open to much vaster realities of Spirit, sinking down into mysterious depths, encountering powers and presences whose manifestations can enrich and ennoble the human search for self-awareness. This opening of horizons will lead the practitioner into the visionary and dreaming basis of human knowledge, will stimulate the imaginative capacities, enhance empathy, increase intuitive psychic perceptions, and open the soul to a much richer, denser, complexity of Being. In alchemical language, this dense complexity of visionary potential is called the Mundus Imaginalis, "the Imaginal World" of collective mental horizons as a primary medium of human expression and self-perception. Presence within that vast, expansive horizon is not reducible to archetypal manifestations only, but opens to a rich, subtle panoply of diverse intelligences whose natures pervade and inhabit the world in a direct, soulful way. The world itself is an ensouled being, a web or network of panpsychic relations constituted differently according to different seers.

However, the alchemy of soul is not simply a process of acquiring a gaze that sees into the Mundus Imaginalis but is more a means for creating a soul that feels, responds, and acts with maturity. Visionary experiences are a genuine part of the alchemical transformation, but not the goal; neither is the goal a mystical perception of the whole, though this too is valuable and important. The goal is to embody soulfulness in an actual way of life, in discrete practices and concerns that enhance human relationships as a source of inspiration for a vital, creative life. The import of the alchemy of soul is the way in which it contributes to the preservation of a reverent, respectful, honoring way of life whose norms are preservation, reciprocity, and collective peace. In alchemy, the goal is the formation of the Philosophers Stone, a symbolic token whose property is a magical ability to transform the material into the spiritual. The Stone of this work is found in acquiring a spiritual heart, a Presence whose transformative capacity heals the fears, wounds, illnesses, alienations, and hatreds that still constrict and bind the earth. The purpose of spiritual work, in its maturity, is not self-gain but a centered way of life that acts on the whole to move it toward greater health, balance, and inner harmony. The Stone of the alchemical work is a sign, a living heart of a spiritual realization carried into the world, through embodiment, that seeks more than self-knowledge or inner transformation. The Stone represents the gift of presence given to others, the capacity to touch a person, a family, a community, or a world with blessings that can heal the fractures, wounds, and injuries of too much violence, fear, and mistrust, of too much indifference and lack of caring concern.

The most powerful challenge is to practice alchemy of soul in order to bring forward an offering that will truly serve the spiritual needs of others. Individual visions, mystical experiences, spiritual communications, journeys, and explorations certainly enhance and add to the richness of our expanding cosmos, but the greatest need is here, in the world, where ordinary people struggle to comprehend the value and significance of their often contracted lives. How can these visions and birthings of soul contribute to a remaking of the ordinary, to a transformative touch that opens the visionary horizon as a resource for the enhancement of the world? This is the primary question. When the soul stops in satisfaction with its own accomplishments and turns away from the world, it denies a yet greater potential and thus discards its obligations toward responsible living. Our care for others is a primary care, not because we sacrifice our own good health or well-being to meet unhealthy demands, but because in caring for others we discover our creative gifts and strengths and use them to enhance the well-being of those whose needs correspond to what we offer. We are not perfect beings, therefore our gifts are relative and in-process, an offering to those who would accept them and receive them with respect. Our personal experiences are secondary to what we offer; our inner vision, only a necessary foundation for our creative work.

World-becoming is a co-creative, interactive, and mutually dialogical process whose visionary basis is the opening of soul to new insights and expression. Sometimes an individual contributes very simply, through the strength of her intuition, through his honesty or commitment, through her values as a loyal and sympathetic friend. Sometimes an individual contributes in a more theoretical way, or through discovery in science, or through artistic contributions. The question is not "What do you do?" but "Who are you?" and "What do you offer?" — to the world, to others, to those you do not know or who think differently. The answers to these questions require us to share our perceptions, to tell our stories as co-seekers, to contribute our gifts to a remaking of world awareness and becoming. It requires an inner truthfulness concerning our soul life, a significant degree of self-knowledge, and a recognition of our strengths and weaknesses. It also requires an offering, a giving from the heart that only you can give. Coming forth with open hands and a willingness to engage with others is often difficult and demanding. It means embodying love as a basis for present-centered, authentic life in order to establish a trustworthy foundation for human communication and respect.

In a complex world, with many alternative paths, a great diversity of cultures, a multitude of languages, an immense storehouse of symbolic forms, rituals, ideas, and beliefs, there is no end to the possibilities of diverse cultural influences on any spiritual path. When we add to this the discoveries of science, the encyclopedic density of recently discovered knowledge, the accessibility of printed and electronic media, the impact of technology, the esotericism of many intellectual disciplines, and the full spectrum of human capability, it becomes clear that all paths are relative. Every alchemy of soul must select; every individual must make choices, must discriminate between what contributes to the process and what does not. Simplicity is a useful guide, but complexity cannot be avoided without denying the full density of what is possible. Every way is a winding way, a path interwoven with other paths, a place where beauty and plurality seek expression through unique human abilities. What does the heart need? What does the self desire for its coming forth, for its capacity to expand into fullness? What offering to the world have we each given in accord with our true gifts, not only in accord with the expectations of others?

Finding an individual way, an alchemical path, is no easy task and there is no forward motion that is not also circular. The patterns that guide us are like geometric forms opening on new dimensions where new forms and mandalas are born and realized as the center deepens. We must root deeply, ground our energies in an earth-based connection that honors our home world, and that values and seeks to preserve plurality, complexity and a richness of eco-spiritual expression. There are many voices lifted in this song of soul coming forth; the dream languages are filled with the potent imagery of emergence and new birth, a descent that brings up the hidden powers that animate our world. This song also calls down the powers of heavenly soul journeys and offers a new home for their birthing. That which is below unites with that which is above, and they join in a new marriage of heaven and earth, a Hieros Gamos, a union of male and female powers, in an alchemical wedding whose children are new soulful beings open to the world, fecund with creative power, and animated by the very forces of creation. We must go down into the depths and reach up into the heights, take a journey far beyond conventional thinking and bring back a new flame.

This work is one such offering of that flame, grounded in direct personal experiences and many years of thought, study and loving relations. Yet, it is only one view among many. Each of us is free to choose what benefits our search, gives direction, or offers inspiration. If even a single sentence moves the reader forward on the alchemical journey, then this effort is worthwhile. For me, the goal is to provide an opening into the alchemical work of soul awakening and its expression in new creative action and relationships. I am not offering a system, but a strategic overview of a creative process which may be interpreted differently by each reader. In this work, I share a variety of perspectives embodied in the life of the author, offered as reflective possibilities rather than as didactic teachings. While I am passionate in my beliefs, the transmission of my insights can only proceed through a correspondent resonance with the hearts and minds of others. Take what I offer according to your own needs, not in terms of truth and falsehood, but in terms of how it benefits your growth or adds to the quality of your human relationships. Soul growth and emergence is a gentle "coming out" process that must tie not only to an individual or a particular teaching, but also to the living cosmos, to the value of love, and to the worth of being human. What is required is to find a means, a strategy to clear away obstructions, and to free the soul to seek its own path and actualization.

1. For an explication of alchemical terms in this text see the Glossary.
2. Mark 5:48
3. James 1:17

CHAPTER ONE
STARTING WHERE YOU ARE

I often find a common attitude held by people seeking a spiritual path or a specific religious teaching they can follow. Faced with a multitude of possible choices, many people believe that what matters is choosing a particular teacher or teaching to give answers to questions that, authentically, the seeker needs to answer for him or herself. One of the most fundamental challenges of a spiritual life is accepting responsibility for answering your own questions. In the alchemy of soul, you are the responsible agent, not an external teacher, guide, book or mentor. Although you may find teachers or mentors and learn from various persons or spiritual writings, the change and inner transformation is going to happen deep within you, within the very heart and inmost depths of your being. You are the one who needs to take responsibility for this change, this inner realignment that brings your daily and working life into real correspondence with a vivid, living spiritual world. It is not a matter of waiting or postponing and rationalizing apparent lack of direction or purpose. Instead of setting up external criteria based on intellectual values or emotional hopes created by others, why not take a different attitude? Learn from every teaching. Learn from every person you meet and every situation, starting right where you are this very moment.

In this process of taking responsibility for your own decisions and spiritual commitments, it is important not to be overly self-critical. Starting where you are means creating a clear inner space of self-acceptance and honest self-appraisal; it means developing a sense of clarity about your goals and desires and not simply seeking a doctrine or teaching which answers questions before they arise within you. A questioning approach is natural and good; it means your soul is engaged and that your assumptions are subject to scrutiny and evaluation, as they should be. However, at the same time, it is also necessary to learn openness and receptivity to the differences that create diversity and plurality in the world. The goal is not a predetermined ideal as much as a a process of inner discovery that seeks to refine and adapt a teaching to the real needs and aspirations of the individual. In that process, we change; we discover new ways of understanding and acting in the world. This means that wherever we start, we must be prepared to undergo metamorphic changes which may well result in discarding formerly held beliefs or values.

1

The tendency in self-criticism, often disheartening, is to see the weaknesses that seem to inhibit development or to divert action into older, regressive patterns or to imagine an inner barrier where there is only doubt and uncertainty. Alchemies of soul require working with the raw material at hand, with what is, rather than with what might be or should be. It is not a matter of judging what is, but of knowing it and clearly accepting the bound or partial or inhibited condition of what is, without devaluing its potential. Working with the raw material in the alchemical process begins with accepting the exact condition of what is: the goal is to transform the what-is into what-can-be. It also requires knowing what-is without illusions and rationalizations, without barriers or buffers that cushion self-perceptions. The primary mode, the basic alchemical attitude, is positive and supportive, knowing that any psychic pattern (or "prima materia"), however crude or partial or incomplete, is a basis for spiritual transformation and inner awakening. In the history of alchemy, the alchemists recognizes the most ordinary, crudest material as the very stuff of transformation, as the basis for carrying out the Great Work.[1] This base material, the existing soul state, is the content with which the alchemist works, constantly refining, developing, breaking down, reshaping, and seeking to bring to realization its deepest hidden potential.

It is important that the alchemist acknowledge the inner potential and have confidence that through work and refinement new birth can occur. It is also important not to have an overly inflated sense of potential or accomplishment. Alchemists of soul are not highly visible in the social world. This is because the Great Work, that is the work of creating an illumined soul, requires inner focus, solitude, introspection, and a genuine sense of personal strengths and limits. We are all limited in some ways; we all have areas of greater and lesser ability. However, there is often a tendency to hold an exaggerated sense of self-importance or ability or to cling to emotional states and conditions which blind a person to his or her actual abilities. The alchemy of soul does not require surrender to the authority of others, nor does it require being a master or authoritative figure with personal followers. In many ways, the greatest barrier to inner transformation is the tendency to believe that a personal point of view, a socially supported status, or a variety of external accomplishments and social successes are a valid testimony to a person's spiritual potential. If self-criticism is a barrier to inner work, dismissive criticism of cultural differences or of non-conformity is a far greater danger to soul development, reflecting as it often does a pride of position or intellectual, cultural, or ethnic vanity. The importance of stripping away the excesses of pride and identification with external accomplishments is a critical part of soul development, proceeding not from intellect but from the heart.

Alchemies of soul do not start in the same phase nor with the same first steps; every person comes to the task carrying a variety of predispositions, tendencies, beliefs, attitudes and inner resistances which strongly condition the present. This is where we each start, at the place we are when we begin to awaken to the task of self-transformation as a spiritual practice. Individual capacities are highly variable, as are the strengths and weaknesses each person struggles with to find inner integration and alignment. Finding the center in this process can take many years, and finding the means to sustain that center and to encourage its growth and expansion is the work of a lifetime. So it is important to lay aside the sense of urgency that often drives people into excessive patterns of inquiry and dissatisfaction. Sometimes we move ahead quickly and then fall back, and sometimes the change is very slow and not even perceptible. What is required is consistent effort, a clear sense of purpose, and a willingness to learn and grow. Limitations can be overcome, inner resistance can change and dissolve, new horizons can open new questions, and the resolution of certain concerns can act to generate new concerns. The Great Work is a cyclical process, a way of life directed by an inner willingness to seek metamorphosis and to undergo the rigor and challenge of ongoing transformation. It is not a matter of beliefs as much as practice and inner realizations that constantly realign perceptions through increasing expansion and enhanced awareness.

Opening to the full beauty, depth, and wonder of the sacred character of the world requires us to take a journey into the deepest mysteries of life and death, of being and becoming, by overcoming our own weaknesses and inner constrictions. The twin tendencies of over-inflation and self-denial, of excess or imbalance in self-perceptions, must be subdued and sublimated in order for deeper energies to flow freely and creatively in the Great Work. And this work concerns more than individual transformation; it also includes world transformation because the evolution of soul is a basic ground for the transformation of our shared humanity. When soul expands, it meets the world; it takes in the world and the world becomes the true arena of the soul's strengths and weaknesses, the true ground of soul's learning. This is because the Great Work is a co-creative work; it unfolds through human relationships that draw out of us our deepest potentials and capacities. In this work, the soul is an image of the world and the world, an image of the soul, and both require sublimation and refinement for full realization.

The revelatory ground is seen in the quality of our human interactions, in the love we carry with us into the world, and in the reciprocity by which that love is returned. And this ground extends further, into the diversity of all living creatures, all plants, animals, birds, insects, mountains, trees, streams, oceans, and forest hillsides. The Great Work is a work of world transformation as an index of the maturity of our species wisdom and our creative kindness. Starting where we are includes starting with a vision that embraces the world, all of nature, all cultures and civilizations, all times past, present and future, without denying the limitations and boundaries within the individual human psyche that still does not comprehend the meaning of the Whole. It is not because we understand the Whole that we embrace it, but because the richness of the Whole offers unlimited possibilities for future growth and development. And we embrace the Whole as the full dancing ground of Spirit, as the place where creation and creative becoming play out the dramas and comedies of human ignorance and wisdom. Alchemy of soul does not reject the world, does not seek transformation through world denial but through world affirmation. The place of creation is here, in this place, now, and includes the full panoply of all created beings, both seen and unseen.

Starting where you are means starting with your life in the world; it means not reducing spiritual practice to a private arena, to discrete disciplines and strict habits of body or mind. Discipline comes in its own time and own way; it teaches many valuable lessons and provides fiber and inner strength. But living in the world is the greater spiritual discipline; bringing the practice into the market place is the greater challenge. Not all professions provide a good ground for such development, but even the most ordinary activity can be a ground for manifestation. My own perception is that occupations which support violence are the most difficult ones in which to cultivate an alchemy of soul. I am not saying that someone in the military or police cannot bring his or her practice into action within the world he or she inhabits; but that place which is controlled and structured from the outside, by rigid authority, or based in compelling acts of defense or aggression, is a contracted ground of soul. This could be a place of business, a home, an alternative community, a political party, a religious institution. We must choose our place for growth, and the more there is aggression and external control, the more insistent the structure of authority, the more difficult the task of inner transformation and the more demanding the effort. Choose your own ground; do not let others choose it for you.

Where we are is not always where we want to be, but here we are! And that place is where we start. Perhaps you will change location, or events will move you toward unseen consequences and unexpected openings. But where you are is where you start, where you open to the possibility of change and new direction. Change is the very nature of the process, so starting where you are does not necessarily mean staying there! Perhaps the change is slow and reflects growing affirmations of new directions; or perhaps the changes come unexpectedly and with shocking suddenness. The concern is not the rapidity of the change, but the adaptation that holds to a center of authenticity. This is crucial. Whatever comes calls us to meet it with inner flexibility, with freedom and, at times, abandonment; it calls us to be true to the inner process of following the soul's promptings. The true alchemy of soul requires that we not injure others, not abandon them or deny responsibility, but that we listen to the soul's call, test it, and discover what is hidden beneath that call. To live authentically means to live according to the deeper urgency to open to a more complex, full world of becoming. Starting where you are means being open to change and new possibility; it means gathering energy to shift both inwardly and outwardly.

BECOMING YOUR OWN TEACHER

In a complex world, it is not surprising that people feel a need for guidance and direction. Many alternatives mean many choices, and making those choices is not always easy, nor is the consequence of a choice always foreseeable in the circumstances of the choosing. But there is a way to choose and a way to uncover direction, if we learn to live authentically in all of our relationships. This means cultivating honesty, perhaps the single most important quality required for being your own teacher. Being honest does not mean simply reporting on how you feel or how you are affected by the actions of others; this is simply a description of actual feelings or thoughts. Honesty is much more and requires more effort because it seeks to express the "why" of those feelings and reactions and to evaluate them in terms of core values. It is almost impossible to be honest if you do not

5

know what your core values are and why you hold them and how they relate to your everyday circumstances. Many people mistake describing immediate or long-held feelings as an act of honesty because they are caught in a superficial image of "honesty" that correlates the description of inner feelings or thoughts with a certain quality of sincerity, often mistaken for real understanding. But honesty as a virtue, as an authentic aspect of a committed way of life, one growing from clearly held values and shaped by intentional actions, calls for a deeper self-report that uncovers the formative conditions of feelings and thoughts. The question is not "What do you feel?" or "What thoughts do you have?" but why do you have them, why do you feel what you feel, and how did these thoughts and feelings come to be in the first place?

Such honesty requires being able to see our own limits and boundaries and to also be able to evaluate how those limits may shape our perceptions of others. The conditional aspects of self-awareness are not fixed or permanent; they are only relative conditions that can be changed and transformed. Becoming aware of an inner limit or boundary provides a sense of who we are in relationship to others who may also share those same boundaries. And we can move beyond our boundaries through courage and an inner determination to enhance understanding. But this advance requires an inner correspondence with our deepest values. It is not a matter of change simply as a response to a boundary but change motivated by inner values that support a meaningful reason for crossing a boundary in order to enhance our spiritual development. Some boundaries are self-protective and others are limits that are natural and which we may choose not to cross because we wish to maintain a certain focus or circumstance. Boundaries are natural, and honesty requires that we recognize those boundaries that constitute our identity as spiritual beings. There are many spiritual paths but we cannot walk all of them; we must choose and what we choose means we must also choose what not to follow. This does not mean that others who choose what we have not chosen (nor understood) are any less developed or any better — they are simply different.

When we relate to others, in a spiritual practice, we want to seek a correspondence that brings our values and beliefs into some meaningful relationships with the values and beliefs of others. By honestly assessing our own values, we can determine how consistent, how intentionally clear we are in actualizing those values. And we can relate our choices and intentions to those of others through an ethic of love and acceptance — regardless of the values of others. But only if we hold love and acceptance of others as core values and actually enact our commitment to those values honestly, knowing our boundaries and yet remaining open to change. Love can teach us to be receptive and yet honest about our limits so we can move forward through a willingness to grow and change, without denying the freedom of others to take a different path or to make different choices. In assessing our core values, it is best to be utterly honest in evaluating how well we actually *enact those values* in real life situations. This requires honesty in assessing the gap between thoughts or belief and real action and behavior. The standards we apply to ourselves are not always applicable to others and our struggles are often individual and unique to a particular situation. So this process of evaluation and self-honesty is ongoing and part of a spiritual path, to be alert to the continuity between our core values and our actions.

We may not always be able to love to the degree we might desire or to live according to an abstract, non-judgmental stance. We do make judgments; it is better to be clear and honest about the fact that we make those judgments in relationship to others, our own circumstances, and in terms of our expectations and values. Here the link should be strong between honesty and humility. It is not so much a matter of what we know as a matter of what we believe, what we do, and why we do it. What motivates our actions? Starting where you are means starting with serious self-assessment and, being as honest as possible, beginning to articulate core values in terms of how you act, how you speak, and how you think and judge. The Hermetic teaching here is: self-honesty in thought, word and deed.[2] But honesty means a clarity that matches words, thoughts, and deeds with deeply held values. When we can honestly articulate our primary values, and bring our thoughts, words, and deeds into alignment with those values, then we are moving forward into a life of integrity and directness. Humility means seeing the limits where our actual behavior does not live up to our spiritual ideals. That is why "starting where you are" requires an effort to clarify beliefs and aspirations in terms of actual behavior and to begin making efforts to bring those aspirations and beliefs into harmony with actions.

Thus a first step is to start with an evaluation of core values, to investigate how closely you actually live your values, to know what those values are, and to assess the gap between your ideals and actual practice.

7

On the alchemical path there is no wholesale adoption of a doctrine or of values in a systemic sense. Each value has to be developed and refined in actual practice; each ideal has to become a clear goal that is authentically embodied. Here a root metaphor is helpful. Root metaphors are image-ideas that consolidate and compress the ideal into a relationship between visual image and verbal idea, thereby providing a central focus that can be elaborated through interpretation and new insights.[3] A good root metaphor is the image-idea of the pilgrimage or a journey to a sacred place. On the spiritual path we are on a journey, and this journey requires a certain degree of commitment and preparation. Thus, we can reflect on making a pilgrimage: "How do I prepare for this journey? Can I just walk away from all my commitments and relationships? What is my intent in making this journey? What is my purpose? What do I hope to gain? Do I need help to make this journey? Will others support me in my journey? Which others would I want to support me? And what support can I give to others while making this journey?" Answering these questions helps to give priority to your values and to place your aspirations and values in a context of the metaphor.

The journey metaphor is best symbolized in Hermetic traditions by the Grail Quest, the search for the sacred that results in a transformation of those who are able to pursue the quest to its very end. As in the many Grail stories, often the seeker may actually encounter the Grail without recognizing it or being able to receive it in the full transformative sense. One of the earliest Grail narratives was recorded by Chrétien de Troye (c. 1170), a courtly poet and singer in the French court of Marie de Champagne. When the hero Perceval encounters the Grail in the castle of the Fisher King, carried in a procession, by a beautiful woman, he fails to ask the King about what he has seen. His failure to ask the appropriate questions means that the Grail King is not healed of his wounds and that Perceval must set out on a long quest to gain maturity and experience to prepare himself for a future encounter with the Grail.[4] So asking authentic questions is appropriate and necessary on the quest or on pilgrimage; the quality and attention given to these questions will in many ways determine the nature of the journey. The Grail quest is a journey of maturation that requires mastering many difficult situations and thereby acquiring skills and wisdom that can deepen the realizations of the goal. The pilgrimage, the quest, requires us to ask heartfelt and meaningful questions about our journey, our values, our goals, and about who we are and what we encounter. It is not simply a matter of gathering experiences, but of being able to grasp the fullness of the moment in such a way that it opens our minds to new understanding and insights.

The journey metaphor works well with another root metaphor, and that is seeking or following a spiritual path. Some people in making their journey want a path or a road that is well-marked and structured in a way that gives them a sense of security and membership in an established community. Others prefer a path that is less well marked, perhaps only a trail through the forest, one they can walk at their own pace and not necessarily as members of a community. And there are those who prefer no path, just an open wood that requires them to use their utmost in skills and abilities to master whatever situations or challenges may arise. At different stages of life, the path may change and evolve from more to less structure or from less to more structure. The Hermetic path of alchemy is a path of individual efforts; not a path of community in the collective, mass sense but more a fellowship in Spirit, an unbound community of highly diverse practitioners. As a "middle path" it holds the journey as a root metaphor and then seeks to actualize the path in an individualized, unique way suited to the temperament and abilities of the seeker. It is not a path of communal sanctions and strict guidelines, and yet it is not entirely without form or focus. The communal affinity between practitioners is based on an inner correspondence in root metaphors and in commonly held ideas and practices. Yet, like the Grail Quest, the path must be undertaken by each individual under the power of his or her own inner motivation and commitment.

If we start where we are, then we also start with the intention of making a spiritual journey, a pilgrimage that will change our lives and change the way we see and experience the world. First, it is necessary to prepare for the journey and one of the first stages is to ask appropriate questions about the journey — the goals, the requirements, the degree of inner preparedness. An index of this stage is to remember and reflect upon dreams, dream images, and the flow of free imagination, its contents and visual forms and metaphors. The core of motivation for a spiritual journey does not come from a purely rational need, nor does it depend only upon an ability to rationalize the process. What must be sought is inspiration, an inner sense of direction that leads to greater freedom and personal fulfillment. This is not always a rational process! One of the great challenges of the alchemy of soul is to discover the ways in which our normative, rationalized lives limit and inhibit personal development. Rational analysis can paralyze the will; it can offer uncounted "reasons" why an action should be avoided or denied. I do not wish to suggest that the path of transformation is therefore "irrational," but only that conventional rationality has its limits and is bound by the logic of its own presuppositions. Part of the spiritual challenge is to find new guidelines and resources for living, new inspirations that are not bound by the logic of ordinary reason.[5]

On the spiritual pilgrimage, dreams, visions, intuitions, imagination, and creative inspirations all play a significant and central role in helping the pilgrim to find the path that is unique to his or her needs. So questions must be asked about the value of dreams and visions, the role of intuition and imagination, and the importance of acting in terms of guiding metaphors rather than in terms of rational discourse. In starting this journey, the resources include all aspects of our awareness and being. As we set out on the pilgrimage, seeking the holy places, seeking the Grail, the Sophianic cup, the stone or waters of transformation, we will move deeper and deeper into the language of metaphor, into poetic image-ideas as resources for guiding the journey. The alchemy of soul, as central to Hermetic teachings, is a process of discovery, of a journey into an unknown land, an exploration of new worlds and new ways of being. The Grail of that quest is spiritual maturity leading to visionary encounters and illuminations that open the horizon of ordinary seeing and allow for deep inner awakening to a fuller and more aware life. But it is also a process of shaking down, of getting rid of excess, of shedding unnecessary burdens and false responsibilities. It is a journey testing the depths of commitment and the true willingness of the individual to shed the old outer skin for a new inner life.

Starting where you are means making a mental and emotional inventory of your own strengths and weaknesses, learning to evaluate your own goals and desires apart from the expectations and demands of others. It also means honoring commitments and relationships as part of your present condition. This requires honest evaluation of obligations you have willingly taken on. It means identifying your core spiritual values and altering your life in such a way that you can begin to exemplify your values. The root metaphor of the journey is to start from where you are; it is not a journey to postpone, but a journey to actualize in the present. It is a journey that moves in two directions, each increasingly in resonance with the other.

One direction is inward and the other direction is outward. The inward journey requires attending to all the signs and intuitions, all the personal indications that point you in a direction consistent with your spiritual ideals and values. The outward journey involves your engagement with others, with the world, with your particular culture, time, and with your social circumstances. These two directions are inseparable but, increasingly, they come into harmony and balance as the necessary steps are taken to fully actualize the journey. The discovery of the sacred is not just inward or just outward; it is the union of all that is within with all that is without, the above and the below; in the process of this union, the world and the soul are transformed.

The journey begins when the individual makes the decision to seek this harmonization of inner and outer being — not simply to follow one or the other. But the world as it is seen and the self as it is known, at the beginning, is not the same as the deep union of soul-and-world that results from processes of alchemical transformation. The alchemies of soul are many, but they share a common process of discovery in the value given to embodied and incarnate being. The value of our embodiment of the sacred is found in the ways in which that embodiment enhances and adds value to the world and in the ways in which the world is transformed by inner spiritual awakening The Grail of this quest is not an other-worldly goal; it is not a denial of our embodied life, but a celebration of this life as the ground of sacred being. The alchemy of soul, as another root metaphor, is our capacity to transform our present state, whatever it may be, into a more worthy and sacred condition that reflects the unrealized, deep potential within us, within other beings, and within the world-cosmos. The water of the Grail Cup is the Water of Life (Aqua Vitae), that is, the water that gives us the increased ability and sensitivity to fully honor and appreciate the gift of life in every creature, great or small. What I have written here is only one such alchemy, but there are as many alchemies as there are practitioners; what I offer here is a guide to general principles, but each person must choose and create the path she or he would follow.

Thus the alchemical journey is a transformative journey that teaches each person to see the temple of the world as a divine image in which he or she may serve as an acolyte to a great mystery. Our role in this world is to act as agents of change and transformation that sustains and nourishes life, that adds the value of our wisdom and maturity to the processes by which all life is enhanced and developed. The consecration of the journey comes from within, as we awaken to a Presence within the world that is co-creative in guiding and inspiring our actions. This Presence is a powerful, creative source, a deep and holy mystery whose embodiments are creative expressions of an immeasurable potential, a potential great enough to create the entire visible cosmos and all invisible worlds inhabited by a vast panorama of beings. Thus the journey is a journey to the Heart of the World, to the Soul of Creation, and into the density of a mystery that is far greater and far more ancient, profound, and holy than any single human being can fathom. If we are honest, we will recognize our own individual limits and will come to understand that this journey requires an inner simplicity and stripping away to prepare us for our encounter with deepest mystery.

The journey also requires a making, a creating, that seeks to evolve a new depth of personhood, a new kind of Being-With as a co-creator in which our individual gifts are recognized and fully valued. Each person is a unique embodiment of that sacred mystery, each creature a testimony to diversity and difference that does not contradict but enhances and adds value to the Whole. This contribution can be simple: an honest, loving way of life, a willingness to care about others, and an inner capacity to share and to learn with others. As co-creators, we each have the uniqueness of our individual being as a resource for contributing to the well-being of others and to the coming into maturity of other beings. As we set out on the journey, it is important to recognize the value of each pilgrim, of each seeker after sacred transformation. And to make this journey successful, it is important to consecrate our actions and intentions for the good of others and not just for our own good. But the realization of that good for others comes through the inner awakening of each individual, through a process of mutual discovery and inner sharing. We cannot share the vision of the Grail fully or truly until we have each experienced it directly in a state of receptivity in which we ask the right questions and accept the responsibilities given with the inspired response. This takes continual work, honesty, and willingness to change in accord with inner rhythms tempered by continued self-knowledge and learning.

LEARNING FROM OTHERS

The world is full of teachers and we are all students. Our teachers are not just designated leaders or guides for various traditions or esoteric pathways. Anyone can be a teacher to the student who is ready to learn from every situation. A child can easily teach an adult and the uneducated can surely teach the educated, who still have so much more to learn. The elder can teach the younger and that same elder can learn from the younger. Animals can be our teachers and so can the plants and elements of nature. The very small can offer a great lesson and great individuals may have very little to offer, but even there we can learn. So we should consider ourselves to be always on a path of learning from others and in particular from the daily lessons of our human interactions and our animal relationships. A useful esoteric metaphor is that the whole world is a book, a text to read and interpret, a manual that teaches us correct interactions and skills if we can read and understand the meanings. The natural world is not an obvious text, emblazoned with human reasons, but a divine calligraphy written in a language that often we barely comprehend. Everywhere around us, there are teachings, teachers, and lessons to be learned.

Some people feel they have to find a teacher or master to guide them and sometimes such teachers can be helpful and inspiring. But teachers cannot do the work that is necessary to bring forth the inner luster of our own being, nor should a teacher become a substitute for our efforts and decisions. We are each our own teacher; this is fundamental. The alchemy of soul, on the Hermetic path, is an alchemy carried out by the seeker and not by someone else in his or her name. But this alchemy affirms the value of others and the necessity of human relationships in the alchemical process as central to the task of world transformation. So while we are each our own teacher, we are also each a student of the teachings of others. A test of our development is to see how easily the teaching and the learning flow forth and back between individuals able to be both a "guest" and a "host".[6] The key is reciprocity and not being caught in only one role — either as student or teacher — but being able to be either at any time, with ease and relaxation. Persons seeking a teacher who then expect a teacher to give them the guidance and directions they need are not serving themselves well; they are abandoning responsibility for the realizations of others. They are becoming imitations of other images and realizations that may be far removed from their own inner gifts and abilities.

This does not mean that there should be no teachers, but only that others should be treated as teachers and recognized as having gifts and insights, a style or method or means, that only they can offer. But do not hold on to your teachers and do not let your teachers hold on to you! Be your own teacher, now and always. This is a harder road than the road of finding a teacher and then simply following his or her teachings. Perhaps for a time you will find such a teacher, and perhaps for a time you make that inner surrender and abdicate your responsibilities by giving them over to the other. But the good teacher will resist this abdication and throw you back onto your own resources and encourage you to think for yourself and to act according to your own deepest intuitions. Teachers who expect allegiance and obedience are often affirming the teaching over the person and the lesson over the learning. I do not criticize these teachers or say they are wrong; I only say that their teachings are based on conformity to principles that do not value the uniqueness of the individual, nor do they value individual differences in a creative spiritual sense. Such teachers can provide discipline and direction and may be an excellent starting point, but the alchemy of soul requires greater self-direction.

On the Hermetic path, the value of being an individual is not paramount, but the very process of transformation is a process of individuation, a becoming whose actualization is unique to the individual. This is not a secondary point, but a central, defining characteristic of a Hermetic pathway. As a "middle path" it teaches that the value of the individual lies in his or her ability to fully realize the unique and sacred capacities that best express an individual realization of Spirit. This realization cannot be made by any person other than by the seeker. You are your own teacher and you are your own path. What we gain from others is insight into their paths; we receive from them the gifts of Spirit that they have discovered and realized in their own self-becoming. What we offer are our gifts and our insights in a process of mutual exchange and sharing. Some are greater teachers according to the very nature of their gifts and efforts, while others are less gifted as teachers but stronger in different, sometimes quite subtle ways. When I say that the individual is not paramount, it is because the goal is not simple individuation, but the realization of spiritual potentials whose nature and being exceeds and surpasses an individual manifestation. The individual is like a lens with a unique focus that sharpens the light or a prism that refracts the light into a unique band of colors and gives that light character and quality.

Finding a teacher is like finding a guide to help you navigate a particularly difficult terrain with which you are unfamiliar and in which you may feel that the experience or perspective of another, one more familiar with the territory, can help you find your way. In a sense, this depends on the nature of your path. You might want a teacher because you are too lazy to find the answers to your own questions, or you might want a teacher because you are anxious and do not trust your own intuitions. Even in a difficult terrain, it is important to remember that your guides can only show you the way they know, the path they have walked. And when a teacher or guide says that all of his or her teachers taught it the way he or she teaches and not some other way, that is only an articulation of a specific tradition and not of all possible ways. Sometimes you have to cross a terrain that is difficult and sometimes you have to do this by taking the long, difficult route rather than the short and easy one in order to learn the necessary lessons. And sometimes, it is Spirit choosing for you, urging you to go this way and not that way and to trust this direction and not that one. Not all guides through a particular terrain show us what we want or need to see and sometimes, only years later, do we realize how easily we were misled or how we misconstrued the lessons of our journey.

The greatest teacher is Spirit, the inner guide that prompts us to follow a particular way and tells us which teachings can help us and which hold us back or only lead us to a narrow ledge. Sometimes we think we know the way and then, after climbing up a slope, we slide all the way back to the bottom and scrape a knee in the process. Or we come to a dead end and have to retrace our steps and find an alternative route. Yet, on reflection we may realize that the blind alley taught us something important, and how we deal with that lesson is part of training the heart-mind in patience and perseverance. Soul is not simply there, waiting to be discovered in all its beauty and fullness. Instead we have only a glimmer, only a flash of intuition, concerning its presence and nature. This is because the unique and seeking soul, in the alchemical sense, is yet unperfected and, like coal embedded in layers of rock, has yet to undergo the pressure and formative, shaping influence of life that will bring forth the particular beauty of its diamond sparkle. In speaking of such a soul or deeper self-identity, I am not speaking of a transcendent entity that hardly connects with your real being in the world. I am speaking instead of your deep, incarnate identity that is in the process of forming, perhaps through many lifetimes, the essence of your own higher realizations in Spirit. This is a slow and gradual process and like the transformation of coal into diamond, it is long in the making.

Knowing that Spirit is the inner guide means learning to listen and observe the presence of Spirit in others, to seek that presence in their being through an inner awareness and developed sensitivity. When I say everyone is a teacher, I do not mean in an explicit sense; in an implicit sense, each person IS a manifestation of Spirit-in-process, engaged in acts of becoming. No matter how "unconscious" or unaware the person may be, Spirit is there, at work in each individual, acting as primal source or deep well from which the individual draws energy and vitality. The fact that many people do not experience this source in a direct and primal sense is irrelevant to its function and its capacity to be present in all moments as undiscovered potential. Who lives up fully to their potential? Only those who spend a lifetime cultivating their capacities as multifaceted beings and who are not reducible to any one skill or unique ability. When we look at the skill of another, or a particular talent or capacity, we are looking into a mirror that reflects the human potential and shows us what we might actually become if we undertake the full discipline and training necessary for its realization. And when we see someone who is very limited and not very aware, we are also looking into a mirror, seeing an image of what we might become without that discipline or inner desire for realization.

We are linked in subtle ways to all the many beings who are incarnate with us, and many who are not incarnate as well, and together we create a wide variety of worlds and conditions through which we can explore facets of our potential or ability. We can become obsessed with one particular skill or capacity and seek out others who also dwell on that capacity or facet of human behavior. Because our human capacities are highly diverse, we can drift from one kind of experience to another, from one fascination to another, being conditioned by our own lack of inner direction. Events and persons we do not really choose can create an energy that momentarily gives us focus,e which is later dissipated through a lack of inner clarity and sustained purpose. This is life lived on the margins of free choice, not life lived at the center of our human freedom to genuinely choose a path and then to actualize it through creative efforts and long-term commitment. Alchemies of soul require a lifetime of effort, and devotion to a process that does not offer quick, easy gains. We have to become rooted in the process of self-development as a way of life, not as a sudden response to tragedy or unexpected flux and disturbance in an otherwise unreflective momentum lacking direction or spiritual purpose. What we want to seek out are exemplary individuals who have lived life devoted to creative development — in the arts, in science, in business, or in any way of life

16

that promotes peace and self-development.

What we want to avoid is the situation that requires us to drop our search and our commitments only to take on a social persona that masks our real personhood. We can only learn from others insofar as we are able to be authentic in living our own lives. Otherwise, how will we recognize authenticity? How will we value uniqueness if we feel that we have to sacrifice our individuality to conform to an external identity because that is the normative expectation? Leaning from others requires being authentic, and being authentic means having an inner sense of individual freedom to explore and to discover as yet unrealized potential. We must change the world so we can change our own capacity as creative individuals; this means we must seek to enact our inner values and to be our own teachers, to be examples to others. We must learn to value those who are different, who seek an alternative way of life and who refuse to play the game of social conformity because of the rewards it offers in supporting an older, less individuated way of life. Those who emphasize conformity in how they live may give to others in ways that encourage human development. But often, they lack the joy and fulfillment of their deeper potential, their unique spiritual gifts; conversely, the artist may revel in individuality but be unhappy and, even as a non-conformist, lack spiritual depth. Self-satisfaction is not an index of spiritual growth but often a sign of inner stagnation and comfort with collective norms or an indication of individuality that is self-absorbed and disconnected from the creativity of communal spiritual transformations.

Seek teachers who are creative, alive, vital in their relationships, respectful of differences and supportive of creative, individual choices. Seek community that fosters individuality and places responsibility for personal development on the shoulders of the individual. Above all else, seek teachers who are firm but loving, rigorous but compassionate, and independent but receptive and caring. Observe the work of creativity in every individual life, see what role it plays and how central creative explorations are at every stage of life. Growing older does not mean losing creativity, it means becoming a vessel of creative energies that reveal a lifetime of inner focus and development. Perhaps such creativity manifests as a very simple inner peace and deep silence that attends well to all that lives and breathes; perhaps it is active and transparent but does not impose itself and exemplifies a centered, caring way of life. Seek teachers who pursue a spiritual path without emphasizing their claims to being teachers.

And seek to be a teacher based on the quality of life you live and the loving kindness of your relationships rather than on what you think, or know, or believe. Teach by example, and learn from those who also exemplify their own values and without imposing their beliefs or desiring conformity from others. And seek teachers within whom you can sense spiritual health, well-being, and fullness.

Such teachers may be good friends, family members, children, or acquaintances who exemplify a way of life that is conscious, individual, and based in principles of caring and love. Teachers without love lack the opening of the heart to inner life, to the depth and presence of Spirit that teaches love in all its variations as an example of deep interrelatedness. As we go within, beginning to explore the hidden depths of our own nature and its inmost capacities, we discover that love is a central and inextinguishable source within us. Such is Spirit's resting place, its resonant center of well-being, even as a single atom of presence within us can offer tremendous energy for transformation. But we must go within the heart, not just within the mind; we must seek teachers with heart, not just intellectual training or mental agility. The heart is the great teacher and mind is the great disciple of the heart. Where the heart goes, there mind follows and when mind dominates, heart contracts and loses vitality. Heart and mind must be balanced, but the center of the Hermetic teaching is the heart, often envisioned as the image of a rose, as the deep center of human spiritual awareness opening and awakening to morning light.

There is a great light of soul as well but this light, as we shall learn, is a transpersonal light that reflects our capacity for transcendent awareness. The spiritual path of alchemy is not guided by transcendence but by transformation. It is a path of the heart, or deep soul, not a path of mind first, but of mind second or third, after love, after responsible behavior and after developed values. Mind is an instrument and not a cause of spiritual transformation; the cause is Spirit, the in-dwelling presence that leads and inspires. Mind is the guardian of a treasure (the awakened soul) placed in its keeping but not a treasure created or caused by mind. Heart is the nurturing place, the womb within which Spirit breathes life and well-being into the world and offers us the opportunity to realize a deep inner creation. Other seekers are an example to us by the qualities of their realizations, not by their conformity to a teaching or by their ability to articulate communal ideas. It is in their capacity to exemplify a way of life that Spirit shines forth as a bright presence and as a luster that inspires us to seek a similar light within. That light does not manifest in identical forms because, as it flows forth through the heart, it takes on a quality and magnitude that reflects the very essence of the person as a unique jewel shaped by his or her individual life, gifts, and efforts. The heart is a great teacher, one that will always challenge mind to release its hold on sensation and perception in order to embrace another who is greater than mind can ever be.

In learning from others, we do not need to make long-term commitments to their way of life. What we need is to put into practice the teachings we receive from them as we learn how to adapt those teachings to our own spiritual development. It is never a matter of imitation but of adaptation, not a copy or a mirror image, but a process of absorption and integration that extracts the nutrients and washes away the unwanted excess. The heart as the Vas Hermeticum, the "hermetic vessel" in which the essence is distilled, requires continual warmth and heat to regenerate the teaching in forms that serve the needs of the individual. The heat is our commitment to be an authentic example of the values we hold, arising from passion, desire and effort. The distillations, done over and over, reflect the work of transforming a particular teaching, making it our own, truly understanding it. On some occasions, a single exposure may result in a whole new vision of life — and repetitions may diminish the original insight. Look into the heart of each person and you will see there the alchemy of the inner life, clearly visible to those who practice the Great Art. This is why we can learn from every person, because as the heart opens we begin to master the ability to share and reciprocate the intensity of the spiritual transformations. For we are each a teacher and we each reflect exactly that degree of self-realization that we have actualized in our daily lives, not in theory but in practice, not in ideas but in an actual opening to the deep wisdom of the heart where soul becomes increasingly individuated and uniquely formed.

DISCOVERING YOUR IDEA-BELIEFS

Let's start with a brief descriptive phenomenology, that is, an analytic description of any "object" of consciousness, a description that lays out the basic elements of the phenomenon (object) and discusses the relationships between the elements. Most phenomenology is analytic in the sense that the observer tries to describe the image or thought or content in terms of various qualitative aspects as he or she experiences the phenomenon. Our experience of the object adds subjective character to the object of perception, thus delineating not only the object but how that object is perceived by the observer. There is no phenomenology without this subjective character as an intimate feature of the observing subject, including a description of the experiences of others. I can observe the emotions of another but my perceptions are colored by my own subjective attitudes. Thus a phenomenology of idea-beliefs begins with a description of the inner relationships between my ideas, beliefs, images, and feelings — all of which I observe as intrinsic features of reflective, self-aware life.

The alchemy of soul requires a certain degree of introspective phenomenology, an ability to analyze one's own feelings, experiences, perceptions, ideas, beliefs, dreams, imaginative states, memories, intuitions, and somatic and psychic conditions. We are complex beings, physically aware, sensing, emotionally perceptive and reactive, imaginative, thinking and believing, inter-related, socially conditioned beings. The alchemy of soul requires that we know what we feel, believe and think as clearly as possible in order to institute changes and continue with our personal development. First, it is necessary to cut through the illusions of inherited beliefs and ideas, or culturally active patterns of thought or action that result in collective behaviors driven by unreflective habit and identification with collective norms. By "illusions" I mean the phenomenal quality of shared or collective ideas and beliefs that simply pass from one generation to another as uncritically accepted norms. Some collective ideas or beliefs may be quite appropriate and valuable, but their value comes into focus and meaningful acceptance when the individual grapples with these idea-beliefs and personalizes them through a process of conscious internalization, through a willing assent to their validity, rather than simply accepting them because others accept them. Our phenomenology requires that we proceed through questioning (not through simply accepting answers), a deep and thorough questioning.

Thus questions arise: What are the ideas and beliefs that I hold as an individual which I regard as truly my own? What values best reflect my personal, committed, willing assent inseparable from the inner coherence of my actions and behavior (and not just my thoughts)? What are the core ideas-beliefs I hold that are crucial to how I orient and respond to life and all of its opportunities and possibilities? What is the phenomenology of my beliefs and ideas; how would I describe them and articulate them to myself and to others? And how have my idea-beliefs changed over the years and why have they changed? What has motivated me to retain those ideas I hold and why have I dropped others or changed their intent or significance? It takes serious effort to answer these questions. An unwillingness to answer them often reflects both the difficulty of the task and the fact that this practice takes time and consistent effort because these questions must be continually asked and answered as one proceeds on the journey. It is a questioning journey, a quest-ioning search for insight and understanding. The real "answers" do not come from without but from within. Failure to attend to the inner coherence of our thoughts and beliefs results in a continuing participation in the illusions of collective distraction and indifference.

The phenomenology of idea-beliefs begins with a recognition that I am not speaking of abstract ideas, of not just "thoughts," as we have a multitude of mental activities constantly providing awareness and varying degrees of self-consciousness. It is not the "stream of consciousness" per se which I want to consider, but the content that is lifted out of this stream and given some special attention and priority in living. The location of these idea-beliefs may not be in the brain or head, but may have strong connection to other centers in the body such as the heart, or stomach, or genitals, or muscles, or other organs. Idea-beliefs, like perceptions both physical and psychic, may form a complex of feelings-thoughts-images with diverse locations and strong invocations under specific emotive and interactive relations. There may also be strong associations with whole body postures, like lying curled on one's side while sleeping as compared to standing stiffly at attention or of sitting in meditation as compared to running or walking. Let us avoid the fallacy that ideas are something we discover by sitting down and thinking. In fact, such thinking may simply be an exercise aimed at generating diverse alternatives or exploring relationships between abstract thoughts and a controlled stream-of-consciousness.

The idea-beliefs I am describing are the junctures between motivated actions, postures, and behaviors, and the conscious beliefs or ideas that shape those actions or responses. They are not based just in thinking, but in the connection between the thought and the belief that a particular thought is true and valued, an accurate guide for a response to a given situation. How conscious are we of the idea-belief that lies within our reactions to others or to situations which challenge or throw into question our idea-beliefs? This description seeks to break through the static assent of collective norms by looking at the individual character of the idea-belief as it acts to motivate meaningful behavior within the subject regardless of collective opinion or normative behavior. What are your core beliefs and what ideas do you hold as central to your life as a creative, intelligent being? In an alchemy of soul we do not proceed by ignoring or discarding idea-beliefs but by transforming those idea-beliefs into ever more clear, guiding, inspiring principles and inner resources for a complete and full spiritual awakening. This is a process of crystallization or distillation in which the idea-beliefs are refined over and over through experience and thus purified, distilled, sublimated, and re-birthed into ever more luminous attributes that enhance the quality of life.

What is the connection between your feelings and your ideas? This is a crucial juncture, the ways in which your ideas impact and are supported or resisted by your deepest feelings. In alchemies of soul, the link between ideas-beliefs and feelings should be increasingly clear and interrelated, consistent and mutually supportive. Where there is tension and conflict between ideas and feelings, between beliefs and emotional responses, there is an incompatibility, an energy of resistance that may well reflect an artificial link between ideas and feelings. For example, a woman believes she should be caring and supportive of others but she also wants time to reflect and explore her own inner nature or some form of personal spiritual practice. But the practice conflicts with her idea-beliefs that she should be available to her family or friends, so she postpones or denies her own need for meditation, art, music or self-reflection. Thus her idea-beliefs conflict with her deeper feelings about others and about herself. This can result in a kind of spiritual paralysis, a static compromise that inhibits her ability to move forward and results in a lack of growth and development which in turn will impede her relationships. Or, a man has a commitment to his children and to his job but there is a competition between the demands of each and his ideas of spending time with his children are contradicted by his compulsive work ethic, his belief that he must put the job first, even though he suffers feelings of emotional guilt or doubt about his work ethic.

The conjunction between belief-ideas and feelings is a critical threshold for evaluating the degree of spiritual integration. And here is another criterion: how consistent is your own perception of your feelings and beliefs with the perceptions of others? First of all, do you act according to your promises to others, is your word consistent and dependable, and do people trust you because they know that if you say you will act, you do in fact act as you promised? Or is there inconsistency between your thoughts, your words, and your deeds? What ideas do you hold of your commitment to fidelity in relationships, a fidelity of your word, or your promise, or your willingness to be present with others in their needs? The idea beliefs we are seeking are not just intellectual ideas, but engaged interactions that demonstrate the qualitative excellence of integrity and intentions. These are idea-beliefs connected to will and deed and promise, not just detached "ideas" afloat in a sea of abstract possibilities. And the perceptions of others are a crucial test of your integrity and clarity of mind, not because you conform to the expectations or demands of others (you may well resist such demands) but because your thoughts, words and deeds are truly consistent and create an honest portrait of yourself in relationship to others.

Another phenomenological aspect is found in the perception of how clearly your thoughts and beliefs link with your imagination. How does your imagination reflect consistency and inconsistency with your core idea-beliefs? By "imagination" I mean the free and spontaneous play of imagery, the visual, aural, and sensate experience of visual events seen in the mind as they spontaneously arise, revealing unexpected openings into the stream of consciousness. The point here is to look at the inconsistencies (acting in imagination in ways that contradict your real beliefs) as an index of the gap between your ideals and your actual psychic reactions to events and persons you encounter. Also it is important to look at the ways in which your imagination reflects consistency or inconsistency with core beliefs— perhaps inflating or exaggerating your self-image or expressing some confirmation that helps you to act consistently in an encounter. It is not a matter of overcoming all inconsistencies and counter-imagery. Personal growth and spiritual development depend on inconsistency! Without perceiving our imperfections and limits, we cannot move beyond them; we become caught in the illusion of our own accomplishments and in the false notion that we are more mature and more aware than others. This is a very dangerous and imposing barrier. Discontinuities are places of growth, they are the boundary where newness flows in and alternatives become meaningful because we seek to move beyond a limit.

The power of the imagination is great; it can reveal and it can conceal, open or close capacities and provide new ways of being, or reinforce fear and anxiety. Like all abilities, it can be abused and misused or be a means for transformation. On the Hermetic path, imagination plays the central and crucial role of providing the visionary basis for opening to new worlds and perceptions, not in an unreal sense but in actuality through a spiritual use of imaginative ability. The first step is to pay attention to all spontaneous mental imagery both while awake and while asleep. It is important to practice being as fully conscious of mental activity as possible, particularly spontaneous and uncontrolled activity. The stream of consciousness is broad and active and a keen observer of consciousness will quickly learn how active mind is on multiple levels of awareness. Even as I write, the imagery flows around the words and beneath the meanings and opens into powerful currents of visual association through images and spontaneous connections, all of which have particular meanings and significance. Self-knowledge requires real awareness of this inner activity and the ability to control and direct it without forcing the stream into channels cut by purely rational logic or communal beliefs that inhibit the spontaneous growth of mind and soul. To grow and develop, there must be an inner cultivation of perception, not a passive acceptance of norms or external beliefs. Continuous awareness is the goal, a free-flowing attention that works within multilevel consciousness to promote ever deepening integration and inner continuity.

In this process, imagination is one of the key integrative factors, not as abstract ideation, but as a visually constructive process by which we see the possibilities and vividly create the ideals we wish to embody through the integration of our thoughts, feelings, words and deeds. We must learn to envision the potential of our own nature, to give it substance and form through an inner process of imaginative construction, deconstruction, and reconstruction. We are each our own creator, and the power of the imagination is a great gift that can be used to focus consciousness in a free play of images directed toward a spiritual and visionary cosmos which we inhabit through inner inspirations. But these visualizations, coming through dreams and imaginative exercise of consciousness, are rooted in core idea-beliefs whose creative effectiveness depends on their degree of integration and interconnectivity with full feeling, full commitment, and full engagement of the will. Only when we can truly engage our whole being with our imaginative constructive power can we actually create the world in a new image. And at the depths of this empowerment through integration is the moving presence and inspiration of Spirit as an indwelling capacity to birth co-creators. The intensity of spiritual realization flows from an inner depth that goes far beyond the stream of consciousness and enters into the Mystery of All Being, into the ontology of deepest being and the inner transformative power of the sacred.

The quest is to find this power through the constant and creative recapitulation of our core idea-beliefs, not as static and fixed forms, but as central motivations to inhabit the fullness of our humanity in a living and holy cosmos This means that core-beliefs and feelings must undergo a transformative process, must be subjected to the warmth and heat of change and inner growth. This supports the inner nurturing of life as the spark that creates a new being. The cosmos as a living being is itself a core idea-belief; the soul as capable of transformation into a more aware being is another core idea-belief. The central role of human relationships as the testing ground of inner integrity and of the person as relational and interlinked to others are core idea-beliefs. The multilayered nature of consciousness and the interrelated correspondence between these layers and the human person is a heart-centered construct that may take many generations to fully comprehend and integrate as a core idea-belief. Spirit as a living presence, as an internal, immanent depth giving inspirational support and energetic content to maturation is a profound basis for human development. The Mystery of Spirit as an all encompassing and multidimensional basis for life and profound experiences of transcendence are also belief-ideas that may take many lifetimes to fully comprehend in a direct personal sense.

On the alchemical path, idea-beliefs are resources and tools for carrying out the Great Work of transformation. The key is not to adopt a certain set of these ideas or beliefs, but to evolve your own personal and individual view of the alchemical path that is receptive to and in search of the full potential of humanity and not just a search for personal fulfillment or inner peace. This is an ongoing, open-ended process, a quest that each person makes and must resolve in the depth of his or her being. In this work (and in my other writings), I introduce many such core idea-beliefs. But it is the responsibility of the individual to develop a unique synthesis, an "alchemy of soul", through the internalization of these and other idea-beliefs that can become the axis around which personal and interpersonal growth occurs. We dwell in an evolving cosmos at the local level and at the level of human global life; alchemy is a highly creative, energetic, and evolutionary process that takes great attention and inner consistency to fully realize. Thus idea-beliefs must be examined continually as part of the developmental process; these engaged, interactive idea-beliefs will undergo many stages of development and refinement. Starting where you are means discovering your core ideas and beliefs and beginning to subject them to constant review and consideration in terms of the quality and maturity of life lived. Every alchemist of soul must do his or her own work and that means finding the ingredients that work best for you in contributing to a world process of spiritual awakening and integration.

FEELINGS FROM THE CENTER

Finding our personal center is a crucial task. In carrying out this task, we must journey inward to the center and then we must bring those inner realizations into the world, into our creative relations and interactions. This is the dialectic of soul, to go within and to go without, and to mediate that process through a heart-centered way of life. We can start with the observation that the center is the spiritual heart, the human, individual heart, and thus there is a center for every being, a heart of felt and lived relations within an expansive world of feeling others. I say the heart and not the mind, but I do not exclude the mind nor deny in any way the role of mind in supporting the heart with direction, ideas, and a critical ability to think and reflect on alternative possibilities. But it is the heart that must amalgamate and alchemically join these possibilities into a committed way of life. The heart on the Hermetic path is the crucible of refinement and integration, the Vas Hermeticum, the vessel in which the mental and emotional aspects unite the psychic and the spiritual to give birth to the unique inner essence of soul that is the distinct creative realization of each individual. The alchemy of soul is a heart-centered process of inner transformation that leads through progressive stages to an ever-increasing subtlety of awareness and expansion of consciousness. Eventually, this expansion embraces the entire macrocosm, seen differently by different souls.

The heart and center of feeling is informed by mind through a healthy body and an active and creative will. These aspects of will, mind, heart, feeling, body and soul form the basis through which there is an interweaving that leads to an increasing illumination uniting the individual with an ensouled cosmos inhabited by soulful others. Soul in this case refers to a deep, feeling relationship with the world and with all its inhabitants. Soul is the medium of interconnection between beings, infused with Spirit, and personalized through unique characteristics of individual development. Soul is not an impersonal or "universal" quality, but a highly individual set of characteristics best described in terms of felt relationships with others. Feelings of compassion or kindness for others are soulful qualities that are distinctive for each individual. The basis for those feelings is Spirit as a life-presence that connects us through shared, creative energies. Soul mediates the felt-relationship to others, through individual qualities of psychic and mental-emotive ability, directed by will, in ways that may enhance or diminish soulful relations with others. Spirit infuses all life and creation with a full spectrum of possible creative relationships in a living cosmos and soul selects, responds to and personalizes those relationships.

Soul connects us to the souls of others; qualities of soul are reflected in the quality of our relationships with other beings as well, with animals, with the vegetative world, with the full range of organic and inorganic life. In a living cosmos, soul is the personalized, connective medium that sustains relatedness not only through individual intentions but also through our collective being. Soul is the medium of connection with the less visible and deeper stratum of psychic life — individually, collectively, and transpersonally. Groups of individuals may unite to form soulful relationships that are reflected in developing group consciousness, and a collective association may impact and influence the soul life of its individual members. This same principle is also true in connecting us with various alternative realms in human development, with various heavens, hells, Pure Lands, and psychic worlds and shamanic planes, all constructed as soulful projections of collective thought and belief. More expansively, soul is a medium through which we can know Spirit directly as well as the transpersonal magnitude of the Divine Mystery. Soul is the qualitative medium of relationship to all being and to all creative processes.

The soul has a mind just as it also has perceptions and feelings, as reflected through the body. It has memory, intelligence, imagination, self-awareness, and a capacity for self-transformation and deep communion with All-Being. But the heart of the soul is its capacity as a medium of relationship, a capacity to share soul with others, and an ability to explore the worlds of creation through soulful, visionary experience and co-participation in multiple realms and embodied existence. Soul is a feeling center and to know soul is to know the heart of creation through a sharing of perceptions and deeply felt concerns. It is also possible to know through mind and to experience All Being as a purely noetic reality, as a mental or intellective aspect of inner contemplation and transcendent knowledge, but this knowledge is often disjunctive, unconnected to the ensouled world and the world-making processes. Mental paths, those emphasizing the Jnana Marga, or path of mental realization, enter a realm of noetic being that has been emphatically transcendent and often result in a teaching that regards the human world as "illusory" (maya), a teaching similar to that of classical western Gnosticism. However, in Hermetic alchemies of soul, the path is one of world incarnation, emphasizing the value and centrality of embodiment and the immanent manifestations of divine life. In Hermeticism, the emphasis falls on the value of creaturely relationships, on the importance of love and kindness, and on the worth and creative importance of the incarnational process as a God-Knowing, transformative becoming.

Thus, feeling from the center means feeling from the center of soul, feeling through the medium of soul for the purpose of incarnating creative relationships with other soul-centered beings. There is nothing predetermined in this process, nothing coercive other than human traditions, mental habits and rigidities of mind that wish to impose on others a relative vision as absolute. All these feelings are relative! All these thoughts are relative! All these idea-beliefs are relative! Everything written in this book and all my other books is relative. Why? Because we human beings are relative in an infinite cosmos of possibility. But some thoughts, beliefs, and ideas, some feelings and realizations have more to offer human beings than some others, and some perceptions and ideas will have a greater impact and influence than others. And some will come closer to expressions of truth that carry a lasting value and worth. So each person must decide for him or herself which of these idea-beliefs best suit their own path of development and awareness. The Hermetic path as an alchemy of soul is a centered approach that requires cultivating an awareness of the value of soul-relationships, deeply felt connections with others, and with the very sources of creation in an evolutionary process of incarnate, personalized being (not world transcendence).

We are not abstract entities or simply ideas in the mind of a transient body. We are each a living mystery, an embodiment of spiritual energies situated in a complex of dynamic, interactive relationships that can act to enhance or contract our awareness and understanding. The mind-body-spirit relationship is far more complex and intricate than any dualistic theory can even begin to articulate. We are each a multidimensional and multi-energetic being and we are intimately interconnected to a multidimensional, highly energetic world-cosmos. The full spectrum of relationships far exceeds our present knowledge; we do not currently have even a rudimentary grasp of the Whole in all its intra-psychic dimensionalities. We are at a fairly early stage of planetary evolution and our knowledge is highly colored by cultural prejudice, historical conflicts, and bias of many sorts. The full exploration of soul and consciousness lies in the future and not in the present. But here and now we can begin to live in a more soulful way without having to hold anything more than a deep trust and willingness to explore the soulful life and to find, through individual gnosis, how it can lead to a transformation in awareness and in co-creative life. Starting where you are means opening to soul as a heart-centered perception of the world and others and to feel from that center the value and worth of interpersonal, soulful life.

A useful image here is the rose of the heart, the bud of which is closed, sheltered against external dangers, abuse, alienation, and fears. The Hermetic alchemy of soul requires us to open the rose of the heart and allow it to fully bloom, to create the circumstances which will allow for an opening that will not be impeded by the doubt or censure of others. The root metaphor here is the creation of a center that is both a home and a temple, a place of unfolding, of opening to newness without fear or danger. Generally, this is a slow and gradual process, a maturation of feeling and soulfulness that seeks to connect and sustain living qualities of perception in a heart-centered way. In order for this to happen in a natural and gradual way, there must be trust and faith in the heart's ability to perceive more than the simple reactions and responses of others. Perceiving and feeling in a heart-centered way is a path of learning to connect soulfully with every living creature, with life in all forms, with the spirit of place, with the intimacies of Spirit in all the multitudes of indwelling presence. Soul as the medium of perception and interconnection allows us to find relationships through a vast range of interactions that incorporates far more than human relations. The scale of soul-centered feeling has no boundaries in a psychic sense because it opens us to the mental, imaginative, creative life of All Being and a multitude of spiritual worlds and entities. In thinking about soul, the body is only one template, and the inner life of soul incorporates, exceeds, and surpasses that template of present physical life at the same time that it nourishes and sustains the many substructures of that corporeal embodiment.

Feeling from the heart requires opening to the soul of the world, not just to the souls of other human beings. And the soul of the world is rich and deep and dense with life and possibility of relationships and collective identities.[7] The challenge of feeling from the center is not to contract, not to close the petals of the rose because of the harshness and critical judgments of others. Opening from the center requires courage and inner strength and elasticity, a responsive, adaptive emotional life that can open to the hidden currents of the world soul, with all its turbulent, unresolved conflicts, contrasts, and differences. Opening to the world does not mean opening to a purely positive, integrated reality of others but opening to the real currents of pain, sorrow, and woundedness that cry out for healing even in the most rational and detached mind. Detachment itself can be a state of soul contraction or it can be a source of self-protection, a kind of shelter from the feelings and reactions of others. The diverse currents of the world soul are turbulent and challenging and the pain is there, representing the world's unrealized potential as a contracted or un-integrated dynamism that surges into soul awareness as a disequilibrium or counter-current to personal themes of development. Feeling from the center requires drawing from the roots of embodied life as a sacred gift that is nourished by Spirit but fully active in a multitude of beings pursuing highly diverse goals and engaging in actions often destructive and self-serving. These diverse existential currents do not vanish or dissolve in Spirit but retain their character as part of the fabric of creation.

In the soulful life of feeling, there is an alchemical process of grounding these feeling currents through a well-integrated life of spiritual development that is not distracted or contracted by the conflicts and contradictions within the world soul. We are not simply awakening to some ideal spiritual condition. We are creating the conditions for world peace and collective well-being; we are the responsible agents of that creation and our individual lives are a testimony of the maturation of the world soul into a more harmonized and well-integrated global reality. The quality of our life—its generosity, kindness, loving concern, its soulful relationships—is the medium of world transformation. This transformation does not come from some external agency, but from within and through responsible, non-manipulative, caring human relationships centered in soulful being. Spirit is there, a reservoir of power and potential, acting through creative energies to constantly and gently press us toward the realization of our latent capacities through inspired, incarnate action. But we must seek to actualize the potential of Spirit by feeling from the center the deeper needs we have as human beings to realize the as-yet unrealized capacity within us to create a harmonious global community of diverse, distinctive beings. Feeling from the center is not passive, but active and creative; it means trusting those perceptions as a basis for action and social transformation.

Starting where you are means initiating a more conscious awareness of soul life as a feeling relationship to all that lives, to each and every creature, condition, and place. You begin by allowing yourself to feel what you feel—good, bad, indifferent—and to study why and what you feel in terms of others, regardless of what you may think or they may say. What do you feel, in your heart, about this person, this living being, this place, this moment, this event, this action? Feel it from your heart-center without subjecting your feelings to mental criticism or thoughts concerning what you should or must feel. There is no should or must in feeling, there is only the feeling, only the emotive impression, only the empathic contact. What do you feel and what do others feel? Do not let your feelings be obscured or overridden by the feelings of others. Whatever he or she may feel, do not lose contact with your own feelings from the center. Stay centered in your feeling perceptions under all circumstances, no matter how tragic, painful or disturbing the situation. As you learn to do this, begin to cultivate a sense of relationship to all life, to every living creature, to everything in nature and to all beings. See yourself as a caretaker, nurturer, a guardian of life, as a soul dedicated to the preservation of life in the name of human development and species coexistence. See yourself as both a witness and as an active participant in the process of world transformation. Feel from the center the value and worth of your commitment to a healing process, as a peacemaker, and as a co-creator.

We stay centered in individual feelings as a source of perception that cannot be over-written by any collective or individual counter-impressions. Perhaps our feelings bring us into correspondence with others, or perhaps we disagree with others based on our individual emotional reactions. In both cases, we have an obligation in the alchemical process to sustain the integrity of individual feelings as a basis for soul-centered perception. But those feelings are subject to change, variation, even contradictions and conflict. This is natural, a consequence of feeling relationships which are not static, just as the individual is not static but changing and growing. The issue is to have the feeling, to note the feelings, to value the feelings

BUT not to cling to the feelings and certainly not to elevate those feelings over the feelings of others. Feeling is a medium of soul and relationship, not a static condition or a fixation on particular feelings. Like sense perceptions, feelings are a basis for knowing the world and others, and we can trust our feelings to inform our awareness and to provide interconnection and relationship. But feelings are transient. The impressions of soul connection are more lasting if we can allow the feelings to flow without attachment to particular moods and with a freedom that allows and encourages fluid, flowing responsiveness.

Feeling from the center means allowing soul to guide the individual in terms of heart-felt impressions that contribute to soul development. This is not always a matter of positive feelings. Sometimes, soul growth can only occur through challenge, conflict, and feelings of intensity that throw into question or doubt a particular state of soul or soul relations. The soul center is a dynamic, changing center developing through states of expansion and contraction. As we grow, we learn to adapt our rhythms to stages of opening or closing as natural conditions of soul life as we encounter challenges and life-situations that break up complacency and routine. Challenging circumstances are the very conditions that provide new opportunity for growth and insight. Thus feelings from the center may not be positive or simple feelings of happiness; such feeling will inevitably engage with issues of sorrow, pain, anxiety, discomfort, and challenges of many kinds. But those feelings are the very stuff of soul life and are vital resources for spiritual transformation. An excellent index of soul life is to examine how well we handle crisis, conflict, and emotional turbulence, to measure our capacity to flow into every and any situation and remain centered and alive to the feelings of others, but increasingly rooted in Spirit and in the depths of world consciousness. The goal of feeling from the center is to stay open, to be receptive without being un-centered or overwhelmed by feelings from inner depths or from our relationships with others. This is a great challenge and takes continual effort, refinement, and a deeply grounded inner-outer balance.

TRUSTING YOUR UNKNOWN SELF

On the paths of the alchemy of soul, we cannot begin with a conception of the known end. The goal is to explore the mystery of self, to develop unrealized potential, and to actualize a spiritual capacity that is unique and individual. An alchemy of soul is a process of exploration, creation, and self-discovery rooted in our relationship to others and to a living cosmos. In this exploration, we also create the possibility of actualizing a depth of awareness and insight that is often unrecognized by the ordinary, conditioned individual. Most human beings are not aware of the depth and capacity of their soul nature. This depth can only be known through the efforts we each make to actualize our potential in a personal, individual way within the context of a community of self-actualizing others. The Hermetic community is a community of soul and heart whose members may dwell in any culture or time as examples of human beings who dedicate themselves to the full development of their spiritual potential in a personal and non-judgmental realization of interconnective being. Those realizations are diverse and multifaceted, not reducible to a particular image or a fixed set of ideas. They express an inner capacity for multiple forms of self-realization and spiritual attainment. Thus, the path is formed according to the capacity and inner ability of the individual and supported by Hermetic communities of like-minded others.

Starting where you are means trusting that you are more than you presently realize, that you have a spiritual capacity whose depths are unknown and whose actualization will require effort and clear intention on your part. This trust is based on the perception of the greater mystery of life which surrounds and encompasses us If we reduce life to a known quantity, to paradigms of humanity and nature that assume a bounded condition, rejecting possibility or unseen potential, then we mask the infinite within, and we accept our conditioned limitations as the measure of our species or of our individual capacity. But we do not know our full depths and we certainly do not fathom the breadths and heights of creation nor of all other possible worlds, beings, or realities. In an infinite and expansive universe, in the multidimensional inwardness of being, we can discover newness and revelation that far exceeds our "known" perceptions and beliefs. When we engage in an alchemy of soul, we begin a journey into the unknown, into the mystery of creation and into an infinite universe of possibility where the guiding principles of our path help to shape our realizations. How we live and what we believe and think, what we feel and desire, all shape the inner realization of our potential. Therefore it is of great importance that the values we hold be conscious and self-selected as guidelines to the discovery of the unknown. The ancient Hindu-Buddhist adage is certainly true that "the mind becomes that which it contemplates" not through conformity to existing norms but through an active, creative shaping of will, imagination, and thought.

We each choose the path we follow, even in the most oppressive circumstances, and the integrity of that choice produces a result that is marked in the flesh and soul. In the alchemy of soul, this choosing is a conscious act, open to newness and change, qualities which are inseparable from our development as both individuals and as a species seeking maturity. Our freedom of choice stems from an inner courage and determination to change, to not accept collective norms or values as necessarily most appropriate for the realization of our full potential. We are not a "blank slate" on which society or community writes its mandates and expectations; we come into this world with unique and special gifts, abilities, talents, limitations, and inner capacities of Spirit. Insofar as we allow family, community, and society to write on the slate of soul values and goals which come only from without, we risk denying our full inner potential.[8] The narrative we write should be a narrative that is not overwritten by social demands and expectations; the co-creative context is a sharing of perspectives that allows each person the dignity of personal choice in relationship to others. And this process is exploratory, not simply a matter of rote learning and unquestioning ingestion. When we engage the question of soul and self, we begin a process of discovery that connects with all internal states, imaginings, reflections and feelings that we can validate or discard through a constructive process of learning. But first we must be open to the power and potential of individual worth, we must have faith in the unknown capacities of Spirit that are yet unrealized and perhaps even unrecognized. We are not what we appear to be to others, nor are we what we may appear to be to our own introspection. In order to fully actualize hidden capacity, it is important to accept psychic perceptions as relevant and genuinely important. Dreams, visions, voices, intuitions, empathic response, creative ideas — all of these add to the depth and richness of our perceptions and understanding.

The soul as a lived experience is grounded in feeling and connectedness to the world, to others, and to a greater sense of human destiny and purpose than mere fulfillment of social duties. Soul, from the Greek *psyche* or Latin *anima*, refers to the principle of vitality, strength, life, will, desire, passion, heart, and as inscribed by ancient Greeks such as Pythagoras and Plato, "the soul of man is undying" (*anthropou psychè athanatós esti*).[9] The motivating quality of soul most important for development and connection or relationship with others is Eros, love that is passionate and feeling-centered. The soulful individual is one who does not deny the value of feelings, or erotic relationships, that celebrate Beauty in human experience in a non-possessive, nurturing manner. Passions of soul are guided by principled living and clear values. The exploration of self and inner potential requires a continual cultivation of focused attention on issues of development that overturn older ways of thinking and believing. As we delve into the mystery of the human being, into our unrecognized potential, we must engage our will in a process of assimilating what we learn and discover. This is not a matter of control as much as it is a matter of intentional sincerity and clarity of purpose. It is an inwardly directed purpose, an intention to surpass the closed world of self-interest for a more open and receptive way of relationship to others as teachers, as guides, but also as companions and friends who share the journey, who are also on pilgrimage.

It is not necessary to believe in the immortality of the soul. The alchemy of inner life involves the present embodiment, the incarnational creative moment of the present, not necessarily the far future or possible continuation after death. Allow the question of immortality to remain open, unknown, just as the inner depths of Spirit are unknown, and in that state of openness, have trust in the processes of transformation. Soul knowledge is not based in simple, immediate rational perceptions; it is based in pervasive feeling and the cultivation of subtle awarenesses whose contents are linked to dreams, myth, and the invisible worlds of imagination, visions, and mystical experience. Soul knowledge opens onto the horizon of all possible worlds, onto the horizon of the fullness of Being, and into the Holy Mother Spirit as a creative source of inmost awakening to human potential. The space within which this alchemical process occurs is a fullness of potential grounded in all possible ways of knowing. It does not privilege the rational or the immediately observable; it recognizes the rational and observable as resources for growth and development, as rudimentary skills necessary for managing life in a physical, pragmatic sense. But life is far more than a response to immediate needs and physical boundaries, it is rich with potential far beyond the pragmatic moment.

To live soulfully is to live with an openness to the unknown, with a receptivity to all forms of knowing, and with a heart-centered ethic of mutual and co-creative concern for the well-being and growth of all others. To live in this way also means to give up obsessive preoccupation with our own needs, to move into a shared interactive caring that works to sustain the souls of others, including the soul of the world. This requires each person to accept responsibility for soulful living, to choose a pathway that models a soulful way of life. The alchemy of soul moves from the present, the immediate now of who we are, into an emergent process of inner change and development dedicated to the exploration of potential as a creative process. I do not know myself fully. This is a Hermetic maxim, a typological observation that all human beings are in a process of change and they are each capable of being more aware, more soulful, and more intelligently alert to the needs of others. We are growing into a world of mutual concern that requires us to maintain our capacity for individual thought and self-expression even as we grapple with problems on a global scale. We do not know the future; it is veiled behind the shadows of human greed, possessiveness, violence, and indifference to the rights and integrity of others. As long as those shadows fall on others, they will not be able to live soulfully or as freely as necessary for full maturation of soul potential.

Alchemies of soul create pathways of dedication to inner growth and development over the course of a lifetime, guided by an intuitive trust in Spirit and inner life as a primary resource for human development. The knowledge we can access through mind and soul is far greater than is presently recognized or accepted; the depths of human consciousness far exceed the small island of ordinary human awareness. We are like travelers who are fascinated by new experiences but who have no memory, as though only momentary sensation could hold our attention, like "soldiers in the mist" who must everyday reconstruct the recent past because we do not retain or learn from all that has impressed the human spirit with its multitude of lessons. So we live on the island of the immediate and everyday and take refuge in the thought that because we get through the day successfully we are masters of our fate. But all too often we are only slaves to the immediate and to the everyday ordinariness of external events. The alchemy of soul seeks to throw off this cloak of everyday forgetfulness and to embrace a new openness to change and personal growth by listening attentively to the inner voice, the imaginative image, the subtle memory of another kind of speaking. We are called on this journey, not by an outer power, but by an inner urgency to discover capacities latent but active beneath the conventional operations of the everyday surface mind.

We must delve within, undergo initiations, and descend into the shadows of our own soul and into the collective imagery and struggles of diverse human beings over millennial time if we wish to attain a fuller

36

sense of self. We must be willing, like the shamans of old, to die to the younger immature local self in order to be reborn into a more responsible way of life based in loving concern for all, free of blinding self-serving interest and receptive to global insight. We must be willing to change, evolve, and relinquish ideas formed in our youth or in middle years, not clinging to them simply because at one time we became convinced of their validity. Each year is a rebirth; each season, a new opportunity to learn and to grow; each moon, a possible time for new dreams and visions. Starting where you are means recognizing that you are not finished, not complete, not actualized to the fullness of your being. Your accomplishments are transitory; your successes, only steps along the way; the recognition of others is merely an affirmation of certain capacities, but not an understanding of the whole of your being. The whole of your being is veiled, cloaked by the energies of social life, relationships, commitments, patterns of actions, habits and recurring emotional states. To move beyond the pattern, to move into newness and emergence means to strip away the known and to open to the unknown, to a possibility within that has not yet expressed Spirit.

Trusting your unknown self is like the unwrapping of a precious gift given to you by an unknown admirer; you are cautious, but curious, alert with interest, wanting to know directly who it is that gives this gift. The gift is mysterious; it is a gift of unique ability, a gift that only you can fully actualize. And the giver of this gift is embedded in the very making of the world, in the coming-into-being of this creative moment. In accepting the gift, you make a bond with the giver to explore its potential, not because it is required of you, but because you freely and willingly choose this exploration. And the uncertainty is natural, a function of limits and boundaries that have not yet been crossed. As you move into that unexplored country of soul, into the felt world of living beings and intertwined, co-creative exchange, you will discover a new potency. It is up to you to shape that potency into form and intentional expression, and the more you can draw on the full range of your capacities, the greater the shaping and making. We go through stages of making and unmaking, creating and recreating expressions that seek to incorporate ever deeper awareness and insight.[10] We seek to embody, to incarnate our soulful being, into forms of life that are truly expressive of our full capacities. What we create, our words, actions, relationships, are tokens of this process that touch several surfaces, that penetrate a few dimensions, but which constantly call us to yet more expression and being.

Trusting your unknown self means cultivating a faith in your own potential and in the potential of others to assist and inspire you toward greater self-realizations. It is a gentle process, a long initiation of gradual empowerment punctuated by sudden visionary leaps and spiritual encounters. Some others that you meet can, in fact, assist you on your way; they can act as teachers; they can give initiations, help you to unfold your potential for inner growth and spiritual realization. But the greatest teacher is within, Spirit abiding in the heart of creation, an inner power and presence that is the incarnate activity of utmost potential. The creative energies of Spirit are everywhere active and alive, flowing forth and back within the world of soul, carrying with them immense possibilities in currents of shared and transpersonal perceptions. We may expand into a living cosmos of multidimensional being or contract into an isolated world of self-preoccupied sorrow, pain, and alienation. Both experiences are possible and actual, even within the heart of one human being. But the challenge is to trust in creative inspiration and, with humility, to search out a soulful way of living that opens to the mystery and hidden capacity of being human. We begin with trust in this unknown self, this uncertain possibility and direction, and we begin our journey with the first step — to accept our limits, where we are now, and to trust that we can move beyond them to a better and wiser way of life.

1. Lyndy Abraham, 1998: 61-62.
2. See Glossary for more Hermetic definitions.
3. Jane Kopas, 1994: 32-51.
4. Roger Loomis, 1991: 32-34.
5. Tobin Hart, 2000: 31-54, "Inspiration as Transpersonal Knowing."
6. The terms "host" and "guest" are from Ch'an Buddhism where the roles are sometimes reversed in a single action-dialogical encounter between master and student; see Master Sheng-yen, 2001.
7. See Robert Sardello, 1992, for more on the soul of the world.
8. John Locke popularized the idea of the Tabula Rasa, mind as a "blank slate" or "dark closet" waiting to be filled by learned social values and behaviors; Leibnitz thought of it as a block of marble waiting to be carved and borrowed from scholars the saying that "there is nothing in the intellect that is not first in the senses." See: Jonathan Dancy & Ernest Sosa, 1994: 503, passim.
9. See Plato's *Phaedrus*, 246a-212; also Walter Burkert, 1985: 321-325.
10. On the visionary processes of making and unmaking worlds, see Lee Irwin, 1996.

CHAPTER TWO
REVISING COLLECTIVE GROUNDWORK

Engaging in the practice of the alchemy of soul is a process of differentiation that leads through a separation from more embedded, unquestioned values and practices to a more conscious, self-selected orientation. This is not a matter of wholesale rejection or denial of inherited values, but it is a matter of sifting through the present and past in order to bring to the surface just those values that affirm and further human development in a direct personal sense. It is also not a matter of simply indulging in personal passions and pursuits in the name of individual freedom or autonomy. The alchemy of soul is a relational alchemy; it is not an isolated activity of strict inwardness, but a twofold dynamic that heightens inner awareness at the same time that outer awareness expands into a living cosmos of multiple other beings, all of whom are part of a creative, interdependent process. What must be broken up is the tendency to petrify and formalize relationships based on inherited values that act to suppress or deny individual spiritual development or creative exploration in social relationships. This is not an appeal to anarchy, but to creative, living development that values the worth of the individual as a primary center of human good. In turn, this positive valuing can lead to more fluid and dynamic human communities in which commitment to group life is truly balanced with the pursuit of individual creative gifts and abilities.

We are born into a family, we have parents and siblings, friends, community, work relationships, acquaintances, and distant relatives, as well as soulful resonance with like-minded others. We are also part of a particular cultural time and place, an existential circumstance that is highly influential and further embedded in a variety of communication technologies and electronic, global networks opening onto very expansive international horizons. We are no longer isolated by nation, language, culture, or strictly ethnic identities, as these continuously interact and reform with increasing international and global impact. Our history as human beings is no longer the history of one nation or one segment of culturally dominant others. Our history is now the history of all humanity, stretching back into aeons. Through an ever-branching series of pathways, our shared histories lead us toward a multitude of probable futures where, increasingly, the actions of any segment of humanity impacts all other segments. We are no longer separated by seas or oceans, mountains, deserts, or miles. Today, the impact of a single event is felt on a global scale; how much more so, tomorrow? Thus, revisioning collective groundwork is an imperative feature of any true alchemy of soul.

I do not wish to deny the value of the local context of individual life, but to point toward the necessity of bringing that local context into a global framework in such a way that it enhances the whole. What must be overcome is the barrier mentality, the bound world that denies its members the freedom of knowing the whole. No doubt some communities will be inclined to resist and foster an inner group identity (or ethnicity) that has precedence over all global concerns. And, in fact, the value of the individual is an image of the value of the community. It is not a matter of merging or losing identity, but of sustaining and heightening identity through relationships with the diversity of plural cultures and systems of thought and belief. The local and immediate is the living context, not the abstraction of the "global" in a purely mental sense. But do we live in fearful isolation from the whole or do we live with reciprocity and respectful concern for the well-being of all communities? As we sustain differences, as we develop unique perspectives, skills, abilities, and insights due to our community relationships, we also develop a resource for contributing to the balance within the whole because we can offer those resources where they are most needed. Having a place, a center, a home, is good. Sharing what we have learned in relative and conditional circumstances is also good. And bringing that good into the world is a way to help other communities and other persons to evolve and develop their understanding through shared resources and insights.

But the good of place and home and community must also be a creative, individuated good that has been attained through spiritual work and transformation and not simply through an absorption of past ideas or customary attitudes. The task is not a simple reiteration of community life or values, of family perspective, but the alchemical transmutation of those values and practices in a living heart and soul that personalizes and recreates the image of humanity through an individual's direct experience and learning. The good is a fully actualized good in the life, thoughts, words, and deeds of soul; this means that the inherited good is subject to careful examination and reflection that is open to a global horizon of resources and perspectives and not just to the local perspective. The balance required is found in a willingness to value what is local and communal, as well as that which is global and intracultural, in the dynamics of a creative exploration that seeks to foster inner awareness in a more expansive and inclusive horizon. The ground for this expansion is Spirit as the abiding creative energy within all, not just within me or my community. The task of spiritual transformation does not proceed through privileging only one community, only one system of thought or spirituality, but through interactions which include the widest possible range of spiritual alternatives.

The Hermetic perspective in its many-branching pathways seeks to foster transformation in every receptive soul without imposing a particular system of thought; it is an alchemy based in broad spiritual principles whose applications must be individually developed and applied. And this means there must be a close scrutiny of communal values and historical conditions that have informed the spiritual evolution of humanity. And yet, it is inevitable that a Hermetic perspective be a local and relative creation. As a relative creative alchemy, the inner work of development is inseparable from the local and immediate circumstances and therefore the specific community of the seeker. The dialectic is three-sided in the sense that it involves the inner potential and capacity of each individual practitioner; the practitioner's community of direct, personal relationships; and the informative, creative inspirations of Spirit working in and through All to bring about realizations of specific potential. These realizations may well be communal realizations; that is, they can occur only through the combined efforts of various individuals whose interactions provide a new basis for spiritual realization. Thus development is not isolated to the individual nor does it find its locus in strictly individual realizations.

Alchemies of soul are relational alchemies in which each person undergoes transformation in and through dynamic, emotional relationships as well as through inner awakening to spiritual potential. Starting where you are also means starting with your present relationships and evaluating those relationships in terms of how they may contribute or inhibit both personal and communal development. This includes evaluating the larger forum of a particular cultural milieu, looking carefully at the presuppositions and expectations that are embodied in others as carriers of particular traditions, ideas, or systems of value. A key question here is how we each distinguish ourselves within a cultural framework that we may not fully embrace or that we may consciously seek to transform. This does not mean necessarily adopting radical attitudes or actions, but rather forming genuine commitments to creative change and a consistent pattern of contributions, both positive and critical, to on-going communal development. The alchemy of soul calls for something more than a simple affirmation of culture and community; there is a need for an ongoing process of self-other evaluation that seeks new manifestations of potential in ways that exemplify the deepest possibilities within human nature.

The great challenge of social life is not to be caught in the widespread assumption that normative values are best or that collective assent is a reflection of moral or spiritual truth. Assent may well be a barricade against seeing inculcated prejudice and bias as well as a type of collective reinforcement of privilege and position or status. Normative values may marginalize the less empowered and deny rights or freedom to those who do not share such widespread assumptions. Further, collective norms may well inhibit spiritual growth by denying the value of inner life or by dismissing alternative values and more marginal explorations of human potential. The challenge is to face the unknown by cultivating an inner trust in direct perception and experience that can then be brought into the public forum as a resource for communal exploration. Continually, we are seeking to break the normative pattern that sees only the obvious and denies the value of the improbable or the personal and subjective. The alchemical test is to bring forward the inner work so that it can contribute to collective life and so that it may be further refined through dialogue and personal interactions with others. In this process, the social world undergoes the challenge of integrating diverse individuals into a rich and creative context of interaction and learning. This can only happen to the degree to which we can let go of outer expectation and embrace the value of inner spiritual work directed by an ethic of loving kindness and creativity.

OLD ORDER THINKING

I describe "old order thinking" as basically hierarchical and authoritarian with a strong emphasis on expectations of conformity and obedience to norms that are external to individual needs and/or unique abilities. The good of old order thinking is that it provides a framework and a structure within which the individual and a community can live with a clear sense of the external demands and expectations of social life. But this kind of thinking is often a cultural artifact of social privilege and status usually inaccessible to all members of the culture or community. In general, such thinking has been done by men and reinforced male social and religious status in the form of religious teachings that privilege male-centered spiritualities. The normative structure of such a cultural pattern is a top-down hierarchy of institutional control dictated by the elite members of those institutions and carried out by legal, political, and customary rules often protected and enforced by militant punishment of those who violate such laws. In the context of religious institutions, penalties for such infraction have been historically aggressive and dictatorial, ranging from arrest, torture, and death to fulminations against non-conformists and censorship in local communities against those seeking alternative spiritual directions. This type of thinking emphasizes conformity to male sanctioned law that does not recognize the rights of all members of society to seek spiritual growth through personal choice and inclination.

Another disturbing feature of old order thinking is its tendency to hypostatize, or over-value, its ideological concerns under the banner of immutable revelation or claims to absolute truths and to assume the universality of those truths for other human beings. Neither of these claims can be proven to be true in the face of multiple religious traditions whose diversities call into serious question the exclusive over-valuation of any particular form of spirituality. Religious truths are relative and, like any truth claims, demonstrate through comparative analysis a partial good whose cultural and historical context limits the universality of its ideals and goals. In old order thinking, alternative values are rejected for an exclusive, local cultural truth closed to the impact of genuine comparative thought and study. This comparative analysis of truth claims does not mean that all such claims are equally relative. In fact, some claims may be more valuable and more significant than others, but which claims are those? Such values cannot be dictated by others, nor can they be genuinely valued unless they can be understood in a context of free choice and inner affirmation through personal exploration and commitment. It is not a matter of an external authority determining the values each person holds, but instead a new order of thinking that fosters freedom of choice in the pursuit of spiritual knowledge. Revelation is not a past event, but one that takes place now, in the present, in the heart of living individuals who honor deeply the emergent processes of continuing creation.

Old order thinking is caught in the structures of its own authority. This is true in science as well as in religion. The issue is not authority, but free investigation of matter, nature, and spirit unbound by aggressive denials or haughty rejection of alternative truths by those all too often completely ignorant of religious history or comparative philosophy. Most science does not offer spiritual truths but material proofs based on highly formalized methodologies of observation and testing. These methodologies are not grounds for moral or spiritual development; nor are they grounds for the rejection of religious claims to truth. The work of those in science may well contribute to our future understanding of spiritual life, but not through the basis of scientific authority or methodology. The alchemy of soul is not based in the strict investigation of the material world but finds its center in the heart of a moral, spiritual, living being whose relationships with others are not determined by strictly material causes or by simple external conditioning. The soul cannot be observed scientifically, but this does not mean that "soul" has no value or meaning simply because it eludes the grasp of scientific materialism. The scientific orthodoxy's denial of soul and Spirit is an expression of old order thinking when it posits its own authority as the only valid criterion for knowing life or nature or human community. Like religious autocracy, scientific thinking can easily make truth claims about its own "revelations" that undercut human freedom and the integrity of a personal search for understanding.

Old order thinking rises through a communal sanction based in unreflective, collective conformity to values or goods that reinforce institutional and economic norms that benefit the few and not the many. In old order thinking, privilege is primary, personal power is an extension of control over others and is not unilateral or dialogical but coercive and dominant. It does not hear, does not listen and respect the beliefs of others, but insists that its own truth is more significant than any voice from the margin, that a dominant majority is more valuable than a non-dominant minority. Old order thinking loves the sound of its own voice and speaks over the voices of others; it dictates terms that support its own good and way of life, often failing to see the consequences of its aggression and denial of others. Thus Christ is crucified by the Sanhedrin, in the name of a collective truth, and yet this death becomes the seed for Christian institutions which will also deny and condemn others. Old order thinking makes claims about the superiority of one race over others or celebrates a particular culture as superior to those of the "third world" or develops weapons of mass destruction in the name of progress. Old order thinking is based in a lack of awareness; its vision is focused on a narrow horizon of self-interest and power that does not consider the long-term consequences of its actions nor care about the impact of those actions on the free life of others. Old order thinking is caught in the paradigm of competition and dominance, and enacts a tragic parody of human development as a Darwinian drama of aggressive relations.

In moving beyond old order thinking, it is necessary to start with a fundamental principle that all beings have a right to freely explore, but not exploit, the world and its life affirming alternatives. This principle requires respect and love for others as primary over any and all economic or material needs or wants. Integral, more progressive science is based in furthering our understanding of interrelatedness; it values the part as much as the whole and seeks to understand complexity as differentiation and creative emergence. Such science may offer multiple paradigms for considering the spiritual value of human relationships and can take an open-ended view of the spiritual world as a horizon for possible study rather than simply rejecting it on the basis of material or ideological preconceptions. In religion, comparative studies have also opened the doors to complexity and diversity as a source of human creative understanding. The relative value of religious authority does not undercut the value of religious experience as interpreted by practitioners open to the diverse claims of other spiritual traditions. The real values of spiritual teachings, like those of science, are the ways in which they enhance and deepen our understanding of the creative processes of life in a direct personal sense. In revising collective groundwork, it is necessary to accept a certain degree of relativity in all truth claims without abandoning values which truly enhance human life and relationships. The relativity in science and religion is a creative foreground for exploration that allows for differences and yet seeks to ground those differences in genuinely compassionate thinking and care for others.

While complexity may introduce relativity, it also brings about greater correspondence between diverse parts of the whole. Rather than seeing the world as polarized into simple opposing forces or organizations or belief systems, it is more coherent to recognize that in a relative world, these large scale tensions tend to collapse into a great diversity of shades and colors that reveal many partial correspondences. So while there may be points of difference, there may also be points of similarity, particularly at the level of individual relationships. The new integral thinking values diversity while also seeking to understand wholeness and completeness, to see how complexity creates points of contact that support larger scale development. Thus Indian Buddhism may impact Chinese Daoism and produce Japanese Zen; or Islam and Christianity may interact and result in various forms of alchemy or Rosicrucianism. Yoga may impact many non-Hindu spiritual traditions and Chinese herbal medicine and acupuncture may offer additional benefits to spiritual healing in America or Europe. In the increasing complexity of global relations, old order thinking must collapse into new integral models of science, religion, and spirituality through a complex integration of soul on an individual level. The central value is not competition, but the preservation of life, nurturing our global future as cooperative participants in a long term, sustained effort.

Valuing diversity and human relationship restructures the nature of institutional power as well. Perhaps this is best illustrated in the institution of the family. Creative growth and development requires respect and appreciation for difference, not conformity to a dominant norm or to the demands of an intolerant parent or relative. Breaking down old order thinking requires establishing a new priority that seeks to foster creative development and allows for differences in temperament and taste. Power in the family should be reciprocal and interactive, not dictatorial or based on aggressive punishment for failure to conform to another person's attitudes or practices. Spiritually, freedom of choice in terms of religious interests should be no less than freedom of choice in studying science or history. Personal interest should be given encouragement that fosters appreciation of diversity and teaches respect for differences rather than condemnation for lack of conformity. Children have rights from the moment they are born (and before birth); they are not simply there to be shaped by external control of others. They have a right to choose a pathway that fosters individual growth and development. The role of parents in this process is to provide a loving environment in which trust and affection support a diversity of interests. Parents certainly offer strong models for development and this is a situation in which children can learn to develop tolerance, respect for others, and diversity in perspectives.

Another important, and perhaps central, feature of integral development is the role of the feminine. Feminine, woman-centered values are greatly needed to foster appropriate attitudes of tolerance and respect, and they are also needed to foster a sense of independence that does not deny that same independence to others. Women, perhaps more than men, understand this need for independence without denying the independent worth of the other. The history of oppression of women is the history of old order thinking that sought to elevate men while denying to women their autonomy and freedom of action and choice. In the integral cultures of the future, women will certainly model a new tolerance and support for diversity. Power in terms of intuitions as well as in teachings of all kinds can benefit from womanly perspectives that share power through trust in cooperative action and dialogical decision-making. The truth claims of such leadership will not rest on authoritarian, unquestioned assumptions, but will emerge through the trials of human relationships to fashion supportive networks in which diversity, not conformity, is the rule. Such networks of shared ability and authority can create interconnections and cooperation where old order masculine thinking tended to polarize and establish dangerous and violent boundaries. Cooperative networks must overcome the tendencies to create advantage for one party over the other; there must be shared power and shared decision making to sanction the value gained for all parties concerned.

Thus the emergence of new integral thinking for spirituality, and any alchemy of soul, requires a path that values others, is receptive and flexible in decision-making, and fully appreciates the relativity of individual and communal perspectives. In revising collective groundwork, the responsibility for these changes requires each individual to contribute to a variety of networks that support mutuality and cooperation in order to induce change in the community at large. In a daily sense, this means cultivating attitudes of respect for others, particularly others who may think quite differently or have a different cultural perspective. It also means standing forth as a loving presence that seeks to transform a violent and competitive worldview into more loving and tolerant spiritual perspectives. This requires courage and commitment that understands how to deflect and transform negative intentions and denials while also knowing how to cultivate a positive and growth-oriented outlook in others and within oneself. Alchemies of soul require that we each take a soulful approach to present circumstances as agents of change and transformation. We are each a presence of love and care if we choose to inhabit a more integral space open to shared relationships and mutual respect. Overturning old order thinking is a slow process and it takes great consistency and inner determination to provide the new model of integral spirituality.

LEARNING FROM THE PAST

The past is rich in teachings and events which can inform a present-centered spirituality. Individual lives are also rich in incidents and encounters which have contributed to who we are in the present. The places in which we live and develop and come to maturity also have a past and a history that is part of us. These three pasts, the past of humanity, the past of the local environment and culture, and the past of the individual are all linked through patterns of interpretation and embodiment. In order to learn from the past, it is necessary to see through the veils of immediate concern and need and into the multiplicity of influences that have shaped our humanity over thousands of years of collective interaction. The visionary poet William Blake once wrote that a man's kingdom was all the countryside he could survey from standing on the roof of his own home, and there is a truth in this observation worth remembering. Human perspectives are too easily shaped by the immediate and local; we tend to imagine our world in terms of our current place, a particular circle of friends, a specific work environment, or a certain cultural present. There is a strong tendency to generalize our own experiences as the experiences of others, to draw parallels where there are only the most tangential relationships to our own subjective world. The present all too easily becomes a substitute for the past and is not understood as a creative ground of differences.

The other side of Blake's comment may be read quite differently. What we perceive in the local sense is indeed the boundary of our understanding, and immediate perceptions become the defining characteristic of our own stubbornly held limitations. Then we may read the metaphor as if we are at the center of our own universe and mistake the local for the cosmic and the immediate for the eternal. But we are rarely cosmic or eternal in the local, everyday sense. We are shaped by a multitude of influences that far exceed our immediate perceptions or environment, and yet we grasp onto the local and immediate as through it were unquestionably real. We are far more deeply connected to horizons of perception which we often reject as illusions or mere imaginings. Lacking historical knowledge, lacking a genuine sense of human experience outside of the local, we tend to deny the value of alternative perceptions and to dismiss the fine, subtle edge of perceptions that lead us beyond the everyday. We miss the lessons of the human historical struggle to realize and integrate alternative awareness into an emergent understanding of what it means to be human and fully perceptive. We too often truncate perception in the name of rationalism or common prejudice and deny the value of alternative modes of awareness as marginal and eccentric. But the heart of human development has long thrived on a cultivation of perceptions that go far beyond the normative, rational, everyday mind. Such cultivation requires breaking free of the binding prejudices of the local, and learning to truly see. As Blake also said, "He who sees the Infinite in all things sees God but he who sees the Ratio [reason] sees only himself."[1]

History is valuable because it teaches us that that which is local and immediate is not the only truth and what we may experience as individual human beings may be experienced differently by others. Learning from the past we clearly see that the local is constantly held up as universal and imposed on others as a truth greater than their own. Thus missionaries of religions, political doctrines, economic theories, and scientific thought have all too often asserted their own prejudices as good for all and as surpassing the value of what others may hold to be also true and worthy. Further, history also teaches that overall, people resist strongly the imposition of an external and often alien "truth" that denies the value and worth of their own way of life. Colonialism, economic opportunism, aggressive capitalism, and political dominance have all proceeded on the assumption of the superior value of one way of life over another. Those less empowered have suffered tremendous deprivation, loss, and denial of their rights as human beings in the name of profit, religious truth, or scientific advancement whenever it is imposed from without rather than embraced from within. War, destruction, and death are the consequences of the imposition of one way of life on another; the greater the force, the greater the resistance. There is no one way, no one truth that all humanity can embrace as valid in the context of human diversity and cultural-spiritual differences.

What is emerging is a global context of shared truths, truths whose value do not serve one interest group through the denial of others. Valid truths of the future will be truths grounded in the realization of relative values in application; such truths will be, by necessity, modest in claiming to represent others. It is not the absolute truthfulness of the claim, be it the laws of gravity or the saving grace of Christ, but the relative value of those truths in a particular context of living, in specific circumstances that require choice and freedom of internal decisions and outer actions. This does not mean that the truths that we hold are of any less significance as guiding principles by which to live; it only means that such guiding principles are open to change and development based on interaction with the truths of others. What history reveals is the damaging impact of absolute claims, the destructive and corrosive effects of willful, ungracious assertions of truth that override the values and concerns of others and thereby create resentment, opposition, and hardening denials and resistance. History provides innumerable lessons in the destructive impact of absolute denials of the truths of others and it shows the aggressive lines of conflict and division that continue to destroy the inner fabric of human connection and shared vision. Learning from the past requires us to learn the hard lessons of oppression, denial, and bigotry that have suppressed human creative freedom and failed to honor the diversity that gives humanity strength and inner creative vitality.

The recognition of diversity in perspectives, of the value of the unique and creative vision that opens a vista on new perceptions, requires no absolute claims. It requires only a relative claim — that throughout history many tens of thousands of human beings in every generation have "opened the doors of perception" and beheld a more complex, diverse creation than that attested to in the local, normative sense. Such seers have been a part of humanity from the earliest time to the present; they are explorers of consciousness and spirituality, in religions, in arts, in science, in literature, in all aspects of human life. This creative frontier of perception is not a single horizon of being, but opens onto multiple horizons of being in a relative, transformative universe of diversely gifted individuals. History holds the records of a vast multitude of individuals who have claimed to see into the Infinite and to be transformed by that perception. But these perceptions are by no means the same and on close examination reveal many distinctive and unique features that resonate with the perceptions of others but are by no means identical with them. Esoteric traditions of spirituality are found in all religions and many are found outside of any religion. These are traditions of mystical and mythic, visionary perceptions grounded in the intersection of specific spiritual teachings and unique individual experiences.

Learning from the past means learning to appreciate the differences and the interconnections between diverse views of reality. In an alchemy of soul, we are not seeking to amalgamate all truths into our own truth; we are seeking instead to learn from the truths of others how to better value and fulfill the potential of our individual gifts and abilities. We are also seeking to contribute to the truths of others in a modest but sincere sense. This means having a sense of discernment and humility in learning from the truths of others; and it means that sharing and the exchange of views is central to fostering communal and collective development. This is why the alchemy of soul is a process of individuation and personal development; it is a process by which each person can make the select truths of others part of his or her own discovery of truth. What we are seeking is not an absolute, but a relative maturity that is part of an ongoing plurality of interactions and relationships. It is immature to insist that truth have an absolute context because such an insistence springs from two sources: a naive insistence that truth is reducible to simple, dogmatic assertions; and, a sense of deep insecurity in the face of the actual complexity of life and its multiple horizons of meaning. But real security comes from gaining mastery of the inner processes of knowledge and affirming our relative understanding without denying the capacity we each have for further learning and development.

The past provides an immense resource for future development. This past is not simply the "historic past" as recorded in material, visible forms, but also the "psychic past" as experienced through dreams, imaginative works of art, or visionary experiences that bring to life past events and persons. The past is not a material phenomenon, a mere excretion of visible remains, but an inner *noumena* (or vital essence) of the living present. And access to that past does not occur simply through a rationalizing about objects, records, or places. It occurs through a vivid inner presentment, through processes of mental representation in which the subject is able to experience, in imaginable and vivid ways, events once lived and known by others. Some persons are more gifted in this ability than others, but everyone has some capacity for this kind of knowledge as witnessed by the immense popularity of written recreations and various forms of "historical drama." In a more developed psychic sense, it is quite possible to acquire even more vivid impressions from places, from objects, and from visionary experience that places the subject into a very powerful experience of the past (that is actually experienced and known in the present). The foremost examples of this kind of knowledge are the recovery of past life experiences, various types of psychometry, and a wide variety of intuitive impressions catalyzed by specific places. All places carry latent psychic impressions, embedded through emotional resonance, that form subtle currents within the collective memory.

Learning from the past is not simply a matter of studying records and historical documents, but knowledge of the past can certainly be informed and grounded in such study. But what is the purpose? Claims of objectivity in the study of historical events are highly suspect. Inevitably, individual interpretations assimilate historical materials and shape them according to individual bias, psychic predispositions, and collective, subgroup ideologies. Rarely do we discover that history reconstituted by non-participants in the events analyzed actually conveys the experience and awareness of the real participants, an awareness that is highly diverse, multifaceted, and by no means congruent or necessarily shared. All history is a history of interpretation, and interpretations are often influenced by ideologies or bias unrecognized by the interpreter. This does not mean that historical interpretations have no value; it simply means that human experience cannot be easily reduced to a fixed notion, nor can human events be summarized as reducible to simple, one-dimensional ideas of cause or consequence. There is something elusive and ungraspable about human existence, and this elusive quality consists of the inner meanings, the inner values of the individual, that cannot be known with certainty by others. It is these very values which often motivate actions and responses in the visible, historic world. Thus, the value of historical studies is found in their capacity to reanimate a circumstance with depth and nuance that allows us to participate in some degree in those events, and thus, to learn from that participation.

We can learn from the past through factual information and imaginative recreations, through a willingness to engage past events both inwardly as psychically constituted collective impressions and outwardly as recorded, visible materials. The suffering and joys of others cannot be known simply by observing photographs and reading documents; there must also be an inner connection, a willingness to allow the experiences of others to inform and acquire resonance within us, to touch us emotionally and deeply, before we can claim any real understanding or insight. By the past, I mean the past experiences of others that still live within the collective memory, that still resonate with place, with objects, with persons, with ancestral and genetic consciousness within us. Opening to the past means opening inwardly to past events as a personal journey through multiple lifetimes and as a collective struggle resonant within the present lifetime. The ground of learning now, in the present, is opening to this resonance of the past within us and within the world around us; it is a visionary knowledge, a participant receptivity to imaginative regenerations within the World Soul. The mental, emotional, aesthetic, and intentional structures of noumenal history are not lost, but continue to live as impressions within us and within the world at large. What is required is a deeper sensitivity to these impressions, a deeper rapprochement with the depths of consciousness that sustain life as a global phenomenon.

Learning from the past is a matter of study, travel, and inner awareness. To gain insights into the actual history is an interpretive project, a search for relative knowledge that cannot be reduced to an unquestionable quantification. Every person has a right to freely interpret the past, but some interpretations are shallow, misguided, and self-serving while others are confused, superficial, and purely imaginative. The real work, the real effort, lies in accepting responsibility for genuine, mature relationships with past events. This means not to subject those events and persons to manipulations for self-serving reasons, but to open to that past in order to be informed by the experiences of others, to reach that plateau where we can experience something of the heart and mind of others. But to do this, we must practice hearing and allowing others to speak their differences to us in the present. Only as we gain facility in truly hearing and receiving others with love, respect, and care, can we hope to gain knowledge of the past with that same respect and care. Then the past can speak to us because we genuinely listen to its voices and receive impressions that are not subject to immediate shaping and manipulation. When we learn to hear the stories of others as they wish to tell them, when we can respect those stories however different they may be from our own, then we can hope to learn from the past.

DECONSTRUCTIVE PARADIGMS

One paradigm, or collective model or basic pattern that needs to be deconstructed is the concept of the "spiritual path" as an individual pursuit whose rewards are primarily for the good of the individual. At the introductory level, this is true, and a spiritual path that does not help to guide individual development is in danger of becoming a communal ideology. The spiritual path of alchemy is a path with many byways and branches; it is not a single walkway that is laid out as a directive for a conformist or collective development. Divergences are basic to fulfill the needs and temperaments of different individuals. However, at another level of development, it begins to dawn on the individual that a spiritual life is not simply self-serving. Spiritual path work is multifaceted and an alchemy of soul is not simply a directive for greater personal mastery. The goals of such development are by no means limited to patterns of growth

54

that serve only the benefit of the seeker. In fact, spiritual development requires genuine engagement with others, a necessary sharing of insights, and an authentic communication whose goals are mutual and shared, not simply personal and for self alone. In this sense, the alchemy of soul is an alchemy of human relationships, an alchemy of concern for the well-being of others, and an alchemy that seeks to sustain and honor relationships in the context of world concerns beyond the personal needs of the individual. It is an alchemy that fully values nature, a healthy social world, a reverent way of life in which it is possible to cultivate the transpersonal aspects of soul while still valuing and working in the world. Another way of putting this is to say that the self in me honors and respects the self in others and our connections as human beings. As spiritual seekers, we are linked to the well-being of all. The alchemy of soul is a path of working within the world, of discovering the value and depth within human relationships. If we honor a teacher, it is because the teacher helps us to discover our humanity through our human relationships without denying our differences. The spiritual path then becomes a way that intersects with the ways of others, not as a confrontation of differences, but as an opportunity for sharing and an exchange of views.

As we come to know the deeper self, our layered being that penetrates and is penetrated by the world and others, we can develop ever greater sensitivity for how our development corresponds with the aspirations and ideals of other paths and other ways of life. In deconstructing the alchemical path as something more than a search for personal knowledge and mastery, we open to possibilities of growth that depend on the creative interactions between many paths and ways. But this requires learning to think about our spiritual work as a contribution to world development and not simply as an extension of our own personal experiences or insights. The alchemy of soul is a path that receives from others a good that enhances our own abilities to contribute to the whole and not simply a good that helps me resolve my own inner struggles. Such a path offers the good of individual insights for the development of the whole, not just for other followers of a particular teaching. There is a constant challenge to deconstruct the personal need while not denying the value of the individual and our unique differences. The emergent model, the new paradigm of the spiritual path, is non-exclusive and does not proceed through a required conformity to a communal doctrine or a rigid set of ideas. Paradoxically, such a path must challenge the assumptions and unexamined attitudes of each person in order to help him or her acquire a more authentic realization of individual potential. And, at the same time, such a path also challenges the individual to manifest the benefits of his or her development as a contribution to the development of others, including those who follow quite different paths.

As we move away from the paradigm of a self-serving spirituality, we must also deconstruct the hierarchical basis of authority in matters of spiritual leadership. Leadership in spiritual path work is not an issue of power or control but of insight and compassion. The hierarchical paradigm that wishes to exalt either the teacher or the teaching by insisting on absolute conformity to the directions and teachings of the teacher are rooted in an age-old pattern that emphasizes knowledge through authority and control. There is some reason for such an emphasis, for many seekers are lazy, dismissive, and vain about their own sense of "freedom" in all aspects of spirituality. To say that the teacher does not have to be followed submissively is not to say that the teacher has nothing to offer! But the emphasis does not fall on the power or authority of the teacher; it is rather the humanity and spiritual insight of the teacher that matters. Further, the idea that the seeker is part of a group that sustains and privileges the teacher must also be deconstructed. The teacher may have extraordinary insight and clarity of mind in helping others, but students have a responsibility not to bind the teacher to their own immediate needs and unrealized ambitions or fears. Teachers, in a mature sense, are there to guide and encourage, not to control and dominate. Nor are they there to receive the adulation or approval of others who have not traveled the teacher's road. In the alchemy of soul, the responsibility for personal development, as well as for communal contribution, falls onto the shoulders of the individual practitioner.

The responsibility of the teacher is to be a resource and inspiration for further development and a model of inner realization without holding up that realization as a supreme example or as an epitome of human accomplishment. Good teachers places themselves below their students, but they often know the mind and heart of others far better than others know themselves. The role of the teacher is to encourage and direct the student toward the realization of inner potential, not to control or to assume complete responsibility for another's growth. In the alchemy of soul, the real work must be done by the individual, not by the teacher, and this means that the true teacher is within each person. This inner teacher is the presence of Spirit, the unbound potential of the inmost self, whose capacity to guide is a function of the maturity and insight of the individual. The teacher whose development has ripened to inner clarity and deep perceptive insight can act as a correspondent voice, as a presence whose very being is a calling to others to realize that same maturity within themselves. But this is not a matter of control or authority; it is a matter of Presence, of authentic inner realizations whose invisible actions radiate into the world of the everyday and create there memorable and, at times, remarkable consequences. The true teacher is a source of inspiration, knowledge, and practical experience in the realm of inner development. But the value of this experience and insight cannot be transferred to the student; it must be earned by the student within the context of his or her own struggle for inner illumination. This is an ongoing process of relationships between students, teachers, and every living being who crosses our path.

Another paradigm that must be deconstructed is the belief that the spiritual path can be delineated by fixed stages and stations of development. Such formalized patterns do exist in many traditions, but they are primarily heuristic — that is, they are a means used to teach the student, to help the seeker learn through formalized steps and stages. Many of these paths are embedded in traditional ways of thinking and often taken to be ontological in nature, that is, to reflect the actual structure and nature of reality or of being. However, in the alchemy of soul, there are no such formal structures. Whatever structures may be devised are seen as a heuristic means toward an end that lies beyond all such structures. In the alchemy of soul, the goal is to seek inner illumination and a more compassionate and creative way of life that enhances the value of life for others. But it is rarely possible to predict the experiences or stages of progress of others; each person, through temperament, personality qualities, education, personal history, and cultural and social influences, will unfold and flower in unique ways. Therefore, each person may follow a pattern of development that is unique to his or her qualities and past experiences. In the alchemy of soul, there is no one path and no one pattern or fixed stages. The emergent pattern is a co-creative one, one that is adaptive and shaped by a threefold interaction between the student, the teacher, and the larger communities which sustain each of them. There are stages and transformative experiences that mark those stages, but they are by no means the same nor identical for all; the more complete the individuation, the greater the differences.

This raises a question concerning the role or place of community in spiritual development, a question I will address later in this work. However, I want to emphasize that this also raises another deconstructive concern. Community, in the alchemy of soul, is not a matter of a closed society; nor does it require secrecy, hard boundaries, or a hierarchical order of teachers and students. Many spiritual paths have emphasized the issue of secrecy and there is a significance to secrecy in the sense that the inner life is not simply open for display or commentary by others, particularly others who are simply spiritual dilettantes and non-participant, intellectual analysts. The inner life should be protected and nurtured within a context of trust and sharing that is not violated through the external, insensitive probing of the non-participant. There are particularly vulnerable stages or developmental periods which require a secure environment for inner discovery and opening to light. And, much esotericism has been persecuted by an unsympathetic, externally-oriented and often aggressive majority who are themselves threatened by teachings which honor and value inner personal freedom of thought and belief. Nevertheless, alchemy of soul is not something to be pursued in the dark, nor hidden away by purposefully obscure language, ritual stages, or hierarchical orders with advanced degrees, all of which may decline into externalized forms with no real inner meaning. The goal is not to form an external organization or to develop an esoteric order that substitutes organizational structure in place of genuine inner development.

There may, however, be initiatory experiences or practices which are not accessible to all simply because these practices require a certain degree of inner preparation and development. A person does not learn to become a theoretical physicist, medical doctor, highly developed musician, or artist without disciplined practice, work, training, and a series of learning experiences that lead him or her to an appropriate state of mind where certain sophisticated concepts or techniques or insights are fully grasped and appreciated. This is particularly true in spiritual development. Such development requires significant learning, study, and practice to fully comprehend the nature of illumined being that is regarded as a goal in the alchemy of soul. The spiritual path as a true alchemy, a true process of inner awakening and development, is an advanced practice and not simply a framework for ethical compassion and sincerity in human relationships, both of which are preliminary aspects for more developed alchemical inner work. The spiritual path, as a many-branching path of inner development, is a work of a lifetime, a long-term process of learning, and one which requires the deepest and most dedicated commitment. And the greatest challenge on such a path is to discover the unique, expressive forms that best convey understanding and insights to others. This requires genuine creativity, a commitment to communication, a capacity for symbolic interaction and a certain degree of internal and social analysis. These are not learned simply by engaging in an ethically sensitive lifestyle, nor by occasional moments set aside for ritual or communal activities.

To become a spiritual teacher requires an even more significant degree of inner work as well as the cultivation of intrapersonal skills and group interaction leadership that can spark development in others without imposing upon them the internalized structures of one's own developmental path. The highest degree of such leadership can set aside entirely personal history and individual struggles, to engage fully with the needs of others through an inner communion of illumined understanding that corresponds directly to the inner life of others. Yet, such a correspondence may require that the teacher act only as a witness, only as an observer who encourages, through attention and love, the necessary development in the other. Such a witnessing is not a mere passive listening or detached observation; it is rather a deep resonance with Spirit that sets up a conditional atmosphere of loving concern that heightens and quickens the inner unfolding of the other. Like a flower opening in light, the illumined heart can provide a supportive context for growth in others through a transparency that acts directly on the other and creates a resonant harmony of co-relation. In such a relationship, there is no pressure to designate a path or stages, or even guidelines. What is required is to be a vessel of Spirit, a loving presence that holds an open space for transformation, creative insight, and spontaneous realizations.

THE COURAGE NOT TO BE

There are many paradigms in spirituality that require deconstruction, that is, a new evaluation that seeks to place those paradigms into the context of a creative alchemy of soul that is tailored to the specific needs and requirements of the individual. This does not mean, however, that the needs of the individual should override the deep requirements of the spiritual path. Nor do the "needs of the many" represent an authentic basis for formulating a course of spiritual action, particularly when those collective needs are in fact a consequence of ill-chosen modes of life or self-indulgent and destructive patterns of social or economic existence. Collective desire for revenge, hatred, ethnic and religious bias, nationalism, party politics, and various types of collective and sub-group arrogance have all contributed to disorientation in spiritual life. Collective bias has malformed much spirituality and has resulted in many justifications which have reinforced existing social privileges, particular status ranking, and gender, race, and age discriminations of many different degrees and types, some quite subtle and secretly self-serving. The alchemy of soul requires a balancing and harmonizing of inner life with outer social existence, based in principles of spiritual growth and development that are not arbitrarily subject to the momentary needs of either the individual or the collective-communal.

The courage "not to be" is a courage rooted in being an authentic spiritual seeker whose being and identity are not fashioned by collective norms or by exclusive group identity. The courage required is the courage not to be submerged, not to be simply a follower of externalized social norms, nor a conformist to party or communal, ideological expectations. Integrity is a mark of an individual freedom that acts with a courage that can resist conformist expectations when generated within a context of simple ideological, political, or religious doctrines. The law is meant to serve man, not man to serve the law. This saying requires integrity and compassion to understand; it leads to integration and maturity, not to chaos or anarchy. The courage not to be submerged is the courage that leads to individuation, to the realization of inner potential as a unique gift of Spirit. Such courage requires an inner resistance to the norms of a more material, external, mechanical life of habit and identity rooted in unreflective appreciation of potential. Yet, it is not a matter of the wholesale rejection of a way of life or of a radical dismissal of a communal or collective view. Each of us must choose, consciously choose, the values and beliefs we hold as paradigmatic to our personal and collective development. Therefore, we may well find within any particular ideology or belief system certain ideas or values we can cherish or hold as a true. But what we choose, on the spiritual path, we must choose consciously and with an individual conscience that is inwardly developed according to internalized and deeply held values consistent with a specific spiritual path.

Thus, we do not ask, "What must I believe to become X?". Rather, we ask, "What do I believe and hold to be true in order to value the beliefs and teachings of others?" We seek an inner affirmation of personally held values and inner ideas that are worthy of full commitment and dedication, regardless of the expectations of normative, usually unreflective, collective beliefs. Spiritual identity does not come from membership in a particular organization nor by subscribing to traditional beliefs received externally; spiritual identity comes through inner work and a search for personal integrity that is grounded in direct inner experience. Part of the task is to bring that inner experience into meaningful relationship with others, not always in the communal sense, but in ways that enhance and contribute to human development. In any alchemy of soul, the task is to co-create, to contribute through individuation to the collective transformation. This requires having an individual center, having a clear view of one's own values, beliefs, practices, and insights as distinctive contributions to ongoing spiritual dialogues between mature beings. It is a task far more demanding than simple conformity to a communal doctrine or a traditional path with high expectations of conformity or obedience to norms (or teachers) created independently from the actual needs of the individual. Yet, individual needs must be moderated and guided into higher patterns of inner development, a process which, indeed, requires a certain degree of sublimation and self-surrender.

The spiritual goal is not simply the pursuit of individual needs or even inner aspirations. In an alchemy of soul, each individual faces the challenge of engaging in inner transformation. This means, very decisively, that where you are now is not where you will be at later stages of development; through various experiences and insights, who you are will change and evolve. Part of this transformation requires dropping certain attachments, false expectations, artificial longings or desires, exaggerated ideas of self importance, and learning to shake down the grain and wheat to a measure that truly represents your real being. Usually, this is a process that ranges from dropping inflation and excessive self-interest to recovering self-potential from fear, anxiety, and contracted feeling of insecurity and worthlessness. Often, this range is found in a single individual—overly inflated ideas mingled with contracted feelings of worthlessness, emptiness, or despair and meaninglessness. The depths of self must be plunged, each must find the courage not to be who we think we are or were and not to be who others may tell us we are; we must not be simply the product of a process from outside that has been internalized to the detriment of our full development. We must seek for the deeper authenticity of soul that speaks to us from the heart and illumines our identity at the deepest stratum of being. But this requires change, an inner overturning of old habits, unreflective collective thoughts, and a clearing out of partial and fragmentary beliefs that do not serve to guide or direct.

Thus at the very outset, it is important to realize that the raw material (prima materia) of the alchemical process is both the internalized world of individual identity and the externalized world of collective attitudes. The path is not one of passive consent, but of active, engaged, and questioning exploration and careful assimilation of just those teachings, beliefs, attitudes, and practices that facilitate the processes of spiritual maturity. The will must be actualized to accept the challenge and the burden of a vastly complex world of potential beliefs and paths and not flee this demand simply for the sake of personal ease and comfort. Each person must define the limits and the possibilities of his or her quest. Like seekers of the Grail, each individual must search to find those circumstances which will best lead to insight and development. This requires a willingness to strip away the externalized layers of inherited beliefs or collective assumptions; it requires the courage not to be what others may expect or demand. And it requires an inner surrender that will allow for transformation that does not result in an aggressive, inflated sense of self-worth. It requires the will not to be caught in secret self-admiration rooted in supposed independence or haughty criticism of mass thought or collective mentalities. Such thought and mentalities serve other purposes connected to the evolution of human consciousness and the problems of adaptation to rapid change and growth. Fear is often a root cause in collective thinking because there is a threat of dissolution and social chaos; and this threat is not just imaginary. The history of revolutionary movements clearly shows the dangers inherent to counter-ideologies that threaten a particular social order but result in the imposition of often inhumane and cruel destruction.

In alchemies of soul, the courage "not to be" is a step toward a new being-with, a being-with that is not simply based in conformity and normative duty, but emerges as a co-creative engagement with the problems and challenges of creating a more just, harmonious, and peaceful world. This being-with is marked by a willing, cooperative engagement with diverse others through an inner center of values and self-knowledge that guides the degree and nature of personal commitments. While these values may overlap and resonate with the select values of others, the key is not the degree of collective identity in co-creation, but a keen awareness of how such relationships further communal life in harmony with personally shared spiritual goals. One of the manifest results of such alchemy, at times, is a magical quality in which diverse others join together to create a consequence that exceeds every individual contribution and yet furthers the quality of life of every participant. This "synergy" of creative energy and spiritual commitment is a consequence of each person's co-creative contributions to the process of collective work that results in a heightened manifestation of potential because there is no grasping after consequences and personal rewards. Thus being-with can result in an opening to greater Presence, enhanced by communal receptivity to the needs of the present but also engaged in a "karma of service" such that no benefit is sought by a particular individual. This requires deep detachment from the consequences of authentic action as well as genuine and co-creative love for others.

The courage "not to be" springs from the depths of an inner resistance to accept what is normative as fully adequate to explain or justify a particular way of life or practice. Such justification may be adequate to the life of ordinary familial, social, and cultural concerns but in a culture of material preoccupations and constant striving for external stimulations and comfort, there is often a genuine lack of creative spiritual values. Or spiritual values have become so petrified by static mythologies or by authoritarian structures of tradition as to provide no guidance based on the real spiritual needs of increasingly complex individuals. We are in a historical era of great change and complexity. This requires new strategies for personal development that frequently exceed the normative boundaries of most traditional religions. Yet, those very traditions have a wealth of insights, practices, philosophies, and cosmological reflections that can enhance and nurture the processes of inner transformation. Thus, there is a need to approach the spiritual teachings and traditions of others with respect and humility. The task is to learn respectfully what those traditions have to offer each person in the alchemy of his or her inner awakening to spirit, life and illumination. The courage "not to be" requires a willingness to sustain a certain creative tension, a conviction that honors fully the spiritual values of others and yet maintains the place of individual integrity as a center from which a new understanding can emerge.

The creative work of the alchemy of soul is truly a Great Work, creating a luminous soul through the transmutations of incarnate life, but one that cannot be accomplished by another for one's self. Each person must undertake the necessary work and disciplines of inner purification, development, and new birth. Each person must be willing to cast out the unassimilated echoes of collective thought and belief in order to discover within a genuine depth of maturity that flourishes through inner individuation that seeks to contribute to the good of others. This contribution is not made through any demands for conformity to a collective ideal, but through a steady encouragement and recognition of the value of each individual. Every person has his or her unique gifts and abilities and these gifts are a means by which we can actualize new expressive insights and forms of human potential. And we can do this by learning from others, by truly valuing what others have learned, developed, and actualized in their lives. Our being-with is a condition based in shared insights, in respectful dialogue, in a loving consciousness directed toward integration and maturity. This requires courage, a courage that can accept its own limits, realize the relativity of self-development, and have the patience and determination to sustain the necessary creative tension for further development and insight. This requires a capacity to stand apart, but not stand alone; to walk a path that leads toward a full realization of potential, but also to be willing to sit with others, to listen, and to learn.

There is no end to learning. We may spend a lifetime or more, even many, seeking to answer some of the most profound and difficult questions. But in this life, now, there is a necessity to be open to the diversity of potential development without seeking to resolve the conflicts and tensions through simple conformity to a collective norm. The courage "not to be" has a counterpart in the "courage to be", that is, to be true to authentic inner being that constitutes identity through our relationships and through inner integrity and inner spiritual vision. The alchemies of soul are many, not one. Therefore, it is the task of each individual to learn the techniques, teachings, and skills necessary to craft an individualized alchemy whose radiance is a contribution to the World Soul, the Anima Mundi, to a purposeful unity of diverse individuals working together to create a more radiant humanity. This is a dynamic process of continual learning, development, and maturation whose goals can only coalesce if we can truly learn from each other in our differences. And there is an inner spirit to this process, a sacred quality of spiritual realization that provides an interconnective medium, a psychic and spiritual resonance, that flows out of the depths of Being for the betterment of our understanding. In the alchemy of soul, one goal is to become fully conscious of those sacred currents that unite us in a greater harmony of understanding without

64

denying the value of each individual gift.

WEAVING NEW WORLD PATTERNS

Alchemy of soul is a process of refinement and inner transformation that leads to a discovery of deep potential. This potential is not immediately accessible to the conscious, momentary "I" or to the simple, inward meditative gaze. We can look "within" but what we see will often be no more than a cursory, momentary, reflective awareness, an immediate sense of seeing in the moment. Inner stimulus enters through the senses, reflective memory evokes images, imaginary circumstances, memories, and thoughts, but this is by no means a portrait of the full human spiritual potential. We are veiled from that potential by the self-protective energies of our own limited sensory awareness, mental and emotional habits, and a variety of collective and cultural attitudes and values. Often, these values and attitudes do not condone or support an image of inner development based on unrecognized or unaffirmed deep potential. Too often, members of contemporary cultures, highly influenced by "western" ideas, conceive of themselves as nothing more than the immediacy of their own mental and emotional habits and patterns of perception, an attitude reduced to colloquial sayings like, "What you see is what you get." But too often, what we see is only the surface, only an image projected back through the mirror of a social order obsessed with material control, comfort, and conformity to highly limited paradigms of human existence.

The depth of human potential must be delineated from the history of human experience in the full spectrum of religious, philosophical, spiritual, psychic, occult disciplines and in all arts and sciences. There is no experience which does not reflect human potential, however positive or negative the experience. In the history of human exploration of consciousness, there is a vastly complex record of the human capacity for altered states, trance, out-of-body, near-death and after-death perceptions, a wide spectrum of psychic, visionary, and healing abilities, and many diverse types of supersensory perceptions. This history also records many remarkable dreams, visions, and various types of ecstatic knowledge, and sophisticated states of higher consciousness explored extensively by traditions in Hinduism, Buddhism, Daoism and other mystical traditions such as Sufism, Hasidism, and esoteric Christianity. Only by including all of these in our explorations can we say that human potential has within it a capacity for self-transcendence and self-realization that unite us with

65

the very foundations of spiritual wisdom and a wide variety of transpersonal insights linking us to an expansive cosmology that is only very narrowly perceived by the surface "I". The depths of human potential are hardly recognized by a majority of collective subgroups of humanity whose primary interests are limited to the pursuit of wealth, pleasure, control, domination, and who hold a very limited and minimal concern for the health and well-being of others or for global and ecological harmony and balance.

The depths of human potential are not simply "psychological," nor are they limited to our biological or hereditary capacities. Such capacities do play a role in human development and psychology is an important discipline in understanding mental-emotive life. But the depths of self are depths that connect us with the foundations of Being, with numerous onto-theologies of human evolution in the most cosmic sense. The ground of self is the Ground of Being, and that ground is an infinite potential of creative inner awareness whose expressive forms and outer manifestations are found in the full range of all life-forms on this world or any other worlds we may discover. And that same potential links us to all created forms, to the subtle energetic worlds of every created thing, from stars to planets, mountains, streams, oceans, minerals, plants, animals, and beings both visible and invisible. The model that looks at human potential as a strictly social or psychological capacity is far too narrow for a mature alchemy of soul. The alchemy of soul is a Hermetic Alchemy, an alchemy that seeks to foster awareness of the interconnective relationships between individual existence and cosmic Being and to do this without insisting on a strictly univocal teaching.

New world patterns for human development require a more expansive sense of human potential that can relate to the organic, biological, social and psychological in a framework that does not deny the higher values of awakening to expansive states of human consciousness. To weave these patterns through an alchemy of soul is to open horizons on the incredible capacities that we have as spiritual beings in a living and dramatically evolving cosmos. But this requires finding the foundations for self awareness in the very depths of the human soul, in the depths of psychic and spiritual capacities that are yet dormant or undeveloped in most human beings. It also means affirming the existence and reality of supersensory perceptions that go far beyond the local, immediate sensations of the physical self, and opening to psychic capacities that are latent in every person. These new patterns are patterns of soul-work, individual creations that capture nuances of light, color and energy to bend them into new expressive forms through creative living and visionary, co-creative manifestation. The prism through which these lights and colors are refined and then refracted into new patterns of illumination is the lucid, clear, crystalline self, purified of dross and outer layers of denial, doubt and indifference. But the development of that clear inner sense is itself an evolutionary action; it is not simply the discovery of a given potential, but a conscious shaping and making into newness.

The inner potential is not a form or a particular state; nor is it some arcane "level" of consciousness in any specific map of visionary states. The inner potential is a dynamic capacity in a residual state of containment, only partially actualized and capable of expansive openings whose contents and horizons are shaped by the unique capacities and gifts of the individual. Thus, rather than a model of development that seeks to draw all individuals into conformity with one standard of development, the alchemy of soul is an exploration of inner capacities whose actualizations reflect a multitude of models and possible directions for future human evolution. The "spiritual soul" is rooted in a shaping whose formative powers are a co-creative fusion influenced by the universal qualities of Spirit and the unique individual capacities of the spiritual seeker. The weaving of a new world pattern is a weaving that may be only a nuance on an older pattern(s) or it may be a completely unique and highly individualized realization created in the open space of a particular historical and cultural period. What matters is not the pattern per se, but the clarity and light that such a pattern brings into focus for the contemplation of others. The alchemy of soul is a process of sublimation that acquires greater and greater richness and content through multiple exposures to higher states of awareness and increasingly expansive horizons of inner-outer being. The crystallization is an inner responsiveness to a living cosmos whose energies can be refracted into the thoughts, images, and words of others. This is as much an art as it is a science.

The weaving of new world patterns means that each individual, through an alchemy of soul development, contributes to an ever more complex and diverse process of world transformation. Our individual efforts are part of a larger pattern of shared insights and realizations, and the various experiences and states which support those insights are the creative ground of human evolution. As an evolving species, we have within us a capacity for transforming our world through the quality and cooperative insights of our human relationships. In this process, individual potential is a manifestation of our spiritual capacity to realize a greater wholeness in which diversity and difference is a creative source of development, not an impediment. But this requires that we also embrace an authentic ethical sense of cooperation and tolerance that will guide our human relationships toward a more synergistic, interactive world pattern. The new world pattern is not one thing. It is an evolutionary transformation, a crossing of the transhistorical horizon in which we discover our citizenship as world-embracing while still rooted in the local, ethnic, and culturally specific. As we cross this horizon, we can discover that we are not bound by our historical past in the local sense but share a species history that seeks a new temporal horizon beyond the rudimentary awareness of sensory, rational, and pragmatic thought.

This new temporal and transtemporal horizon is grounded in a spiritual capacity that is able to embrace the cosmos as a living, sentient ground of ensouled beings who directly sense the interconnective energies that unite us within a single integrated Whole. This Wholeness is a spiritual reality and is directly perceptible to those whose spiritual senses are open and receptive to a higher kind of seeing, hearing, and subtle perception. And we are each a part of that Wholeness within our own being, in the depths of our own potential, through a heart-centered opening from within. The inner effort to weave new world patterns is made by an opening of this heart-centered being through an alchemy of soul. As we open our hearts, minds, and wills to the depthless source within, to Spirit, we can discover radically new means by which to transform our world into a more balanced and harmonious communal life. The efforts involved in realizing this opening horizon are considerable and require of each person a full and sincere commitment to the work of spiritual transformation. Yet the spark of the inspiration is a free and fluid inner presence, like yeast in dough that activates expansion and fullness. It is not a matter of will alone or strong intention and determination; it also requires inner surrender, patience, humility, and a willingness to shed the skin of surface learning through many stages of development.

As a species, we cannot survive without a cooperative union of creative individuals who find the inner freedom to explore their unique potential without bringing harm or injury to others. It is not a simply a matter of control or intervention. The opening of this trans-historical horizon, this horizon that opens to a multitude of worlds and to a deeper continuum of interconnection with others, is a creative action within Being, an opening outward that gathers an entire world into a new stage of development and perception. But this only occurs through willing commitment and attunement with a deeper soul process within the whole of humanity. It is not because we strive toward a particular synthesis or doctrine or philosophy or teaching, but because we begin to understand the interrelationships and deep connections between ideas, worldviews, cultural differences and collective diversities. As we develop into this new horizon of Being, we do not merge in our thinking or interpretations as much as we sense the deep affinity that unites us as embodied souls seeking transformation. Alchemies of soul are refractions of this inner realization that the cohesive unity of our species life is linked psychically to all life, to all species, to all beings. The transpersonal horizon is a vast and extensive horizon within an infinite cosmos of living beings and our own place in that horizon is determined by the acuity of our perceptions and a soulful capacity to join with others in the shaping of a more mature and integrated world.

There is no dominant ideology in this horizon, no favored nation, no political order from above, no imposition through force or coercion, no determination from outside. The opening of this horizon into new world patterns requires a the necessity of cooperation and the sharing of visions. This transformation is grounded in an inner spiritual revolution that no longer abides the controlling domination of any sub-group or any political or religious institution. This is revolution from within, where the prime material of that transformation is not the transformation of the other, but the transformation of the self. The impact of true spiritual awakening, its subtle and sometimes miraculous consequences, flows out from the heart of the individual from the depths of Being into the creative worlds of others. This light flows not simply from the reservoir of individual capacity but from the depths of creation. And this deep well of Being is accessible to every person in the process of awakening to a more expansive horizon of perception and awareness. The work is to seek the gold and light of inner spiritual presence, to undergo the alchemy of inner transformation to become a light to others, a source of inspiration. However long this transformation may take, the goal is not the creation of an ideology or teaching, but the living manifestation of Spirit, the opening of the horizon of perception for a remaking of human relationships. This can be very simple and yet, very profound and radiant. What matters is the quality of the gold, its purity and magical quality, its radiance as a source for new world patterns. The words and teachings are only relative; the light, far more lasting.

1. William Blake, 1968: 78, from "There is No Natural Religion" (1788).

CHAPTER THREE
UNBECOMING, THEN REBECOMING

One of the most difficult aspects of the alchemy of soul is letting go of beliefs, habits, attitudes of mind, and emotional attachments that have been carried for years, possibly from childhood. Often, these habits and attitudes are unexamined because they are taken in as normative for members of a particular sub-group, community, or cultural milieu. Or these beliefs and ideas have been propagated as authoritative in the education and development of the individual while he or she is struggling to formulate a meaningful worldview. Further, there is rarely a single group with which a person shares some degree of identity and interaction. Most individuals share identity with many different groups from family to a wide variety of communal, vocational, political, religious, and social organizations. In the process of assimilating the beliefs, practices, or values of any one of these groups, there is often a high expectation on the part of other group members that there will be a significant degree of similarity in values and ideology among group members. While these patterns of group membership are partially responsible for providing varying degrees of stability in social, collective life, they are also a basis for a conservative retardation of group members when such groups resist creating varying degrees of interface with other, alternative groups. The degree of receptivity in any social group for others oriented differently is a significant index of its potential for creative development and growth.

Yet, in all this, where is the center for the individual? Do we find our identity only in the groups which constitute our social life, or can we find a deeper and more personalized center from which to evaluate the worth and significance of those same groups? Are we identified with the collective, with the sub-group, with a particular family or communal pattern as our own fundamental identity? Or are we capable of divesting the self of its identifications with dominant social collectives that only act to preserve a normative and closed society indifferent to the diversities of human life and a more cooperative world orientation? Where is the center of our spiritual identity? Where is the root and heart of this identity in terms of our unrealized human potential? In order to answer these questions, it is necessary to step outside the normative frameworks that value only the good of the collective in terms of fulfilling a role that, in service to the collective, fosters selfish goals, personal wealth, or unjust social values at the expense of diminishing the lives of others who only serve to support an imbalanced, often destructive, social order.

In the alchemy of soul, it is not a matter of imposing one order over another, nor of substituting a favored political, religious, or economic perspective through a questionable process of majority consent. It is a matter of individual conscience guided by an ethic of compassion, creative love, and a deep knowledge of human potential no longer shaped by strictly cultural, collective norms, practices, or beliefs. And it is a matter of working together to create a more just, balanced, and healthy world of creative individuals whose collective efforts are a function of mature deliberation and clear, intentional, self-aware choices and creative synergy. This is not a path based on conformity to group values or of forming an identity bolstered by party affiliation or group membership that seeks a submergence of individual differences. The alchemy of soul is a path that each individual must walk in his or her own way and whose goal is the development of inner capacities that can creatively interact with the creative capacities of others. Spiritual authenticity often requires a divesting of inherited values and beliefs in order to discover what it is that we as individuals truly hold to be of utmost value and importance—regardless of what others may insist should be important for all.

The central issue of this development is attaining an inner certainty, centered in a value orientation that is stable and effective as a basis for action in the real world. But in order to know the self as a creative, spiritual agent of change, it is necessary to first divest that self of its inherited and externally acquired beliefs. We must first unbecome so that we may then more authentically rebecome, as unique individuals whose goals and beliefs are consistent with their inner development and outer skills and with the practical application of those skills. So we must start where we are, become our own teachers, and work to revise collective thinking, not because we cannot learn from that thinking but because the creative ferment in human development is found in the inner transformation of each individual and not simply in collective norms. The contribution of the individual is not necessarily an earth-shaking insight or revolutionary idea; it may be a just, kind, and compassionate life, a caring for others, or an admirable and modest insight into human needs and hopes furthered through individual actualizations. It is not the scope of the newness as much as the quality and beauty it engenders in human relationships and cooperative life. It may be a joyful humor, a sparkling wisdom, or a humble sincerity. What matters is not excessiveness from the norm but a genuineness and authenticity of being, a radiance that inspires, a smile that enlivens the world.

The process of stripping away the accumulated layers of inherited beliefs and attitudes is not easy or immediately accessible. We are often blinded by our own predisposition and our place within a community of relationships which, when questioned, may well threaten the stability and support of those relationships. This includes the family first of all, then friends, then general communal relationships. Integrity in the enactment of a spiritual path requires that we access a level of inner honesty that can question even the most cherished beliefs and attitudes, no matter who may hold similar beliefs, whether a mother, father, child, friend or teacher. Yet, in divesting the self of artifice and accumulation taken on without self-evaluation and testing, we do not have to reject the beliefs or attitudes held by others. An individual worldview is always partial and relative to the worldviews of others; there is no absolute worldview, no "one way" that can authentically supplant the views and beliefs of others. The challenge is to create a climate of respect that allows for individuation and a giving up of all unauthentic attitudes when they no longer resonate with a genuine development of inner understanding. And this understanding is a personal realization, an inner exploration of potential that takes on more specific content and signification as the individual seeks to individualize and adapt what is taught as right and true by others.

The unbecoming process is not always painful nor does it always result in a loss. Often it is a discovery and a joy found in new thoughts, insights, and an opening of horizons, a feeling of breaking free. Further, this process does not lead to isolation, but to new and deeper friendships and relationships with those who share an authenticity of self and of soul seeking a more grounded, inclusive way of life. The pattern of development may go through stages of divesting and giving up relationships but it also opens the doors for new relationships and a broader, more expansive view of life and well-being. There is a magical aspect to this process. The manifestation of authenticity is not simply a matter of giving up, but much more a matter of discovery and inner realization of what and who we are as spiritual beings in a spiritual universe. Those who reject this claim are free to explore the territory that calls them, but for those who chose, freely chose, to enter into a deep alchemy of soul, there are wonders and remarkable horizons of being that will affirm the value of the inner transformation. The birth of new insights will confirm a magical view of life that is utterly real and powerfully connected to a multitude of alternative worlds, beings, and perceptions normally closed to a more rational and narrow empiricism. This does not mean that a narrow and stricter empiricism has no value. In fact, it may have very great value in its capacity to produce insights into the world of its focused attention. But for a narrowly focused majority (or minority) to then claim that their insights are the only valid form of human knowledge is not only misleading but profoundly one-sided in its ignorance of inner human capacities for creative imagination, visionary arts, mystical journeys, and the poetry of human life and passion.

The magical aspect is not a mere side affect but is central to the process of an emerging new model of the human being as actually magical in acts of knowledge and power. But this magical aspect must be divested of its collective glamour and superficial trickery, its exploitative tendencies to play on the incredulous, and its fantasy of illusive, excessive effects. It is not the magic of the stage or theater, but the magic of love, the magic of the capacity to create beauty, to see into the Infinite and not lose perspective on being relative and limited creatures with deeply hidden capacities yet unrealized. The magical aspect of the alchemy of soul is found in the heart of the authentic illuminations that infuse mind and soul with a direct awareness of the higher life of Spirit. Authenticity in this sense is not simply the worldview or truth claims that an individual may hold as specific to him or herself, but refers to a deeper stratum of potential that merges with the living energies of creation, that seeks a manifestation of hidden potential as an infusion of deep insight into the living cosmos. This magical capacity lies in the way in which human beings are able to effect change and transformation in the world around them through a clear and deeply attuned will, a willing that harmonizes with self and soul, a willing that is infused with individual character and consequences.

Unbecoming is like removing the bandages from a wound that is healing as it is opened to light and fresh air; it is like unwrapping a present that holds a gift which will require new learning and abilities to fully utilize. This learning can take place at any age and, in the alchemy of soul, it is a practice more attuned to the second third of life than to the first third. This is because in the earlier stages, the individual is experiencing and gathering knowledge about the normative and the possible and then settling into some pattern of relationship with the known. In the second third of life, there comes a time of evaluating the experiences gained, of work, family, play, love, success and failure, in order to establish a new authenticity, a new sense of being the I which can be, rather than the I that is now. This second third of life, after age thirty-five, is a long period of inner development which may take years of inner work to master. In turn, this leads to the final third of life, in which mastery is fully embodied as an illumined center of alchemical realization and as a touchstone of philosophical wisdom and compassion.

An alchemy of soul is not a rapid process because it is not simply directed toward the discovery of higher states or mystical depths. A seeker may achieve such realizations very early, even as a child. But the alchemy of soul is a making and unmaking, a constant process of refinement and purification to reach a series of stages of integrated wisdom and a birthing of magical capacity through a long process of distillation and constant sublimation of outer effects. It is a movement inward toward mystical depths but through incorporation of insights into a creative pattern of understanding that produces visible effects in the world. There is no rushing this process; what starts as unbecoming moves through innumerable stages of development, with characteristic leaps ahead and sliding back, to a stability that must be challenged again and again to keep the energy fresh and flowing. In the alchemy of soul, the process of unbecoming is a stage that we may return to many times, not just at the outset, but over and over. What happens over time, however, is that the unbecoming acquires an ease and feeling of freedom and release as we let go of each previous stage and open to a new horizon of expansion. Unbecoming is itself a magical process by which we give up our attachments to our own accomplishments and let go of our realizations for new, often, humbler realizations. And yet, each step is a step into Mystery that becomes ever more fulfilling and wondrous.

THE WHY OF THE NOT-YET

In the practice of the alchemy of soul, we must learn to use the imagination in a new way, as a creative power of visualization that seeks to embody the emergence of a soulful self in new form and capacity. Many empiricists and rationalists have denied the ontological value of the imagination. Such a denial is based on an artifice of mental presumption, that real knowledge is based in observable, replicable phenomena rather than on the actual contents of human consciousness. This outwardly directed gaze has to be deconstructed so the gaze can turn within and find a new theater of mental presentment in the actual flux and flow of awareness. And that awareness cannot be limited to the simple gaze of the controlling I, but must open to the spontaneity, free play, and creative turbulence of imaginative, dreaming, visionary and extrasensory contents. The alchemy of soul requires a full engagement with Being that manifests in all and every aspect of awareness. Imagination is one of the primary modes of Being; it is an ontological expression of our human capacity to explore a new and not-yet realized possibility or direction or capacity. It is not unreal but the very medium through which the real comes into awareness and seeks actualization.

The imagination is a power of soul, an aspect of Being that resonates with the possible, the improbable, the emergent. In the alchemy of soul, imagination is a means by which we can envision an alternative to our present condition, an aspect of self now latent or unrecognized, a quality as yet unexpressed. Those poor in imagination will find the alchemical processes obscure and dense with imagery that cannot be reduced to a fixed, rationalized set of stages or determinative processes. This is because the work of the imagination is a work of creativity that seeks to explore, to expand, to transform, in the free play of Being, the possibilities of the human. The discipline of the imagination is like the discipline in many arts (and sciences), both the skill and the technique have to serve the creative intuition rather than be dominated by a particular skill, technique or theory. Another way to say this is to confirm the value of the imagination as a visionary power of mind that can transform the world through the lens of a clear, healthy, focused, yet free, attention. Stereotypes of the imagination only kill this ability, the grist for the mills of entertainment foster a death of imagination when it only serves a habituated appetite for entirely conventional imagery, story, and humanity reinforced with sterile dependency on aggression and violence as a solution to all problems.

The alchemy of soul requires a much more subtle, visionary artistry of soul in order to unlock the key to human transformation. And the fluid environment of that artistry is not embedded in violence, aggressive despair, angry rejection, or cynical vanity and distorted views on one's own self-worth. It is born through dreams that have liberated their contents from the collective miasma, that have freed themselves from the torpor and lazy sleep of unconscious identification with collective, stereotyped thinking. This lazy thinking abounds, even in the most intellectual environments, as habits of mind that are closed to truly imaginative expression because the soul is heavy with the imagery of collective representation. The power of the imagination lies in its evocative, revelatory quality of a shift in perspective that opens to new, unseen potential. And it takes discipline! It is not simply a matter of the free play of mind because most minds are only carrying the imagery of the surface, the undeveloped mirror mind that reflects only the external images of human social and interactive life or skips along unintegrated channels of psychic perception that have no center and no clear vision of the whole. This fragmentation of the imagination is widespread; we must reclaim its wholeness as a profound, creative capacity to be truly nurtured and developed.

The power of the imagination as expressive Being lies in the capacity to draw on inner potential for the creation of new forms, relationships, and manifest development. This potential is not a mere passive reserve of energy or consciousness but a primary, vital force, an *elan vital* whose depths are the depths of Being. The "why" of the not-yet is the very why of Being, the interior turning outwardly from implicit to explicit, from envisioned spark to actual form and material being. A painting or song or poem is an image of this process by which an inner possibility takes on visible form, but is only a variant of other possible forms. The depths of Being are a creative reservoir of unrealized moments of merging and crystallization through the inspiration and intuitions of the individual encountering these depths. This means we must as individuals seek to open the soul to the unbound potential of Being, to the Mystery and Sacredness of creation, as the primal source of vital, aware life. These depths are not a colorless unity of passive Being, but a highly charged, multiplicity of creative currents and a blending of various co-creative elements whose emergent properties are brought into focus through incarnate existence. The incarnation of creative Being is through the manifestation of all creatures as vital physical, psychic, noetic, and spiritual centers of emergence. Every being is a nexus, a particular degree of unity differentiated from others by its own particularity.

Our capacity to imagine the soulful self as a creative, transformative being rooted in a divine matrix of co-creative relationships is a necessary prelude to the realization of actual sacred potentials. The true gnosis of self, the true knowledge of our inner capacities, is a luminous opening to sacred depths, to the profound, cosmic energies, life forms, and multidimensional beings that saturate our entire world. The intermediary stages of this realization require us to harness and hone the imagination, to develop an inner visionary capacity by which we can truly begin to see into these depths. It is not a realization of what we are as much as a realization of what we can become. It is an understanding that reaches out past the static image, past the simple realization of inner unity, and attains a transformative vision of opening, of a flowering of potential whose scent is a sign of spiritual illumination. To do this, we must acquire a capacity to imagine, to envision, and to see beyond the limited horizon of the accepted and static image of a less evolved humanity. Yet, this evolution is not predetermined or simply a consequence of past action; it is an emergence based in a new kind of freedom.

Our freedom from the past, our capacity to inhabit a living present, to value the joy and beauty of the now, is not a function merely of overcoming past trauma or suffering. This freedom is also a freedom of the imagination; an imagination liberated from the stereotypes and redundant repetitions of a more closed, fearful, and constrained vision of the real person. We are free to envision a new humanity, a more magical universe whose power to be magical lies in the magical capacity of being human. The magical worldview is not one based in false views or shallow, surface superstitions, such as views that over-value reason or the collective, empirical perception. The power of the imagination is an expression of Being that coexists as a supplement and enhancement of rational thought, as a source of inspiration that can reach out past the visible and obvious into the invisible depths of the not-yet possible. Imagination is the intermediary power of soul that can hold within itself an image of possible perfection or beauty or power and use that image as a source of inner direction. The image, when given the full attention of soul as a heart-centered visionary form, can function to lead the soul into a realization of the image—first within and then, without. The images we cultivate, the images we hold as imaginative expressions of being, are sources of transformation and possible development.

The danger in these images is in the psychic intensity, the emotional strength that we give to the image as a form of self expression. These images can also deform and depress spiritual development, even when cultivated as a spiritual practice. Images which are far removed and ungrounded from actual realized capacity, or which deny or ignore undeveloped aspects of personhood can easily inflate or distort self development. The real spiritual practice of the imagination is not to envision or imagine the soulful self in the grandiose and inflated sense, but to envision the self in the true unvarnished clarity of honest self-assessment. The actual effective use of the imagination is to shake down, strip away, and come to the naked heart of our inmost being as discovered in the image that has no excess, no inflation, no self-deception and no exaggerated imbalance. In most cases, the individual's imagination is suffering from distortion and over-inflated feelings of self importance or self worthlessness. To creatively imagine is to move beyond adolescent images and into mature images as one willing to work in the vineyard without placing the self either above others nor subservient to them.

The balanced, creative self is free-flowing and healthy in needing love and in loving and in being loved. The why of the not-yet is found in a creative, imaginative life that seeks to be a fully loving being in the now of co-creative emergence. This discovery is one that benefits from the insights of others, one that shares a mutual joy and finds balance in community and in service to others. That is the imaginative power, to envision a world of shared responsibilities in which we are each free to discover our role and relationship through the development of our unique gifts and through the inner unfolding of potential, in the deepest spiritual sense, as beings capable of knowing and understanding the unseen and not-yet visible worlds. We have to throw off the false image and the artifice of "heroic individualism" and the self-subsuming cloak of "selflessness" for a more balanced and individuated spirituality that fully values differences while working for the awakening of mutually creative spiritual potential. We each have unique gifts, and no two persons have the exact same path to travel or the same imaginative capacities. The joy and beauty of the creative process is the fractal order of differences that each contributes to the Whole. What we must each seek is to realize those gifts that genuinely contribute to a new awakening of spiritual potential within self and within others. The alchemy of soul is an imaginative journey into unseen potential, into a newly envisioned you whose artifice and externality must fall away and break open for the fragile, beautiful wings of an emergent, creative spirit.

In the process of discovering the imaginative power, it is important to value dreams as a primary source in which the imaginative power seeks to express more fully its unrealized potential. The dream is a not a verbal report but a lived experience, an immediacy of encounter that opens possible vistas, alluring or frightening, and that shows directions for imaginal development. Dreams should be remembered and studied; this is an important aspect of the alchemy of soul. The imaginative life is not simply a protection of the rationalizing ego as much as an exploration of the deeper strata of being, of the hidden capacities of the soul seeking to actualize the not-yet. Dreams are a key to the discovery of the soulful self as expressive witness to inner desires, fears, aspirations and co-reactions. The dream is a visualization of potential, a living out of the psychic life as an imaginative event, one linked to many alternative lives. Remembering dreams, recording them, reflecting on them, and seeing the hidden patterns and interconnections, is an essential means for the development of a grounded and authentic imaginative capacity. In this sense, imagination is linked to the real experiences of the psychic life, not simply fantasy, but actual productions of the dreaming mind. These materials of the dream are a spontaneous source of constant activity that reveals inner life. Dreams impact and reformulate experience in terms of inner needs and reactions that may often pass unnoticed by the waking mind. In the alchemy of soul, both the waking mind and the dreaming mind must be brought into conscious alignment in order to develop greater mental-emotive synthesis.

The imagination is a dreaming faculty, a capacity to create as well as a capacity to perceive. We can look into the dreaming worlds and see there multiple reflections of our own inner capacities as yet unrealized in spiritual life. The goal is to selectively call to mind the dreaming circumstances that best reflect inner spiritual potential and to embody the dreaming aspect in waking life. The dream is a resource, an inner visualizing of potential that opens into the psychic world and into unseen capacities that can play themselves out in dream scenarios. These same capacities can be brought into play in waking life; the dreamer can awaken the psychic potential of the imagination through embodying the dream experience. The imagination, when harnessed to the dreaming capacity, is an extremely powerful means by which the deep seated identity of self can be actualized. But to do so, we must each take our imaginative capacity and our dreaming seriously as resources to form and reshape our identity. We must dream into Being the yet unrealized capacities revealed in the dream state as waking possibility, such that the dream is an index of our not-yet fully attained self. Dream knowledge is a crucial aspect of self development and its incorporation into waking life is a key to inner transformation.

REIMAGING THE FUTURE
Part of the dreaming process is to dream the future and not just the

past. Soulful knowledge is based on that which c
that which already has been. This knowledge is a
the future as a reflection of the soul-life we choose to i
We each attune to various aspects of this future, eac
way, and we are each resonant with the currents withii
themselves into emerging patterns congruent with our i
self-awareness. We do not all see the same future nor do
image of the future as a consistent and knowable becomin, _ future is
charged with uncertainty and ambiguity that reflects our own inner
uncertainty, fear, and self-delusions; it images what might be in terms of
both shadows and light. As we seek to reimage this future we must also
seek to reimage our own inner being as a holder of that light who best
sustains the diverse differences of plural worlds and plural spaces. Our
dreaming of the future needs to be grounded in mature images based on
our willingness to make changes in our own lives now, in the present.
Otherwise, our dreaming will be shallow and awash with all the debris of
unintegrated, immature longings that disregard our deeper responsibilities.

Dreaming the future is not an individual task per se as much as it is
a task of soulful cooperation between individual dreamers seeking to
actualize multiple potentials. This future dreaming is grounded in a new
pluralism that seeks to unify without denying difference. In the alchemy
of soul, such dreaming is part of the process by which we discover emergent
potential through creative relationships with others. Our thoughts about
the future are not isolated from the thoughts, desires, and dreams of others
and dreaming as a psychic phenomenon has collective and relational
aspects. The undercurrents of dreaming life are replete with collective and
personal images passed through a wide variety of media whose impact
can stimulate individual creative thinking. Or that same undercurrent of
imagery can act to reinforce a non-reflective reimagining based in norms
that serve to propagate only superficial or popular ideas, including a wide
variety of destructive and self-serving attitudes. In such circumstances,
we must develop the ability to consciously choose which imagery and
which undercurrents can best be directed to the most creative, cooperative
future.

But first we must establish a soulful relationship with the dreaming
self, an affirmation of the imaginative and creative abilities manifesting
through dream experience. This requires remembering dreams and being
able to voluntarily enter a dream state for the purpose of enhancing insight

ssibilities. The dreaming self is not a reflection of an ...y state, but a conditional awareness that is capable of being ...ed and integrated into waking states. We can remember dreams and ...e can influence and direct dreams toward certain ends through patient and consistent effort that acknowledges the dream as a potential source of insight and revelation. Dreaming is a creative mental and emotional exploration of alternatives; it is a dramatic play of characters, scenes, and situations that reflect emergent as well as regressive possibilities and tendencies. The regressive aspect is also creative in so far as we revisit in dreams past experiences and relationships that continue to need development and integration into the conscious, waking identity. But insofar as we fail to remember, fail to make the efforts necessary to retain the dream image and content, we remain only partially conscious, only in the "raw state" in which the dreaming mind functions unknowingly, striving to maintain a homeostatic balance in a fundamentally divided self. The processing of dreams, through conscious reflection and a sophisticated interpretation of symbolism, metaphor, and analogy, is part of the refining stages of an alchemy of the whole and undivided self.

Dreaming the future of humanity is inseparable from dreaming the future of the individual. The alchemical process of constant refining and integration of the *prima materia* (raw materials) of psychic experience, of dreams (waking or sleeping), or collective and individual imagery, of the charged energies of symbolic expression and communication, requires a constant and ongoing attention to the imagistic contents of mental-emotive experience, including the impact of the mental imagery of others. The dreaming self, in night dreams and day dreams, is constantly receiving stimulation that arises from the environment as well as from the shared world-soul that we inhabit as a species. The developing alchemical gaze must be directed toward this "lunar" aspect of consciousness and not simply toward the "solar" aspects of more lineal, rationalized thinking. This lunar element is a reflected light in which normative mental processes are subject to influences arising from the deeper strata of incarnate being. I do not call this lunar aspect "unconscious" as I do not wish to perpetuate an error in thinking which tends to reify the term as a knowable "thing" when in fact, it is nothing other than a label signifying non-observable contents! We can and do observe our dreams.

Dreams are by no means "unconscious," nor are their contents particularly mysterious or simply products of the unknowable. In fact, dreaming is an art whose contents are like imaginative literature that can, in storied or poetic form, express profound human truths that reveal depths of complexity far more completely than abstract intellective thought. Dreams are a vital aspect of mental and emotional identity that is an integral part of every alchemy of soul. Perhaps more than any other psychic aspect of soul life, dreams are an expression of deep activities in which the soul explores alternative ways of being and confronts the limitations of everyday life. Dreams are an essential key in the alchemy of soul and attaining mastery in dream interpretation is crucial. Such an interpretive skill arises as we study and reflect on our dreams over a lifetime of dreaming. As we carry the dream with us, in waking reflection, we participate in a deepening of our psychic life as lived in an alchemical conjunction of the lunar dream with the solar self-awareness.[2]

The challenge is to absorb the dream experience in a way that allows for its contents to become a significant factor in waking life. When we dream the future, we are free to explore all possible scenarios—positive, negative, or neutral—and in so doing to acquire a subjective feeling for that future that might motivate present actions and concerns. From these dreams, we must extract the meanings that energize positive, creative changes rather than a dark cloud of unknowing, or fearful images reflecting only the "terror of history" and the fallibility of unthinking human ignorance. A crucial part of the alchemy of soul is to attend to the dream life and to do the necessary work of analysis that allows the dream to become part of the waking life and motivating intentions toward a more just, peaceful, and co-creative life. The art of dreaming is part of a process of interpretations whose contents are by no means restricted to dreams, but also apply to life experience in the waking sense. A strategy of the alchemical approach is to regard the waking life also as a dream, one in constant need of interpretation and synthesis in order to clarify motivating tendencies. As in night dreaming, we can learn to reflect on waking experience as also requiring interpretation and integration similar to the symbolic processes of dreaming. In this process, collective guidebooks and symbolic dictionaries are of little use, as they are in all genuine alchemical work, because it is the individual interpretation that matters, not the collective attitude. The work of interpretation has no end; it is a constant aspect of the developmental challenge—to move beyond the dominant paradigms into a freer visionary space that nurtures the soul-life and reseeds the earth with positive, loving intentions.

It is sometimes said that the dream content is incoherent and fragmentary, and in fact, dreams are often vague, opaque, obscure, partial and incomplete. But they can also be highly coherent, revelatory, dramatically detailed and highly plotted, filled with actions which reflect latent and unrealized potentials, far beyond the normative abilities of the dreamer. My own dream life is extremely rich, provocative, mythic and dramatic to a degree that suggests a multidimensional content of consciousness linked to alternative states of awareness such as those articulated in many spiritual and mystical traditions. Many of these dreams are amazingly coherent, extremely rich in detail, and filled with wonderful, provocative encounters, interactions, and profound psychic perceptions that act as a stimulus in the development of my waking states. I attribute this dreaming content to many factors, one of which is my continual attention to dreams on a daily basis for over thirty years. Each morning upon waking, I reflect on several dreams of the previous night; after many years this is a normal and effortless process. There is no struggle to remember and no confusion about the actual dream scenario which is typically vivid, clear, in color, and highly coherent—though not always easily understood in meaning or significance! Attention to dreaming over years of concentrated effort can clearly lead to a daily infusion of dream experiences and events into the stream of waking awareness such that it acts as a counter-perspective and enhancement of waking states. In turn, waking awareness takes on a valence of inner meaning that corresponds to dream imagery and reveals the continuity and value of reflections on experience, waking or sleeping, as grounded in powerful modes of symbolic interaction.

In an alchemy of soul, the model of human consciousness does not bracket out the unusual or non-ordinary but includes an awareness of the full range of experiences that act to inform the individual of his or her own inner potential. What I call the "deeper strata of incarnate being" refers to the full spiritual potential of our humanity as embodied in and embracing the sensuous, emotive, mental, and ethical life of imagination and dream play in a context of human growth and development. We are neither static nor frozen in the social logic of our cultural circumstances. These circumstances are constantly challenged by our own dreams and imaginings, by our storied retelling of our life experiences that honestly portrays the diversity and uniqueness of our struggle to realize inner potential and to be more fully ourselves. The challenge is to move beyond the static model, beyond the closed universe of fixated thought on the immediate and observable and to move into the inner complexity of our own dreaming relationships. And we can learn how to link these capacities with the dreaming muse of others. This is an artful process of sharing, listening, respectfully valuing, and supporting the tentative as it seeks to emerge from its shell of social encrustation.

Lacking dream awareness, we move only in the lineal spaces of the three dimensional order, while a much greater complexity unfolds through the fabric of our unseen dreaming life. Dreaming the future requires us to first embrace the dream life, to honor the imagination as a creative, gifting power, and to celebrate the intersection of dreams among widely diverse dreamers. The dreams of the future are soul creations of shared concern that revere the creative process as it supports a variety of global networks of dreamers seeking to actualize inner potential. This is not new, but very old, part of an ancient teaching that sought to value the dream life as a communication with higher powers. In following the dream images, we undertake a journey or pilgrimage toward a new understanding in which the alchemy of soul is a synergistic union of dreams, visions, and poetic insights with the technical, pragmatic and rational capacities necessary for the recreation of human societies in a new harmony and balance. The imagination, in this process, is layered in varying degrees of accord with our conscious insights into our individual goals and desires. Where we correspond is not in thinking or dreaming alike, but at the intersections where our dreams overlap and stimulate creative thinking and action. The tensions in this process are found at the center where we maintain continuity and consistency as individuals while honoring the differences that distinguish us through dreams that resonate with possible future concord. Dreaming is thus a process, an ongoing search for psychic coordination and symbolic relations with others that does not reduce itself to mere conformity or self-denial in the name of a collective tendency.

To honor the future through dreams and soulful imagination is a creative, demanding task that necessitates constant refinement and development as we come increasingly into contact with other mature, creative individuals. The center of this process is not simply a matter of self-affirmation, but of cultivating the "skillful means" by which we can share and contribute to a viable, supportive future for all. In the alchemy of soul, we discover a great truth about the future—that self cannot reach its fullest development without the reality of self-development for all. As we seek to contribute to this process, each individual has a responsibility to bring into focus his or her unique gifts and dreaming capacities, the special emotive and mental abilities, as they constitute a meaningful contribution to the whole. In dreaming the future, I dream the alchemy of soul as a contributing metaphor to the development of others whose own dreams can also enhance the dreams of those I will never meet or know. In the fractal processes of creative development, the many networks of meaning and co-creation all add their qualitative insights to the actual realization of future events. The task is to embrace the dream and to value its creative addition to an entire planetary evolution in which dreams, visions, and imagination play a crucial, valuable, rewarding, and significant role.

DREAMING THE END OF TIME

In the alchemy of soul, there is no "end of time" insofar as each seeker carries within him or her the capacity to strip away the three-dimensional constructs of historical, chronological time. This capacity, which opens to what I have called the "transhistorical horizon," is a state of spiritual realization in which time no longer functions in a one-directional, strictly processional sense.[3] In dreaming the end of time we are not dreaming of an externalized eschatological end-time rooted in apocalyptic fear and anxiety or in a final immature cataclysmic fantasy of judgment that condemns all other faiths as invalid. On the path of alchemy, the quest of the individual is based in a self-determining, inner discernment that seeks to actualize new perceptions no longer bound by a strictly linear, historical model of human evolution or development. The deeper cycles of the alchemical process engage time as overlapping, interdependent, noetic perspectives relative to various stages of human maturation and emergent cosmological awareness. Our natural human capacity allows us to experience and perceive beyond the bound linearity of an ever-flowing river. We can turn back, jump ahead, or step out of the confining unilinear into a vaster and more comprehensive continuum whose perception is rooted in new states of psychic awareness. Opening the "doors of perception" requires us to drop a judgmental, eschatological vision for new transtemporal horizons that no longer privilege any particular religion or spiritual path.

Dreaming the end of time is right now, not in the future; and it is the "right now" of each and every generation. There is a timeless Now that extends perceptions into a vaster and more complete primal space, or what I call UrSpace, whose contents include all aspects of awareness and being, without exception, and all dimensionality, including the lower dimensionality of tri-part space-time. Time is relative and space is non-linear and multidimensional. Therefore, the alchemy of soul proceeds to embrace the fractal nature of time as a many-branching universe of possible pathways and directions, no longer privileging the archaic destiny of a chosen or select humanity, but instead embracing all the pathways that sanction positive spiritual growth and creative exploration of an emergent, interactive universe. We do not create that primal space through a mental act. Instead, in the alchemy of soul, we seek to assimilate human consciousness into an existent continuum of multidimensional, infolded potential whose actualization will bring us into a much vaster, mutually participatory space. This is the primal spatiality of creation, the UrSpace, the psychically open space of imaginative visions, spiritual ecstasy, and illumination. It is also the primal space of human imagination and visionary truth, the place where the soul journeys in dreams and flights out of the body, and the place of creative invention and discovery, the holy space containing all possibilities.

What we are dreaming is not the "end of time" but the end of lineal imagination, the end of an apocalyptic scenario. We are dreaming the attainment of an apotheosis of insights, leading to a new awareness that affirms the pluralisms of space. The description of external, flat space spread out in all directions and then curved into the relative space of a gravity well or a black hole, is only a forerunner of the deeper curvatures of space as containing all imaginative, visionary, and infolded mental worlds, all the co-created, shared visions of collective truth. The space of an existing afterworld, of the dead or disincarnate, the space of spirits or angels, of archangels or aeons, of archetypes and deities, is the primal space, the UrSpace, of ongoing creation. UrSpace is the great all-containing, living space of the continually regenerative universe that links all mentalities in a shared continuum of psychic perceptions that can collapse the external or quantitative forms of space and time. UrSpace is not separate from the waking and dreaming states of human perception nor is it distinct from the ordinary dimensionalities of height, width, or depth. Like the Newtonian space of the pre-relative era giving way to the new relativity of quantum theory and the multidimensional hyperspace of resonant, vibrating superstrings, the emergent complexity of primordial, psychic space is unfolding its hidden resonant energies and dimensions as reflected in evolving consciousness, in the imaginative, dreaming, visionary aspects of the creative mind.[4] The properties of UrSpace are the properties of mind, matter, and energy synchronized with creative speculations and visionary possibilities of human imagination. This space is the arena of Mundus Imaginalis, the active, layered space of the world soul, the post-collective space of mythic, scientific, and literary interaction, the mental horizons of integrated perception fostered through alchemies of soul that promote new synergies of visionary perception.

Time in this vaster, more comprehensive space of creative psycho-mental and bio-energetic emergence is highly relative. Even the most remarkable global events when measured against the multi-dimensionalities of UrSpace are more archetypal than historical and more qualitatively transformative than any account of lineal time can provide. The poverty of historical accounts lies in the complexity of human understanding of those events as experienced by living subjects, and that experience is inseparably part of UrSpace. An historical account is a mere image, a kind of mental mirage that has been given the documentary authority of varied kinds of evidence which can never replace or equal the actual human experience or its density of emotive and psychological truth. A brilliant piece of historical reconstruction can offer a new perspective, an unexpected depth of nuance that helps one to solicit insights or to appreciate previously unseen dimensionality. But the density of the event is much more a resonance within the layered space of consciousness, within the depths of the human soul and its connection with the living universe of qualitative relations sustained long after the events have passed. Our capacities as incarnate beings can recover these latent memories and resonant energies of past events and we can receive soulful impressions from a future that has not yet manifested. But to do so requires us to collectively accept a non-lineal spatiality, the end of time, as a new kind of awareness that no longer observes the visible world as the only reference for understanding the past or future. This end is a new beginning, a new perspective that no longer privileges lineal time over cyclical or visionary time.

We may dream the past or the future; we may enter into a visionary continuum that reveals events long ago or not yet come into historical realization. We can look into the fractal universe, the ever branching ways of human capacity, and see this emergent continuum manifesting in art, literature, cinema, music, feminist writings, and science as the horizons of the bound lineal universe are broken into new densities of possible worlds, beings, and dimensions. This visionary dream space is the place of creative, powerful encounters whose expansive or contracted character can lead to whole new theories in human development and post-lineal evolution. But it is not a straight line; the symbolic configuration is more a curve and a circle, more a spiral and an impressionistic assembly of quanta whose contents are psychic, emotional, mental or noetic. The gnosis involved in this opening to new space is expansive and functions in a psychic continuum whose temporal boundaries are externally limited by a variety of tendencies that seek to maintain an older order of perception. The cycles of time are cycles of learning, not a measure of some pre-established order or predictable end, but a learning curve whose goal lies beyond the ordinary temporal progression. In the alchemy of soul, there is an emphasis on the dreamtime, on the cycles of human development as related to the greater cycles of nature, not just physical nature, but psychic nature, as related to the depths of incarnate being.

From this perspective, there is no quantifiable distinction between the "inner" and the "outer", as though inner space was only mental and outer space was only physical. Such a division reflects an old mind-body dualism which falsifies the human situation. In the alchemy of soul, this boundary is dissolved and seen as a mythic construct of rationalism seeking to divorce itself from nature. In the cyclical structures of cosmological time, in the spiraling journey of planetary evolution, that sharp division between inner and outer is a stage of detachment and necessary reflection as the individual, along with various communal groups, seeks to stand against nature and its complex matrix of qualitative relationships. But in the emerging alchemy of soul, this barrier is dissolved in the primal UrSpace so we can discover a participation in the blended continuity of body, mind, soul, and spirit. The pervasive energies of this vaster, inclusive space are known through an increasing sensitization for the inwardness of Being, the perceptual opening to the subtle, interpenetrating energies of higher, intermediary, and lower relationships between beings. The all-containing, generative space is not a negation of individuality, but an affirmation of differences developed into highly integrated, communicative relationships with even the most abstract and diverse type of entity. But this requires holding to the personal center; it means not dissolving into the dream; it means standing firmly in the creative space of individual self-realization.

UrSpace, as a primal expression of the Mundus Imaginalis, is structured by the intentional nature of individual awareness. It is not simply a transpersonal space of ecstatic visions, but also the structural space of intentional dreaming projects; this involves whole communities dreaming in interconnective patterns of psychic space — heavens, hells, planes, paradises, after-death worlds, or karmic dimensions of times past, present and future. Visionary worlds of suffering or joy, of sexual freedom and enslavement, are mythic worlds built around transformative themes meant to embody a particular Aeon or Archetype. We see a glimpse of this space in the great Indian classic, the Bhagavad Gita, where the Avatar of Vishnu (Krishna) shows the warrior Arjuna, the "whole universe, moving and unmoving" and containing all gods, goddess, divinities, angels, humans, aliens, others, without end, limitless yet extending into the qualitative formlessness of mystical visions and trance.[5] This space is not simply "inward" or mental, but multidimensional and enfolded into a greater continuum from which consciousness is inseparable and in which lineal, three-dimensional space is a lower and less complex variant. To say that physical space is outside the body is to describe a certain phenomenology of space that is consistent with the perception of the self as body, having certain density and measurable properties. But when we acknowledge the dreaming space of intelligent, self-reflective minds able to reach into the inner dimensionality of others — human, animal, plant, mineral or solar-astral — then physical space can no longer contain the complexity of such intuitive perceptions.

The alchemy of soul requires us to shift our perspective away from a divisive distinction between mind and matter and to embrace a greater continuity of dynamic, energetic interrelationship. The energies of the others are not simply within them but are more accurately part of us through a complex hyperspace that carries three dimensionality within it as a basic paradigm of physical relationship. If we descend into the elemental order, into the molecular structure, we find a complex, multidimensional spatiality and if we ascend into the macrocosm of galactic, large-scale formations, then space changes, bending and folding in unexpected ways. But this is also true between human beings and through relationships with other species. We can enter into a multi-dimensionality far more complex than "outer" space, rich with all the creative mythos of the dreaming self. The dream is an ontological window, an opening into the depths of being that reveal not a mental content, but modes of awareness that are richer and more complete than the simple sensations of physical perception. The physical eye also has a dreaming eye; a visionary eye that, once opened, looks directly into a vaster and more remarkable, primal space, the place of manifest possibility and not simply at what appears through the senses.

Dreaming the end of time means entering into a new perception of space-time becoming where the individual is a visionary center through which Being opens a variety of horizons no longer bound by the historical moment. This opening horizon at the "end of time" is not an end at all, but an awakening to Spirit, which celebrates the interconnective, dynamic communication and insights found within all UrSpace. The collapse of the mental boundary between inner and outer is not a loss but a tremendous gain that requires the utmost in maturity and deep stability to truly fathom. It is as though the separable barrier between the inner and outer were peeled away like the skin of an orange, leaving the perceptive psyche open to, and vulnerable to, the vaster energies of creation and its multitudes of beings. To undergo such a change, as an evolutionary cycle, requires great preparation, patience, skill, and stability in order to sustain individual consciousness and not surrender it in a paroxysm of ecstatic joy, or fear. In the alchemy of soul, we do not seek obliteration or the abandonment of the individual psychic self, but its full development and integration into a higher continuum of perception and awareness. This is a slow and gradual process punctuated by sudden glimpses, mystical intuitions, and visionary journeys which mark the stages of maturation and the very nature of true, individual character.

NON-POSSESSIVE RESPONSIBILITY

The interconnective energies that join us together as a species are qualitatively subject to the infrastructures of Being and Spirit. These infrastructures are seen in evolving patterns of belief and imagination as they are enacted in the social and cultural worlds of diverse communities. Thought itself is such an infrastructure, a dynamic formation of imaginative and logical constructions whose contents help to shape and alter perceptions. But thought does not occur in a vacuum; it occurs in the living mind and mentality of a feeling and sensing being whose nature is veiled from his or her own direct gaze. The path of knowledge, like the path of love, is a gradual unveiling, a seeing into depths at first unseen or not yet recognized. The infrastructures of Being are complex beyond imagining and, in the acculturated poverty of the human mind, they quickly assume conventional, stereotyped, and normative modes of thought that suffer from a serious impairment in visionary ability and higher sensing. In the unimaginative mind, the very idea of "higher" knowledge is suspect because it calls into question the norms and conservative tendencies, the learned habits of mental life. And yet, this conservation of imaginative energy is itself part of the infrastructure that sustains human development.

The paradox of knowledge in the development of our human potential is symbolized by the tendency to embrace a mental perspective that then becomes not only normative but also mandatory and authoritative for further development of that perspective. Perspectives that are exclusive and hierarchical, or methodologically rigid in accepting only narrowly defined parameters, can produce remarkably accurate and perceptive forms of human insight and analysis of both the self and the world. But insofar as such a perspective delimits and denies the viability of alternative forms of knowledge, that perspective becomes an impediment to more integrated and creatively open interactions within Being. Like an expert in ice sculpture who finely carves in a perishable medium that can only be preserved by enclosing it in a controlled and limited environment, so too the thinker who chooses a narrow methodology locks his or her creative insights into a frame that prescribes the boundaries of its applicability. So the artist who uses only black and white photography can reveal new potential and perspective, but is limited by the medium just as a scientist can discover through mathematics new applications but only in a language restricted to those initiated into its use. But to say that black and white imagery, or mathematical logic, is the only true or most accurate knowledge is a falsification of the human capacity to balance multiple perspectives of understanding and insight. To insist that physically repeatable and visibly measurable data provide the only valid base for human knowledge is to create a specter of our deeper capacities, locked into a framework that limits awareness.

In the alchemy of soul, the individual seeks to develop an integral knowledge that recognizes the full range of human perceptual, imaginative, and intuitive capacities and links those capacities to emergent developments within the infrastructures of Being and Spirit. Because these infrastructures are dynamic and emergent, but humanly sustained and created, the task of the individual is to seek an actualization of self that will enhance and epitomize qualitative excellence in human understanding and love. In the alchemy of soul, knowledge is not limited to a particular method nor to a rigidly structured hierarchy of ideas or practices. Yet, there is an ontological foundation that underlies the processes by which individuals seek to know the self and the world. This foundation presumes a fundamental unity within Being that sustains diversity while also acting as a primal source for the elaboration of new modes of understanding and insight. Whatever stages may be articulated in the processes of individual self-realization are relative to the development and discoveries of others. Our capacity to learn from those others and to share our own discoveries is profoundly dependent upon our capacity to love without possessiveness and without excessive attachment to the fruits of our own labor. In this alchemical process, love is the medium through which we, as a species, are able to surpass our own inherent limits and self-interests in the face of the creative activities and contributions of others sustained within Being as an inspiration toward yet greater development and maturity.

As we begin to truly open to our full human capacity, to discover the spiritual depths and richness of our perceptual and intuitive faculties, we can discard the limited and exclusive frames of reference which limit our emergent faculties and open to more expansive and interactive horizons. We do not reject those limited frames but learn to use them in relationships to specific needs and types of knowledge that might serve particular goals or desires. Like a workman with an excellent set of tools, we are able to select those tools we have mastered, for whatever needs may arise that are within the capacities of our skill and ability. The goals of such a process are to sustain emergence, to nurture the emergence of others, and to live in a way that models a compassionate, loving attitude in all the stages of human development. Our responsibility in this process is to open our understanding to the as-yet unseen infrastructures, the underlying currents within Being and Spirit that motivate new insights into the purposes and direction of human life. As we open into the vaster, more primal space of imaginative, creative Being, we become the very means by which those currents assume form and character.

Our responsibility is not to possess those forms, nor to claim a complete knowledge of the structures of Spirit, but to simply contribute our individual insights as they act to stimulate new forms and depth in the quality and complexity of our human relationships. We are not static nor are we fulfilling some greater plan; we are the makers of our own destiny in a universe of wonder whose qualitative depths far exceed our individual capacities. As we seek to emerge into this vaster, more interconnective medium of relationships and psychic interaction, we must learn to sustain a more complex vision of the whole. We must give up seeing humanity as the center of creation or as isolated in an alien universe; and we must realize the limited, relative and yet remarkable aspects of our spiritual capacities. As human beings, we have a capacity to see beyond the immediate and everyday and into the emergent and transhistorical; we are fully capable of entering into a new communion with other worlds, other beings, and other dimensions of space-time. What limits us is our own aggressive denial of these capacities and the conservative tendency to trust only the immediate and observable. The infrastructures of Being and Spirit are resonant with a rich panoply of "others" whose participation within the as-yet unseen continuum is highly active and energetic. Being able to imagine those others—human, post-human, or nonhuman—is part of the task of coming to see more clearly how diverse and creative we really are as a maturing, interactive species.

Each individual makes a contribution in this process; each seeker offers the gifts of his or her insights to the whole of human emergence. The qualitative challenge is to live fully in accord with the insights gained or embraced as spiritually motivated individuals. What we think, what we feel, what we imagine, what we desire, passionately seek and embrace with our whole being, becomes part of the emergent infrastructure. We are each a textured thread in the weaving of new visions; our pattern is a contribution that adds to the whole when we live predisposed to love and share with others the insights that come to us through all manner of perceptions—in dreams, in creative stories, in artful imaginings, in scientific intuitions, in the creative, responsible application of new capacities and abilities. We can offer a gift, not as a didactic necessity for others, but as a creative rendering of possibility that might enhance understanding or insight. This gift is also a gift of Spirit, it comes to us not simply out of our own making, but also out of the density and comprehensiveness of the underlying unity that sustains all life and beings. Insofar as we turn away from others, denying the value of their insights and visions, celebrating only the value of our own community or the bound, like-mindedness of collective identity, we close the doors of perception and block out the possibility of shared horizons.

Within Being, Spirit acts to constantly break down those barriers, seeking to overcome the exclusive, dogmatic, and rigid boundary in order to open the minds and hearts of a multitude of beings to the inner coherence and viability of the as-yet unrealized unity and higher dimensionality. In the alchemy of soul, we are direct participants in that unity as living beings, not as members of a community or subscribers to a creed, but as individuals who embody that unity and coherence in living a unique and gifted way of life. Love, dialogue, receptivity, openness to difference, a capacity to sustain the tensions of creative disagreement, a skillful command of the language and thought forms of others, all mark the way of an inner alchemy that leads directly to the wholeness whose dynamics are constantly seeking new form and expression. It is the way of non-possessiveness; a way of not holding on to knowledge or claiming authority, but simply living skillfully, with courage and determination, to make a contribution to that greater process of emergence. This is the way of the sage, the way of the magical-I that is no longer bound by the collective denial of Spirit but which celebrates a new freedom within the imaginative possibilities of human creativity.

When we act with non-possessive responsibility, we contribute to emergence and becoming; but when we act possessively, we limit the capacities of others to grow beyond our own understanding. This is why love requires courage. To love another is to provide a ground within which the beloved can find that openness to grow beyond a boundary, to surpass an inner restriction, which offers new insights and a more expansive sense of self worth and self-affirmation. Love supports and upholds the growth of others; it provides the warmth and dependability of long-term commitment while also nourishing change and development. But love rebounds; it nurtures love in others and it creates a context of growth for both the lover and the beloved. And this mutual love sustains the process by which we acquire knowledge, the knowledge of life and of others, the knowledge of Spirit, the insights that lead to many diverse alchemies of soul. The higher knowledge we seek is grounded in this process of loving and being loved; it emerges through the mental horizon that is infused with Spirit, sustaining and nurturing mental and intellective insights. The infrastructures of Being are laden with the energies of love, which is why these many billions of beings exist, as an outgrowth of the fruitfulness within each loving person. In the alchemy of soul, we seek knowledge through non-possessive love as a ground of wisdom and understanding; without these, knowledge becomes a barrier and an inhibition to the growth of others.

NECESSARY RECIPROCITIES

In classic alchemy, the "tincture" or the Philosopher's stone, the goal of alchemy, is produced through the correct processing of materials of the physical world in combination with the studies, thoughts, prayers, and work of the alchemist. This work is largely symbolic and involves many stages of refinement, reprocessing, creatively breaking down what has been built up, and a continual subtlizing and sublimation of the Materia Magica (the subtle aspects of the incarnate soul) into a new substance or tincture, one that transforms other substances through the mere touch. The central paradigm of alchemy is the constant work of discovery, assimilation, refinement, sublimation, actualization, and new discovery which continues the process through many, many cycles of development and maturation. In the alchemy of soul, a similar process requires that we fully engage the world as the primary source of the Materia Magica that must be assimilated in the ongoing processes of spiritual life and soul development. We must enter into a necessary reciprocity with not only others, but also with the physical, organic structures of the world, and with the spiritual principles that are revealed through those manifest, incarnate forms.

The alchemy of soul is not simply or exclusively a psychological process; it is also a physical, metaphysical and transpersonal process. The psychology of this process involves a discovery and actualization of soul that is developmental but also revelatory; it is a process of engaging the world through new perceptions that assimilates the very structures of the world into the paradigms of human understanding and compassion. The soul's relationship to the world is not as an actor on a transient stage, but as a creative participant in the exploration and understanding of All That Is, of the entire complex of cosmological life. In the infrastructures of Being and Spirit, we, as living beings, as incarnate, embodied life forms, are participants in a process of ongoing revelations that continually open onto new thresholds of awareness. We are not simply observers in this process but engaged creators whose thoughts, ideas, feelings, imaginings, artistry and visions contribute to the process. In alchemies of soul, we must engage the world, engage each other, and engage in understanding the not-yet revealed, complex dimensionalities of Being.

The tincture we are seeking is an antidote to the ennui or alienation of those whose world has contracted to a diminished circle of self-interest and personal needs. It is also an antidote to the creative limitations imposed by collective thinking unable to move beyond the shadows and anxieties or arrogance of an assumed position that denies the value and worth of alternative perspectives in personal growth and development. There is no one way, only a multitude of ways that suit a complex variety of individuals whose needs cannot be defined collectively and whose inner unfolding requires the freedom to explore new interpretations of the world. And there is no one method and no one strategy for accomplishing this alchemical transformation; it is the challenge of each individual to find the appropriate, individualized synthesis and coagulation, broken and refined over years of work, that leads to a distillation of insights unique to that individual. This is because the infrastructures of Being and Spirit are emergent and co-creative, spatially endowed with vaster horizons than those seen through collective assent. An apotheosis of those horizons might coalesce in a global awakening, but until, or even after, such a time, the task is for each person to find their own contributions and visionary realizations.[6]

The interactive mode of an alchemy of soul is based in a deep and abiding respect for all life—all animal, plant, and mineral life. This also includes a deep respect for the global nature of life and for life forms throughout the Heliocosm of our particular planetary system. An alchemy of soul is based in our relationships to the more complex infrastructures of Being and Spirit as manifested in the balanced whole of both our planet and the Heliocosm of which we are a part. In an even more remote sense, it also involves our relationship to all life throughout the galactic structure or Mesocosm of which we are a part, as well as to the Macrocosm of all life throughout all known and unknown universes. Life is an abundant power that acts as a catalyst wherever it is found, the quickening agent of matter, energy, and consciousness. What we seek is more life, greater awareness, an enhanced sense of capacity that can function in relationship to the emergent life forms of other species, other worlds, other cosmological horizons. The alchemy of soul is both a physical and metaphysical transformation, not into a known and well-defined matrix of philosophical meanings, but an emergence into newness, a process of self-discovery that is creative and revelatory in establishing new meanings and relationships with other life forms and other modes of being quite different than the variants of our present collective life. In the alchemy of soul, we seek the unique vision of wholeness and interactive relationship that fully honors diversity while enhancing appreciation for the inter-workings of the Whole.

In order to emerge in a healthy, interactive sense, it is crucial that we do so by respecting all life and valuing the autonomy of that life so that other living beings have the same freedom that we ourselves seek — to develop fully the capacities intrinsic to evolutionary potential. Reciprocity in this sense means creating circumstances that allow for mutual freedom of development and exploration, grounded in an ethic of tolerance and non-violence. The degree of autonomy of the individual is relative to the freedom of others. This is why the alchemical process is a primarily individual process, one that does not impose on others any strictures that would limit their own alchemical work. The freedom necessary for such work is mutual and relative to the suffering and limitations of others. Because this is an alchemy of engaged world-concern, an alchemy that honors and seeks to promote the self development of others rather than the closed universe of one individual seeker, it is essential that the alchemy of soul be founded in strong ethical concerns for the welfare of all (not just other like-minded humans). The alchemy of soul seeks to embrace the All, the coherent universe of multiple beings whose own autonomy is an index of mutual freedom. And this freedom is attainable through peaceful and cooperative means, diverse and on occasion competitive, but grounded in the metaphysics of a shared and inner unity within the infrastructures of Being and Spirit.

The necessary reciprocities spring from the heart of loving human relationships and an epistemology that is a continuing process of self-revelation through relationships. The irony of self is found in our dependence upon others as a catalyst for insights into our own nature, motives, and goals. To the extent that we interact successfully, open to the insights and perceptions of others, we can move forward into greater self-awareness. Insofar as we fail in our human relationships, we become increasingly alienated and aloof, cut off from the grounding interactions of other real, incarnate beings who might help to illumine our individual perceptions. And insofar as we cease caring about others who do not share our values or worldview, we limit our own potential as loving and life-affirming beings. The metaphysics of love require us to move beyond the similarity and like-mindedness of comfortable relationships and to move and interact in a loving manner with all living beings, all life forms, all instances of life. And as we give, so also do we receive. What we can give is concern and care for others in a way that respects their autonomy and yet maintains an inner integrity and faithfulness to the individual process of self-development, within self and within the other.

The Philosopher's Stone transforms what it touches; so too the self that has attained a high degree of inner realization of potential transforms those with whom he or she has contact. And we are transformed by those who touch us, by those who have attained that higher degree of realization, perhaps through love, or perhaps, through a few words or a witnessed action. The making of the Philosopher's Stone, the secret tincture of the heart, is an art that requires great effort and constancy of practice and attention, to words, to thoughts, to deeds, to goals, and especially, to relationships with others. And yet, the infusion of Spirit into this process is a critical and central aspect of the Great Work. It is not the model of this alchemy to present self as an autonomous being, but as a relative and dependent being whose health and welfare is intrinsically related to the health and welfare of others. Our autonomy is relative; we cannot live without the assistance and aid of others. We are deeply interdependent because it is the very nature of Being that we are created as a species, as members of various communities whose individual lives depend upon the cooperation and successful interactions of others. The energy and dynamics of our human relationships are inseparable from the workings of Spirit; there is an underlying unity that connects us to the greater structures of the Whole. It is not that we must forge relationships with others, but that we must open our eyes and hearts and minds to what binds us in common humanity beyond the demands and needs of particular situations.

Spirit is present in all human relationships, however poorly developed or antagonistic, as a common ground of concern for more genuine communication and deeper appreciation of the intrinsic worth of each and every being. Spirit abides as a yet-to-be discovered potential for more mature love and concern, for a creative response that works toward an authentic understanding that fosters reciprocity. What energizes this process is our receptivity to depths of Being that are potential sources of self-actualization; the relativity of self is such that it can open to multiple pathways toward actualization and learn from a variety of modes and examples. Spirit in this sense is an inspiring presence, an inner sense of the latent potential resonant within every relationship that can act to enhance reciprocity and self-development. We are not simply thrown onto our own resources as much as challenged to realize the potential that we have for a more spiritually inspired life. Spirit acts as a pivot, a center that infuses life with a capacity for greater relatedness and insights into the

Whole. We can turn around this center in a way that gives momentum and direction to unrealized potential if we can honor the life source within us and respect the life source in others.

In honoring the world, we honor each other. To honor the world means to value all of its unique qualities, its diverse inhabitants, its beauty and potential, and to act in ways that preserve and sustain a soulful and heart-felt relationship to the world as a creative place of unveiling. In the alchemy of soul, the materials of the world are resources for sustaining the world, not simply resources for us to exploit. As much as we seek to gain from the world, we should also seek to return to the world through a careful and cautious use of materials and resources. The world is our Mother, our soulful ground of self-becoming, a place we inhabit that sustains us to the degree that we sustain her. The necessary reciprocity is to honor the world, its natural wealth and abundance by developing attitudes and policies that will sustain and nurture that abundance and wealth. The alchemy of soul is an engagement with the world, with its soulful depths, with the materials and substances of matter and energy bound by Spirit and sustained through conscientious and deliberate actions aimed at preservation of and respect for all life. In honoring self, we honor the self of others and the self of the world that ground of Spirit that sustains us in unity and co-creation for the good of all. Without this reciprocity and respect, without this genuine love of the world and others, the alchemy of soul becomes an escape and denial of potential and in the end, a subterfuge for the unwary and self-centered.

1. Robert Sardello, 1996: 70ff.

2.The early modern era of dream research emphasized the normatively unrecognized and unknown character of the dream, but after a hundred years of intensive theory and research in dreams, it can no longer be contended that dreaming is largely a function of the "unconscious" It would be more accurate to say that dreaming does not occur in the normatively waking state and has its own unique phenomenology, but it has become increasingly recognized as a conscious aspect of mental life and will continue to be more integrated into human psychologies of the foreseeable future; see Murray Wax, 1999.

3. See Irwin, 1994: 153 ff..

4. On the multidimensionality of hyperspace, see Michio Kaku,1994: 172 ff.; for the connection with consciousness, see Fred Wolf, 1999: 120 ff..

5. *The Bhagavad Gita*, Chapter 11:7.

6. Lee Irwin, 1994: 168-176.

CHAPTER FOUR
THE MAGICAL UNIVERSE REDISCOVERED

To understand the magical aspects of incarnational being, it is necessary to work creatively with the imagination and to regard the imagination as a primary means for symbolizing the world and its transformations. The sacred power of a symbol lies in its ability to invoke an emotive, aesthetic, and meaningful response to our complex relationships within the ground of Being. Through Being and Spirit, the symbol can become a means by which we may experience the depths of the ongoing processes of creation, sustenance, and dissolution of the world and cosmos. We dwell in the midst of cycles of manifestation and re-absorption, in a present which has no precise beginning or end, within a continuity of Being and Spirit that passes through multiple cycles and rhythms that far exceed a single human lifetime. As we contemplate the vastness of this process, we seek symbols that will codify and concentrate the joy and worth of the ongoing transformation into visible forms for the purpose of enhancing our awareness. This requires imagination and a magical worldview, an understanding in which the unexpected and the improbable are possible and in which the extraordinary is actual and real.

We must unbind our perceptions and strip away the masks that inhibit us from seeing the holy ground of the creation in every aspect of nature, in every living being. The universe is not a mechanical model of mere probabilities, but an acutely sensitive totality of relationships that span ever-increasing dimensions of space, time, and alternative worlds and beings. Matter is not without life and energy is not simply impersonal. There are qualities of life in even the most fundamental quantum or particle. In a magical universe, there is an abundance of life that matriculates through the grades and processes of the theosophical horizons by which that life takes on a changing variety of forms and appearances. Those horizons, from sub-particles to molecules and cells, from simple to complex life forms, from the physical to the psychic being, from the visible to the invisible, from solid earth to the magnetic fields and gravitational flux that surround us, are filled with Being and Spirit at every level of life. It is truly a living universe, a vast sea of interconnected energies and life-presences whose forms and characteristics we barely perceive.

The mystery at the heart of this process is the self-concealing nature of sacred Being as it constantly recedes before the advancing horizon of human understanding, creating in the gap or absence a visionary space in which we may formulate new direction and possibility. But this "absence" is an illusionary feature of the imaginative process; what we can let go of are the anthropomorphic images, the pronouncedly human forms, for a more profound, open horizon in which no form can be adequate to the unfolding nature of Being as it recedes before us and yet animates and fills the visionary space with new understanding. Like a great tide drawing back to expose a new expanse of shore, the absence of visible forms is itself a rhythm, a cycle of opening to new co-creative space, later to be filled with visionary possibilities no longer bound by strictly human images or contents. The nature of Being and Spirit, in a magical universe, cannot be imaged in only human form as they seek to instill within us the self-surpassing qualities that lead beyond anthropomorphic gods and goddesses, beyond the patriarchal and matriarchal images, into a fuller and more luminous space. And yet this space is by no means impersonal, nor does it deny the value of our most intimate relationships with others.

There is an interconnectedness that sustains human relationships in a process of transvaluation that allows us to experience the universe as a mystery exceeding human comprehension, and yet, one that deeply values human love and creative life. In the magical universe, science is one means by which we free ourselves from the strictly human concept but this is also true in art, literature, and studies that value the human and yet look beyond the known horizon into the imagined possibility, into the emergent, newly becoming reality of the undiscovered. In this process, the human being is a symbol of transformation, the means for an aesthetic synthesis of possible perceptions. We are each a living sign in a magical universe of signs, each representing a spiritual capacity, an intellective, imaginative, insightful manifestation of Spirit and Being. Our task, as individuals, is to find the qualities and discipline necessary to fully actualize the inherent potential that flows within and between us as creative, imaginative, skillful beings. But this means we must live with courage and without threatening or harming others so they too can actualize their inmost capacities. In a magical universe, we are each responsible for our individual development and each a means by which others may be encouraged to find their own self-surpassing capabilities.

The gap between our present understanding and our future possibilities, in the face of the receding tides of Being and Spirit, is the space in which we find the emergent vision that can lead us to an expressive self-realization. The courage required is found in a willingness to open to the emergent plurality of worlds, as they intersect and stimulate new thought and vision. The fear to be overcome is the fear of losing a particular world, of losing childhood visions or falling out of harmony with the visionary worlds of others we may love or with whom we share community. In a magical universe, there is an underlying sympathy, a felt sense of interconnection between beings with many diverse ideas, beliefs, and images but who are all motivated by a desire for mutual understanding and shared insights. In a magical universe, the walls are illusory, a crumbling part of the gap in which Being and Spirit seem to recede, only to open new possibilities of insight, imagination and reunion. But this is not a reunion based in a commonly held ideology or in idealized beliefs; it is a reunion held in Being and Spirit as mind and heart are transformed in a deep alchemy of soul. The symbolic nature of this process requires us to discard many external forms and ideas in order to make those we hold real and fully actual in our living and dying. The transformation is deep and penetrating; we must let go of the lesser self and open to new horizons, expanding into an undefined space for the purposes of new creation.

In a magical universe, the self is an intersection of possible worlds, beings, and creative, imaginative, artful projects supported by a credible science of human existence and development. The self in this universe, in this multidimensional habitation of spaces great and small, from the infinitesimal relativities of the speed of light to the maximal solidity of a mountain or a granite monument, is relative and permeable. We are each a perishable work, a continuity of awareness united to a complexity of relationships and bodily interactions that are fallible and limited by the mental and emotive horizons we each inhabit. Our nature is not immortal, but transformative; not simply perishable, but metamorphic and embedded in a vast cosmos of permeations beyond our immediate, incarnate understanding. What we each are, at this moment, is not a static image or an unchanging bodily form. We are each in process, engaging the magical universe to a degree resonant with our development and maturity. The horizon of our understanding is relative to our experience and to our exposure to alternative ways of perceiving and knowing the world. In a soulful, centered knowing, the magical universe is unfolding with incredible dimensionality, revealing an ever-layered sense of infinite capacities yet unrealized through the human form in its full potentiality.

The relational self, as a spiritual being, seeks to communicate insight

103

through the media of written and spoken words for the purpose of illumining the human heart. This is because, in a magical universe, the self is grounded in relationships that foster growth, not just through human relationships, but through ALL relationships, with everything that lives, with the entire cosmos. In the sharing of self, in the writing of words and the speaking of insights, the self comes forward according to degrees of relatedness expressed through a mastery of the arts of communication. Others might choose more visual (painting or sculpture) or auditory forms (music or song), more complex and abstract languages (like mathematics or chemistry) or more physical expressions (yoga or dance), but in all these, the self that comes forward is the expressive self, demonstrating varying degrees of mastery of the communicative forms. The self is a process of reflection and communication, a nexus of integrated energies manifesting varying degrees of wholeness and dynamic connection to the living cosmos. In order for the self to develop, it must open to the complexity and wholeness of all life, to all aspects of ongoing creation, and not be bound by narrow or dogmatic thinking and perception. The self is a mystery in its depths, and only partially aware at the surface. To overcome the limiting condition, we must interact and share insights and our respective degrees of mastery or discovery or innocence.

The communication of insight should be a multidimensional process, not a simple mastery of speaking but also a mastery of hearing and taking-in the other as a partner in the processes of discovery. This taking in must go far beyond the immediate visible or verbal sign; it must move into the subtle energetic realms of shared perceptions, intuitive and empathic impressions, and the full range of our inmost psychic capacities. It is not only how we see the other, but also how we dream the other, how we master the psychic connections that creatively, imaginatively, and pragmatically shape our human interactions. In a soulful seeing and listening, we ourselves are seen and heard; we cannot stand back unobserved, but must step forward into the magical world of relations where we can be seen for what we truly are—living beings in search of a more loving, kind, and mature world, one sustained in the processes of discovery, not destroyed or blindly ignored. In a magical universe, the self is a creative, artistic, and visionary center that fosters exploration into a living cosmos for the purpose of living harmoniously amidst the mystery and sacred depths of Being and Spirit. The universe in this context is not one that is described externally through measurement (though such measurement can enhance our mutual understanding), but through an inner process that validates the human subject as contributing to the mystery and wonder of creation, not merely observing it as a passive witness.

The creative processes of the alchemy of soul are beyond measure or description because each individual must find the exact proportion of creativity, imagination, psychic realism, and calculation that best expresses his or her present capacities. But these capacities are not fixed or predetermined, either by social or psychic processes; our capacities, at the level of our most primal being, are a gift of Spirit that is ongoing, still pouring forth, still there to enhance and enrich our present, limited and relative states. In the alchemy of soul, there are always stages, retrogression, climbing up and sliding back until we can reach yet another plateau of stability and integration. But such a plateau is not our goal; the goal is to continue throughout life to develop and evolve, at a pace consistent with our abilities, for the purpose of sharing insights and capacities, as they come forth, with all those receptive to their positive, creative benefits. This alchemy is not for the purpose of massive or collective transformation except insofar as we can actualize our deepest potentials for cooperative, peaceful, loving interaction and mutual expression and creation. We each bring forth our gifts, we offer them with humility in the face of the infinite universe, in the face of magical qualities that are inherently active in leading us to new, exciting, visionary horizons where we can work, play, and love together.

The receding imagery of a more sterile, violent, distant universe of material interactions must fade as a new affirmation seeks to actualize a living, participant universe of capacities far more spiritual than the material universe can contain. In the emergent and creative self-becoming of human wisdom, the soulful world becomes ever more perceptive to the transforming awareness as it opens increasingly to the hidden, multidimensionality of creative Being. As Being withdraws from the static, limited conceptual forms of the anthropomorphized, "violent" universe, it infuses human understanding with a new capacity for visionary understanding. Shedding the external forms of imaginary space reinforced by tactical laws and institutional codes, the emergent alchemy of soul opens to the imaginative possibility, the creative unfolding of mythic space layered through the processes of human psychic exploration. It seeks a living presence, a presence that cannot be reduced to a shallow image or a dogmatic idea, but a presence that pervades and enlivens even the stones at our feet, the rose so cited by the poet, the moon as an ember of phosphorescent glory no longer reducible to a mere image of lunar reflection. In the living universe, all life is precious, sacred, holy in every aspect, no matter how limited or how profound its awareness and habitation. Our task in the alchemy of soul is to open to that wonder that still lies hidden from dreaming eyes distracted by the liminal forms of daily life or encoded by the narrow messages of pragmatic materialism. In the alchemy of soul, all life is seeking communion, but only the aware soul will understand how profound a call that communion offers.

THE VITAL SOURCE OF LIFE

The vital source of life has no enduring name or form beyond those inscribed by human traditions in dissimilar languages that do not always reference a single, knowable ultimate. The vital source of life may be expressed as the unbound potential of creative Being or as the energetic processes of Spirit, or as an underlying Unity or Wholeness whose grounding interactions sustain an evolving universe of beings and worlds. We might say that the source of life is God or the Divine Unity or the Great Mystery of the Holy Mother Spirit. We might say that it is a vast energetic web of coherent relationships we call Nature or Cosmos. But these words cannot capture the totality nor describe, adequately, the mystery and depths that remain hidden from human understanding, illuminations, and enlightenments. I cannot adequately describe the vital source of life other than to say I experience it as a living presence that animates all creation and is yet uncontainable in any form or in collective physical, mental, aesthetic or spiritual manifestation. It overspills the boundaries of words and names; it surpasses particular thoughts and extends far, far beyond mentally constructed ideas or human philosophies. No image can contain it and no motions or movements fully express it, and yet it remains present at all times, with all beings, without exception.

It seems to me that this vital source of life has an inner content of self-reflected awareness, a depth of intelligence that far exceeds human capacity and understanding. And yet, it seems that these depths of qualitative being are as inseparable from human mental and emotive life as they are from the life-experiences of any and every particular being, visible or invisible, seen or not seen by human beings or by the inhabitants of other worlds. The nature of this vital source is that we cannot see its fullness or wholeness as it is reflected in the totality of all creation. Mystics and saints are fond of claiming that their profound experiences of God or Spirit or Nirvana or the Tao are reflections of this ultimate nature, a reflection of the knowableness of the Infinite. I do not doubt that they have had profound experiences that far outstrip my own, but my own experiences have taught me that the nature of this unbound vital source cannot be reduced to any particular spiritual teaching, nor to a particular hierarchy of spiritual teachings, nor to a specific mystical or enlightenment path without reducing the source to an image of the path or teaching. As an image, it is only able to reflect through the limitations of the human mind, and of the words and ideas communicated. The actual reality is far beyond the ideas or words or images and much greater than even the most enlightened mind or heart.

This does not mean that human teachers or illumined souls are not profound sources of guidance and direction for those seeking to actualize their deepest spiritual potential. But it does mean that the spiritual discourse of any illumined soul is relative and conditional, and that the teaching is always an image of the reality taught and not the actual reality itself. To find the reality is to experience the vital source of life directly and without intermediary guides or spirits, without veils or intervening teachings or abstract ideas or images. To find the reality is to live as a vessel of vital, incarnate Being while knowing that the vessel is a relative assemblage of insights and experiences whose wholeness cannot encompass the full reality of what it can experience in the most extensive vision of, or conscious union with, unlimited totality. But this very fact is the core of our freedom as individual beings, that there is no binding doctrine and no single teaching that is truly comprehensive because the teaching cannot contain what has given birth to its specific forms and manifestations. The teaching may be more or less comprehensive in comparison with other teachings or it may contain its own inner light and brilliance, its own joy and special sorrows, but however luminous or honest, it is still only an image of reflected light. And each person is a carrier of that light, each a modulation of its rays, each an image evolved through will and responsive hearing and acting.

In the alchemy of soul, the vital source of life is an unnamed Mystery, something more than God and something far less than a complete revelation. This vital source is more than a name or word, because no name or word can contain the reality; it is more than a conventional idea or a dogmatic teaching, more than an image or a figure of majesty. And yet it is not a vitality that is rationalized into a particular theology or a strict teaching or graded path. While it cannot be contained in a word, name, or venerable form, it also cannot be compressed or summarized into a fixed or determined system or codified philosophy of exact metaphysical truths without great loss and sacrifice. Some might choose to make the attempt or even to develop a system or language or symbol set that can act as a guiding principle. Such systems may help others to take the necessary steps that will allow them, on merging with that Source, to throw off limiting outer garments, discard the external forms, and to celebrate in naked joy the full intensity of absorption in the unbound seas of Holy Being. In that experience, words and images dissolve, ideas vanish, mental constructs evaporate, and self-awareness collapses into a tiny nova of joy and wonder far exceeding word or thought, yet hardly remarkable or great within the greater extensiveness of the Unbound. The most holy word cannot carry the intensity, and the most solemn thought is a shadow of a truth inexpressible in a light that exceeds all activities of mind or heart or soul.

The purpose or significance of holy words and teachings in the diversity of world spiritual traditions is to provide a multitude of languages, images, teachings, paths and practices uniquely suited for the ethnic and culturally specific peoples among whom those teachings evolved and grew and for whom they acted as a resource for spiritual development. It is an act of grace and wisdom to revere all spiritual traditions that promote peace, cooperation, and mutual harmony and support. In the alchemy of soul, no path is superior and no teaching is ultimate. Every path and every teaching is relative to the maturity and development of the practitioners of that path; every teaching is a reflection of sacred potential, imaged in the hearts and minds of its proponents. Where there is a great soul or teacher, how can we not honor that tradition and its accomplishments in sustaining such a soul? There are many great souls, and every tradition has its exemplars, its Saints and Sufis and Yogis, its masters and its great guides and marvelous workers of wonder and miracles. These teachers epitomize the alchemy of soul, the work of transformation that has led exactly to great-souled being, to a fullness of the vital source manifesting in the hearts and minds of illumined beings through many generations of seekers, initiates, and guides. Matured through progressive illuminations and lifetimes of struggle to perfect a path or teaching, these beings are living expressions of the true alchemy of soul.

The vital source is, however, in each of us, not just in those who manifest a unique sensibility or fullness of its presence. Alchemy of soul is a process of transformation that we undergo in every relationship and every situation that helps us to grow and to develop, to stretch beyond a conventional boundary, challenging and sustaining us in becoming more fully the illumined being that we can each truly be. The vital source is always with us and always working through us and through our relationships to provide circumstances that allow for growth if we have the intelligence and inner will to adapt our capacities to what emerges. Sometimes this takes inner discipline and a willingness to confront an inner boundary or a boundary in others as a matter of integrity and honesty in uncovering the truth of our own principles and goals. Sometimes it takes surrender and compromise in order to foster a deeper sharing or reciprocity; sometimes it takes a sharp and immediate resistance in order to protect or clarify a misleading or dishonest intention. In the alchemy of soul, the process of manifesting vitality and life is not passive, nor is it non-resistant in the face of actions or words or attitudes of others whose behavior might deny or repress the emergent spirit of a genuinely developing life. And yet, the very spirit of that vitality is to act in a loving if firm manner, with compassion and with a disciplined sense of inner values, to guide our human relationships and to lead us to a deeper and more mature mutual understanding.

Relationships as a vital ground of self-development are a manifestation of interconnective being and a revelation of human capacity and limitation. Great-souled beings are not commonly found because social life can easily draw us away from our inmost capacity when we have no vital sense of the life-presence. The underlying unity of shared perceptions and spiritual harmony arises out of the fertile ground of our differences held in tension with our creative potential. Our potential is something deeper than a particular psychological or social condition; it is something much more than the relative culture that constitutes a particular waking world of shared values or ways of thinking. The cultural context provides language, symbols, patterned actions and behaviors that can act to focus and direct the will toward greater actualization, or act as an impediment or barrier to deeper realizations that challenge shared values or ways of thinking. The vital source of life is not the conditioned circumstance, with its recognizable limits and opportunities. The vital source is a far deeper current, moving within a constellation of energies that can carry the individual far beyond the boundaries of present circumstances. In this context, creative, loving relationships act as energetic sources of support that help us to reshape our ordinary thinking into more magical, aware perceptions.

We are surrounded by sources of spiritual inspiration, if we only learn to open our eyes and our hearts to the beauty and power of the ongoing creation processes. In the alchemy of soul, we must work toward a living sense of the underlying currents of vitality that energize and support a more magical, vibrant experience of spiritual awareness. We must work to penetrate the barriers of ignorance and constricted belief that keep us from fully embracing the presence that gives the world life and vitality. This presence is beyond name and form, and in the alchemy of soul, it cannot be reduced to a specific concept that we can hold or examine as a fixed reference that justifies a faith, or that soothes fears or anxieties. We must move beyond fear, anxiety, and dependence on the visible and the concrete. The seeker must move into the unbound world of potential energies that may be defined in various creative ways, not with a goal to control or to subordinate, but with a deep respect that honors fully the mystery and holiness of the Uncontainable. We must embrace the limits of our relative thinking, and yet not abandon our quest; we must have the courage to recognize our conditionality, and yet also pursue the fulfillment of our deepest spiritual potentials. To do this means to walk a different path, one that does not seek power, control, or dominance, but love that earns the respect and love of others through integrity, honesty, and great-souled joy and understanding.

The vital source of understanding is the holy ground of creation, the inner deep unity of Spirit made actual in the particular gifts, abilities and commitments of each individual as he or she undergoes the fire and transformations of genuine spiritual awakening. This process is long and challenging, and requires the utmost sincerity to fully actualize our participation in the ongoing creative process. We can each be a manifest instrument, a pen that writes a new word, or an ideal manifesting in various forms for the good and help of others. Our gifts are unique, but the ground of our spiritual growth is something deeper than any particular doctrine or teaching. The soul opening to light is an image of the particular experiencing the universal. In the alchemy of soul, both the particular and the universal are necessary, both must come into harmony with the specific talent and capacity of individual life. And from the view of incarnate being, it is the life of each individual that must be valued and supported, not simply the universality of a teaching or the pride of the teachers. What must challenge us is the task of bringing to perfection the fullness of each soul. The living vitality of spiritual presence signifies the true alchemy.

BODY-SOUL-MIND-SPIRIT

There are five aspects of personhood that are central to the processes of spiritual transformation, though none of these can be interpreted in an absolute sense. The evolutionary relationships between these aspects are relative and circumstantial rather than systemic or structural. They represent a psychic assemblage or an image of personhood as multilayered and interdependent, having no ultimate subsistence beyond that assemblage. The terms describing these aspects are relative in the sense that they reflect a particular psychic, linguistic history of stages in religious life stemming from ancient Egypto-Greco-Roman-Christian roots and flourishing through Euro-American intellectual and esoteric traditions. The five terms are: body, soul, mind, and spirit which together reflect an embodied self. The relationships between these are more metaphorical than descriptive and yet, each term references a perceptual perspective, an awareness that is dependent on all other aspects for its development and actualization. There is no mind-body dualism. Such a dualism is an outgrowth of metaphysical speculations that are not grounded in an embodied hermetic, incarnational spirituality, but are constructed through a misleading Gnostic distinction made between physical and spiritual life.

Physical, bodily life IS spiritual life; the body is not an imprisonment of soul, but a means by which soul becomes more aware and actualized. The body is a grace, a wondrous complexity of bone, muscle, organs, nerves, fluids, sensory perceptions, and subtle systems and sensations that carry far more information than merely physical, electro-chemical actions or energies. The body is a living miracle, one of the truly remarkable aspects of ongoing creation. It is not a house for a tenant, but a manifest assemblage that can only BE through a life-presence which stimulates its growth and transformations. There is no body without life and sentience; this sentience goes down into the cellular, microcellular, molecular, and subatomic structures and as such, is directly perceptible to mind. Body is inseparable from this life-presence and without it there is only death and decay. The

111

miracle of the body is its complexity and multi-systemic wholeness, the way in which body holds the space of the organic complex in perfect harmony (in health) through life presence, and provides a ground for human growth and development.

The body as self is laden with cultural signs, expectations, desires, and gestural, expressive demonstrations of identity. The shape of the body, its typologies and forms, are not merely physical but also cultural, aesthetic, communicative, and symbolic of a wide variety of states and conditions. Sexuality and health are central to this complex of physical expressiveness, and body has been heavily burdened by the social and cultural expectations of specific societies. The body is a carrier of signs in the shape of a limb or the contour of an eyebrow or in the expressions of face or feeling. Body's beauty is a gift of creation, a joy and a delight that expresses the profound wonder of millennia of evolution and becoming. In the alchemy of soul, we must work to liberate the body from the repressive context of bodily denial and also from social values that place artificial, excessive attention on bodily appearances. The repression of sexuality must be overcome and excessive attention to sexuality must be released in order to give the body freedom and balance in being exactly what it is—a divine creation that is still in the process of transformation. It is not bodily life that we are seeking to exalt; rather, we are seeking to honor the beauty and grace of the body as natural and good. It is not the body per se that is the issue, but emotive, mental, and social attitudes toward the body.

How we paint, prepare, dress, contour our hair, and what we wear as bodily signs are all part of the context of spiritual life. Beauty of movement, graceful control and athletic abilities, expressive individuality, flexibility and supple strength are important features of bodily life in many different alchemies of soul. The body inspires reverence, and its full actualization requires that we attend to the body throughout all the stages of our maturation, from childhood to oldest age, maintaining health, harmony, and sound physical well-being. This also means sustaining a genuine sensitivity and sexual vitality throughout the incarnate experience as signs of honoring the means through which we may know and experience the world. In turn, this means developing habits in diet that maximize health and well-being, eating natural produce, fruits, grains, nuts, herbs, and all the rooted plant life that is itself so beautiful and healthy. It also means avoiding degrading appetites that diminish the bodily life, overcoming dependency and attachments to food and drink that serve

112

only to diminish bodily health and are only products of poor habits and unhealthy cravings. The pure diet is not one kind of diet; it must vary according to the physiology of the body and temperament of the individual and will be, no doubt, more limited for some than for others. But, where possible, we should avoid harming other creatures and not make our health an expression of our dominance over other living beings.

Sexuality is a central issue of the vital being and the life-presence; it is the means by which the incarnate being reproduces and experiences the intense pleasures of uniting with a beloved other. In the alchemy of soul, sexuality is a sacrament and a source of great joyfulness in celebrating the natural pleasures that result from a loving embrace and union. But sexuality is more than physical, and those who only regard it in its physical aspects have failed to realize the soul-centered power of sexual relations. The basis of sexuality is deeply rooted in the life-presence and is thus one of the true spiritual interactions that further the life process. This is a metaphysical as well as physical point; the true union of bodies in sexual embrace is a soul phenomenon as well as a physical joining, and failure to recognize this condemns us to externalized and superficial, only momentary, relations. In sexuality, we encounter the vitality of soul as well as the vitality of body; sexuality is a medium of deep emotional and spiritual perception. The sensate aspects of sex are a stimulus for awakening deeper feelings of connection and love between lovers, and these sensations have an inner plane of awareness that allows one person to share with another an intimacy of communion and connection that cannot be fully expressed verbally or in external signs. In the alchemy of soul, the spiritualization of the sexual is crucial to the process of inner awakening to the creative potential of self and other. The I-Thou relationship is most directly knowable in the sexual and erotic when approached with deep respect that honors the sensitivity and feelings of both partners and proceeds through freely given permission to explore the sexual potential between them.

Soul is the basis of human feeling and heart-centered relationships. Love in these relationships, as well as love for the world, is a soulful awareness that embraces the life-potential in every living being. It is not the soul in humanity, but the soul in creation, the soul in all beings, the soul as carrier of deep feeling, memory, and all the joys and sorrows, all the light and shadow, of our collective and individuated identities. Soul is what allows us to truly connect with others; it is the medium of shared life, the vital center of empathy and a deeply felt sense of an entire world

113

of subtle energies and relationships. At the depths, soul is embedded in a communion with the collective soul life of humanity and all other life forms. It is a heart-centered communion, an inner perception of the subtle and the energetic that contains the body and sustains physical life. Where there is no soul, there is no life. Soul is a sacred energy of human identity passed from life to life through multiple incarnations, and resulting in a multilayered and multidimensional awareness that sustains body as its means for self-development and evolution. The soul surrounds and holds the body through a medium of subtle, expressive, emotive energies whose capacities are deeply linked to body as utterly necessary and inseparable from incarnate life. The soul distinct from body is something quite different than embodied soul because embodied soul is a relationship of great sophistication and complexity. The soul sustains the energies of the intertwined emotions, intellect, and physical body as the very source of creative vitality.

Body does not house soul, but soul contains and houses body through the medium of its unique energetic character and through an expressive intensity of feeling and empathic relations. Soul connects us with everything living and is an open horizon of human perceptions far greater than the physical perceptions of the body. The soul utilizes a psychic spectrum of perceptions that enables us to move through the world of dreams, visions, and various inter-dimensional modes of awareness that can connect us to very distant and removed places or environments. It can also act as a medium of receptivity, taking into itself a wide spectrum of sensitivity to worlds and planes invisible to the physical senses. In this process, mind plays a central and crucial role. The soul has a mind just as mind has soul, the two are really one insofar as mind is a clarity of soul distilled into thought and lucid intuition. The soul has intuitions; these are the intuitions of the soulful mind, a mind that resides in and through soul as the medium of connective perceptions within the life-presence. The noetic aspect of soul life, like the mental aspect of physical life, is a reflection of organized perception and sensation distilled through processes of self-reflection and learning in order to actualize innate capacities. This reflective aspect of self is strongly linked to the use of language, words, and grammar as a means for the expression of ideas, beliefs, values, and ideologies. But mind is far more than a reflected process of socialized grammar; in its depths, mind is a focal point within a field that has extensive range and capacity far greater than the spoken language through which mind communicates. Mind is not a product of language, but a producer of language that reinforces a particular way of thinking; such thinking is only an image of mind, not mind itself, not mind as the vital energy of soul.

The relationship between mind and soul is highly complex, like the relationship between body and soul; mind can act directly on body to alter its health, awareness, and capacities. Mind is primarily a noetic combination of sensations, intentions, memories, beliefs, and ideas energized by the emotional life of soul, through desires, wants, needs, ambitions, and fears or anxieties. And body is the carrier of all of these, sustained by soul through mind's intentions (both recognized and unrecognized), and acting as the physical medium by which mind can instrumentalize its noetic contents. But where is mind's inspiration? The subtle source of mind's intention toward the maximization of its deepest noetic capacity lies in Spirit. In Spirit, we find the pure potential, the deepest capacity for actualizing the unknown depths of incarnate life. In this sense, Spirit is the subtle connective medium permeating all creation, a medium that outreaches soul and acts as a ground and unity for all conscious life. Yet, Spirit is far more than a unitary, collective medium of the life-presence; it is also the astral-stellar energetic basis of ongoing creation whose own nature remains mysterious and unknowable in the everyday sense. Spirit is the deep ground that manifests in the variety and diversity of all living beings; it is the common ancestor of all humanity and all species. In the human framework, it is the very subtle, the very clear, lucid, transpersonal-personal presence that infuses life with inspiration, ideals, and loving capacity for union and mutual explorations. It is the source of our most cherished hopes and the most sought-after content of our dreams and longings.

The place of Spirit within the human being is symbolized by a luminous pearl, the pearl of great price that represents the deep heart of soul, the inspirational center of incarnate life as a luminous gem of startling and unquenchable brilliance. This gem contains a spark which is an interface and slight opening that leads us toward the immensity of a living ocean, sustained by Spirit, containing all life. We must draw Spirit into our incarnate lives and learn to embody Spirit as a soul-centered activity of world transformation. In the alchemy of soul, the goal is to refine and to build up the spiritual life, to give luster to the pearl, as a beacon to guide others toward individual and collective transformations. The goal is to illumine a new possibility in the world of actual incarnations and thus, to provide a safe harbor in the midst of stormy and turbulent change and uncertainty. Spirit is a great blessing that can work through us and within our relationships to bless and guide our development if we can open to it in a mindful, soulful way, with integrity, love, and genuine world concern. We must breathe on the spark, foster its warmth and light, and become a lamp burning with purest oil, a luminous manifestation of inner joy that spreads, like a single candle flame, to others who also contribute to the collective light. Spirit does not work in isolation, but through its own sacred ground; it embraces all, and yet fosters the unique, the extraordinary, and the eccentric.

The alchemical self is a synthesis of capacities and energies, ranging from physical incarnate life, through sexual and emotional connection, to mind, thought, ideas and into the inspirational values and beliefs that constitute our shared humanity. This self references an evolutionary process, not a thing or object, but a synthesis and an expanding awareness that embraces body, soul, mind and social life as the ground of its own becoming. The world, as a place of learning, is fostered by Spirit to provide a multitude of lifeways and experimental environments meant to develop differences and unique distinctiveness. Our task is not to dissolve these differences into a single prototype that claims to represent humanity, but rather to promote and exemplify the diversity within Spirit as a creative ground for emergence and differentiation. The embodiment of the fullness of Spirit must flow through billions of possible channels, each focalizing embodiment, because within Being, Spirit is immeasurable and vast, far greater and more comprehensive than all possible human lives. Spirit is not a mere energy of potential, but a vastly comprehensive vitality whose inner energies manifest not a world but a cosmos, and not a cosmos but a multidimensional universe of uncountable worlds and other beings. In this context, the self is the refracted, evolutionary synthesis, the vivid, glowing image that is constituted within Being as a valuable and unique life, giving itself to that embodiment in order to foster ever more comprehensive understanding, wisdom, and insight.

SOUL-BEING IN VISIONARY MODE

The soul-centered life is a life of rhythmic expansions and contractions, a rhythm that builds on its own experiences and on its relationships with others (and their rhythms) in order to sustain an increasingly open, interactive horizon of awareness. Part of this process involves entering visionary space, entering into the vaster life of the cosmos through an inner capacity to sustain the visionary mode. By this I mean the capacity to enter altered states of awareness, to receive visions, visionary dreams, or illuminations as a means for enhancing human awareness. Simply stated, visions and mystical experiences are valid and highly significant modalities of human knowledge, modalities that can open the horizons of perception far beyond ordinary sensory awareness. The visionary mode is a spontaneous condition of opening, either in waking or sleeping states, that allows the visionary to behold the far more complex dimensionality of the "inner" as it connects and reciprocates with the "outer." In many ways there is no inner-outer distinction other than what we ascribe through conventional attitudes toward the physical and the spatial. But seen from the visionary mode, these distinctions become artificial and redundant; in the visionary mode, the world opens into a vast embeddedness of Spiritual presences, powers, and possibilities. This is the threshold of the Mundus Imaginalis, the Imaginal World of visionary illumination facilitated through inner self-development.

The contact point of this visionary mode does not have a physical location, but is accessed through a shift in awareness, an inner opening to outer wonder, through disciplined habits of mind. Such a shift can happen completely spontaneously, an experience that I have witnessed directly in my own life, and it can be solicited through meditation, prayer and other spiritual activities, which I have also witnessed. It can happen through crisis, through profound emotional needs, in fearful circumstances, and totally without effort in circumstances of perfect balance and intuition.[1] The phenomenology of this shift is quite varied and ranges through a wide spectrum of human circumstances and inner receptivity. But in all cases, there must be a receptivity to shifting awareness from the ordinary to the enhanced state, and a careful attentiveness to the transformation that allows the individual to recover and reiterate the experience. In persons who undergo this shift spontaneously and frequently, the issue is a matter of integration and understanding, not technique or practice, though, at later states of life, practice can provide a stable ground for such integration. For those less inclined to the spontaneous experience, disciplines can be developed to facilitate the shift if the person is well grounded in her or his capacity to re-conceptualize the world in terms of those shifts. The visionary mode is a form of knowledge, not simply an image or process, and as such, requires constant effort (intentionality) to bring those experiences within the frame of a developing maturity that is truly visionary and transformative.

In the alchemy of soul, there is a process of constant refinement and formation that is represented as a temporary frame of reference, and then that frame is dismantled and refined and reassembled. This is an example of alchemical stages: refinement, stabilization, sublimation, calcification, mortification, separation, then more refinement, stabilization and so on.[2] This work requires an inner capacity to adapt and change, to have fluidity and permeable boundaries, to overcome rigidity, defensive resistance, and authoritarianism, to willingly move into the challenging task of making and unmaking worlds, both within and without. The stages of development are not fixed and do not follow a specific order; each individual must undergo the necessary changes and stages in terms of the individual nature of his or her experience, temperament, and social conditions. But a primary goal in this process is to attain the visionary mode and to draw upon that mode as a resource for the reconstitution of the world and its subliminal, shared contents. To enter that mode is to bring body, soul, mind, and Spirit into a state of receptivity to the influx of powerful energies that can be experienced as vastly more real and more potent than ordinary perception and which often embodies a distinctive spiritual presence. In the process of refinement, we can sublimate the forms of these energies into higher and more comprehensive insights that move beyond the specific manifestation into various fields of awareness and intelligibility.

In the visionary mode, a spiritual alchemist may well see angels and archangels, devas, spirits, elementals, the disincarnate, and various archetypal or manifest beings whose actual nature remains obscured by their appearances. Other human beings can be seen as accompanied by various spirits, some luminous and some dark, as well as by a variety of psychic energies, somewhat like a continuous energetic flux surrounding the body. Similar forms can be seen in association with animals, plants, and even mineral and other basic materials like stones, gems, or metals. In the visionary mode, everything is accompanied by its own energies and presences, sometimes very subtle and sometimes very dramatic and even overwhelming. Further, there is a large repertoire of visionary forms that are in direct association with humanly created objects, from handcrafted artifacts to the monumental structures of high technology. In the soul-world, the psychic aspects of human experience and visionary perception are by no means reducible to an archaic or simplistic theosophy of fixed levels and predetermined hierarchies of being. The entire structure of the theosophic visionary mode, the visionary worlds of the Neoplatonic heavens and angelic guardians of the various planetary levels, has been dismantled through the arising of alternative visionary modes tied to scientific astronomy and astrophysics.[3] But that same astronomical science has yet to realize the psychic component or dimension so well articulated by the theurgical and theosophical traditions of the past.

The soul's capacity for visionary experience is not limited to a prevailing worldview, though a given worldview can certainly structure and dominate the psyche of the individual or the collective. We see this constantly in our dreams. The most direct entry into the visionary mode is through dreaming; dream work is a central feature of the alchemical art, one based on the integration and assimilation of dreams into waking experience. Dreams can be a resource for the transformation of the world, and they are certainly a profound source of guidance and inner direction. But they do not simply reflect the normative social world; the advanced dreamer, the true visionary dreamer, can move into alternative worlds of astonishing diversity and power as she or he loosens the bonds of the everyday ego, liberating the psyche from a purely social-centered mode of being. This begins with a deep and profound affirmation: dreams are a primary basis for knowing and understanding the larger visionary reality. Making this affirmation, the dreamer, as alchemist, moves into the dreaming state with respect and appreciation for the contents of all dreams and seeks to develop an increasing sophistication in the interpretation and integration of dreaming into waking life. But this is not dreaming in the ordinary sense, because in the dreaming life certain dreams have astonishing contents and open onto vistas that are truly awesome and inspiring. I have witnessed this directly in my own alchemy of soul and, through transformative dreams and other experiences, I have come to appreciate the wonder and mystery available to us through the visionary, dream mode.

One of the sources of *mortification* in the alchemy of soul is the profound encounter through dreaming with alternative realities that call into question the ordinary life of the dreamer. Such dreams can be vividly transformative, as when the dreamer experiences his or her own death or encounters powerful psychic energies that threaten the normative surface of life through highly charged imagery and emotions. These dreams must be taken as fundamental in the life of the soul; the upwelling imagery is a

119

vehicle that opens the inner world to planes of experience that far outstrip social convention and material beliefs. In the ontology of dreaming, we may take dreams to be revelatory and visionary when they induce a sense of wonder and stark amazement. These are not ordinary dreams, but the dreams of a soul in the process of opening to higher and more complex worlds, to an immensity of visionary possibilities intensely personal and transpersonal. Therefore, the alchemical dreamer must distinguish between normative dreams that simply reflect daily life, and superordinate dreams which reveal new vistas of emotional and psychic experience. Beyond the superordinate dream is the truly transcendent dream, the mystical dream that takes the dreamer into a transpersonal state of awareness enhanced and magnified by total absorption into the deep ontologies of Spirit.

Dreaming is part of the soul's journey into newness and greater complexity, yet, dreams are not simply self-evident; they are often obscure, confusing, and in their non-lineal symbolism, difficult and challenging to comprehend. The art of dream interpretation is an alchemical *separation*, a process of retrieving the meaning from the imagery and emotion of the dream experience. The dream work is analogous to the work of interpreting any life experience, a process of reflection, analysis, and synthesis. But we are working in the dream with contents that are highly symbolic and visionary, so we must move beyond a purely rational frame and cultivate a strong intuitive sense of the value and meaning of the dream imagery and symbolism. Like interpreting a poem, the visionary dream is an artful work of the soul in communion with Spirit whose imagery reflects more than the words describe. We must take in the dream image, the dream poem, and hold it appreciatively, meditate on it, bring it into the waking state, and make it part of our self-reflections. We must allow the visionary contents to act on us and through us as part of who we really are, and not repress, deny, or fear these images. The real dream work requires living with the dream, not simply reducing it to a verbal formula or a particular symbol set. There is presently no adequate theory of dreaming; such theories are only external views on a human ability that far outstrips current theories of mind or soul. Living with the dream takes years of practice and a constant cultivation of dream memory until the dream and waking state metamorphose into something greater than either alone.

Dreams are linked to alchemical cycles, or epicycles, which revolve around the various kernels that constitute the active psyche, motivated by inner intention and aspiration. The visionary dream, unlike the reflux dream of ordinary ego-awareness, is energized by the deep-seated potentials of the dreamer no longer bound by a rationalizing, sensory mind. In this deeper dreaming, paranormal capacities can break through the habitual tendencies to reveal nascent abilities normatively repressed by a less sensitive cultural and cognitive milieu caught in patterns of distraction or dismissal. What is required is a deep inner affirmation, a willingness to explore unrealized potential through an act of sincere determination and receptivity to spiritual dimensions too frequently denied by the habitual dreaming of the collective. The deeper cycles of dreaming are constituted by energetic impulses that stimulate a receptive awareness to a more open, living universe interconnected by a vast continuum of psychic relationships presently unrecognized by the collective majority. These visionary dreams are an opening to that continuum through the unique psychic and genetic constitution of each dreamer, each person's unique capacities to align with and to envision that continuum through the lens of an individual psychic predisposition.

This awareness energized by the visionary dream can carry into the waking state through a multitude of alternative modes, so that the distinction between waking and sleeping no longer carries any ontological significance. The phenomenology of the dreaming subject can be brought into a more mystical context of visionary experience based on individual predispositions that may well neutralize the waking-sleeping distinction. As the great Taoist sage Chuang-tzu taught, there may be little distinction between the dreamer as butterfly or as waking man.[4] The soul's capacity for visionary experience is not limited by the sleeping-waking distinction; the visionary mode can erase the boundary normatively drawn by a collective belief that values the waking, rational observer over all other states. In the alchemy of soul, the seeker must seek to enter the dream to such a degree that its full potential can be brought into the context of waking life and thus, can transform the waking state, opening it to new vistas of imaginal and creative being. Thus another root metaphor in the practice of alchemical transformation is to regard the waking state as if it were a dream that is fully in need of interpretation. Life as dream is a root alchemical metaphor that teaches us to lower the thresholds between our rational, imaginative, and dreaming processes in order to discover the continuum that underlies all three in a unified, Hermetic worldview.

TRANSCENDENTAL DISSOLUTION

Soul knowledge in the waking state is variable and cannot be simply schematized or arranged pragmatically in hierarchical models other than to suggest developmental patterns. The actual developmental pattern, at the level of individual experience, can valorize any number of states as "highest" in terms of the realizations of individual potential. In the alchemy of soul, there is no one model or one hierarchical structure that summaries all possible states. The ontology of an emergent, alchemical Hemeticism is fluid and adaptive, allowing for the valorization and flowering of innumerable cognitive possibilities in the realms of higher gnosis. For example, the imageless, contentless, ecstatic vision is often paramount in many mystical traditions, resulting in an attitude that "lower" visionary states are surpassed by emphasis on a certain type of "transcendent" realization. However, this bias often fails to recognize the creative potential of those "lower" states. Such a bias, based on ecstatic bliss and the dissolution of self, is generally unconcerned with the incarnational project of embodied, creative realization through specific, existential forms and structures. It is similar to a bias that would suggest that one type of art, like music, is higher than other arts because it is the least physical and the most ethereal in its expression. But from the perspective of the alchemy of soul, there is no highest art; every art has value and contributes a reciprocal interaction and exchange that enriches the whole. Each aesthetic form offers different perspectives and reveals various kinds of talent to the world and is only artificially reducible to a fixed hierarchy of values.

All aspects of visionary manifestation are possible elements in the evolution of human potential and there is no "primitive" stratum in this process, only more or less developed individuals with more or less unique gifts and insights. The experiential basis of the individual is not the issue, it is the insight and the capacity to impact the whole that flows out of the visionary experience that validates its worth and contribution. Even those types of experience which may seem remote from current interests or collective aspirations can profoundly contribute to the development of the whole, particularly over many eons of spiritual exploration. Imagine a circle on the circumference of which are a series of points representing types of Gnostic-visionary experience, ranging from highly abstract, imageless, ecstatic dissolutions through varying degrees of visionary manifestation. Experiences will range from animate principles to more archetypal forms and images, from specific entranced states which communicate particular insights linked to specific visionary beings or spirits, from visionary dreams to waking intuitions and psychic perceptions. In turn, each of these can validate a profound unity at the center of the circle that informs all the diverse perceptual possibilities of the circle. In the alchemy of soul, there is no one superior position on this circle, only a progression of states and experiences that leads to an increasing maturity and integration of insights that values and sustains the whole. This is part of the mandalic process of cosmic involution, to embody the potential in actual beings who can then open new vistas of perception within that specific involution.

As such, these involutions are internalized states that draw on a vast potential within the infolded orders of higher UrSpace and seek to embody a visionary truth, a perceptual instantiation of real being. We cannot say the pine tree is more valuable than the cypress other than in a particular situation; in themselves, they are each valuable and necessary. The rose and the lotus are both works of creation whose value is no more or no less than the lilies of the field or the dandelion and the burdock, all of which have various medicinal, healing and curative properties. There is no "appropriate hierarchy" other than those devised for the convenience of human reflection and theoretical speculation. What exists, as an actual fact, is the value of the specific manifestation. Our challenge as equally embodied beings is to discover the full range of what is given to us in each and every embodiment, in ourselves, in the world, in plants, in animals, in every form and structure as an involution of creative energies and sacred potential. In the visionary work of transformation, there is no absolute hierarchy of states or insights; there is only the actual, real experience of the individual that contributes to an ongoing alchemy of soul. In this process, every experience is valuable if we can learn from it, and the goal is not a particular experience, but a highly integrated state of maturity and wisdom.

In the process of awakening to potential, to Spirit and Illumination, there are indeed states that can be described as "dissolution of self." Here again, I speak from direct experience. I have undergone that dissolution, felt the intense parasubjective ultimate of mystical transformations or absorptions that have extended into a vast oceanic consciousness. The contents of that participant experience defy description — it is like an ocean of Light and Being, fully capable of absorbing and transforming all life as we know it, in the past, present, or future, without in any way diminishing its own capacity or power. In these experiences, there is a profound affirmation of the value of life and its manifest, diverse forms that seek to nurture and support that diversity and difference. There is also a profound unity that sustains the whole; there is an ecstasy at the heart of the experience whereby gnosis becomes at-one-ment and illumination. But I would not claim that these experiences, spontaneous and overwhelming, resulted in a profound understanding of human life, its purposes, or evolutionary direction and development. There is a timelessness to these experiences, beyond forms and images, beyond specific contents. Their primary characteristic is a wondrous sense of inseparable oneness that dissolves static boundaries, yet harbors the living soul as a sacred vessel of creation. This dissolution does not negate life and incarnation, but affirms and sustains incarnation as the very purpose and central act of Being.

In the alchemy of soul, there are innumerable ways through which the higher self can be dissolved into the primacy of Being and Spirit. This is an alchemical act of *sublimation* in which the identity of the individual passes through the boundary of discrete being and personhood into the larger and vaster reality of the unbound totality. There is a human capacity for this experience, an inner ability to merge with the primal foundations of mind and soul, to be fully at-one through an ontological union, a holy marriage of soul and Spirit. Just as body supports soul, so too, Spirit supports soul, for soul is the vehicle of individuated awareness passing through innumerable cycles of life and death. In a moment of ecstasy, both body and soul may be surpassed by an awareness whose contents are purely energetic and cosmic in subtle scope and dimension. There are no forms, no images, no abstract notions, no ideas, no voices or thoughts, only the extensive multidimensional depths of self-in-Being, of a profound I-Thou whose sacred depths cannot be contained in any theology or meta-psychology of soul. The very thought of "containment" is a paradox because this is the experience which affirms the uncontained potential through an expansive lens of specific personhood. The individual becomes, alchemically, the means by which this depth is validated and known, becomes the Hermetic vessel in which the work of transformation is carried out as sign of cosmic involution. It does not privilege the individual as such, but it does privilege the incarnate state of personhood whereby any individual being is a means for the expression of a latent cosmic potential.

This process of sublimation to greater presence and depth is by no means the goal of spiritual life, but it is an important stage along the path of maturation. In the alchemy of soul, the attainment of mystical illuminations is not the goal, but a means by which the path and goal are validated and made real. The task is to embody the illumination in the unique forms of insight and expression that those illuminations provoke in the psyche of each individual. Such forms may not manifest as philosophical or reflective thoughts, but may well manifest in artful forms and aesthetic expressions, in a quality of life that is generous and compassionate, wise in a pragmatic sense, or simply stands forth in humble dedication to values rooted in co-creative life. In the same sense that there is no one higher form, there is no one higher expression of the experience, only the unique forms that each individual synthesizes in and through meaningful relationships with other living beings. The sublimation of soul to Spirit, of self to Being, of inner potential to outer cosmic reality is only a stage in the process of full, enduring embodiment of principles that reflect a valued, ennobled way of life. The goal is to bring the full potential of embodiment to a spiritual realization of incarnate capacities which affirm and value the transcendent without subordinating those capacities to the ecstatic state.

There is also a shadow side to this process of sublimation by which the inflated personality, under the influence of the immensity of cosmic potential, takes his or her own experiences to be ultimate and supreme. There is no ultimate or absolute realization. There are only the necessary cycles of maturation that work toward a flowering of potential in and through the individual, a flowering that is a union of truth and beauty in a relative, co-related sense. From the perspective of the individual, the experience of this dissolution of self-into-the-whole may well be "supreme" —as though one had plunged into an ocean and found that his or her salt body was in fact, transparent to the sea in which it dissolves. But that is a record of one individual union with the All, not a record of the All as it is in and for all others. No matter how profound the experience, each individual account only adds to the complexity of human understanding of the mystical event; it does not solve the problem of human purpose or meaning. But such experience does validate human potential and the sacred relationship of humanity to the Whole. It also establishes human experience in a context of cosmological life and opens a horizon on the future development of species potential. But such a validation can be easily distorted by human ambition and self exclamation, allowing for a falsehood to mask the openness of the horizon.

The ontological capacity for human development is non-lineal and cyclical by nature. We tend to repeat and reprocess insights and experiences based on the insights and experiences of others. In the ambient sea of Being, in the alchemical solutions of higher awareness, there is a need to exercise a cautionary self-discipline that seeks to bring all mystical experiences into a context of dialogue with the experiences of others and to affirm the relative nature of shared mystical insights. While there may well be a "transcendent unity" within being, such a unity is not an ultimate as much as it is a relative truth based on how the experience is integrated into a worldview or how it may motivate actions (or inactions) in the world.[5] In the alchemy of soul, we may affirm a higher unity without subordinating the pragmatic application of such unity to projects of world development, social justice, peace and non-violence, or a wide range of individual modalities for the expression of such unity. Such unity is a fact of cosmic life, not a pinnacle or absolute in-itself, but a factor that does not negate the temporizing possibilities of other modes of human knowledge. In the alchemy of soul, this unity is the pivotal foot of the compass by which we inscribe a full 360° circle including all forms of creative, spiritual life without devaluing in any way the diversity and complexity of those forms.

We live within the boundary of the circle, but we also affirm the reality of the center as relative to our purpose and intentions. The center does not overwhelm the circle and the circle does not deny the center; both are necessary for the inscription of form and realization. It is easy to be overwhelmed at the center and difficult to know the center at the periphery; therefore we must strive in a true alchemical fashion to synthesize and unite what is within us with what is without and seek to each become a center with a new, elementary boundary. The shadows in this process are those that inflate the center by denying the value of the periphery, or allow the center to subsume the circle as though only one path or one way were true or real. As living embodiments of the alchemical process, we need to accept the power of the center as a profound affirmation sanctioning our task of individual realization. The hard work of that realization is to fully embody our insights and their creative demands while yet illuminating the work with the light of the center. This is a profound spiritual art—not merely a mystical event, but a living process of integration that moves beyond the ecstatic truth into the fabric of creation as a weaving, creative presence. This weaving involves our full capacities as embodied, incarnate beings using all skills and abilities to create a positive, enlightened world of co-creative beings—and not just in celebration of our personal realizations.

BRINGING IT ALL BACK HOME

Embodiment is an act of creation. To truly embody the experience means to absorb the qualitative influx of energy, light, and illumination and to transform it into actual practices, relationships, and manifestations in the visible world. It does not mean to generate words about the experience, but to generate insights in the minds and hearts of others. The language we use is a relative effector, a medium of verbal and imagistic forms that seeks to evoke a resonance within others. It is not the words that matter as much as the effects, the ways in which the words are empowered by an understanding that generates awareness in the mind of another. To empower our words, it is necessary to have the requisite experience, the primary substance, the prima materia, that is alchemically transformed through reflection into coherent ideas and insights. The dissolution of self, as a mystical encounter, is one more step on the path that leads to a reformulation of self, a new synthesis shaped by the deep characteristics of individual soul life. Soul is the medium of the transformations, the living entity that undergoes cyclical purification and insight through embodying those insights in tangible forms.

The relationship between self and soul is more metaphoric than phenomenological, more interpretive than descriptive. Consider the image of the pearl that is illumined from within because thought is directed towards its beauty and luster; mind and awareness can hold the image but it is soul that gives it sustenance and vitality. Soul is the animate presence, the vitality that energizes and sustains awareness, a medium of consciousness bound by habit, desire, and variable attractions and repulsions. Soul is a carrier of feeling, passion, and empathy as well as a medium for mental processes of thought, memory, imagination, and intuition. We separate mental processes from feeling only by ignoring the unity of soul life; mind is an aspect of soul and feeling is the soulful medium of relationships with others. Mind and soul are one entity, not two, and not separable except through an act of interpretive violence, a dismemberment that denies the coherent unity and completeness of being fully human. The body is a medium of soul-life, a complex, systemic correlation of aspects and attributes that are reflected in soul images as necessary developments of psychic capacities actualized in visible organs

127

and senses. The process of embodiment is a process of materialization by which organs and senses become increasingly attuned to subtler and more expansive perceptions, intrinsic to the inner capacities of soul.

Thus, images of mind are a reflection of soul capacity seeking embodiment in visible form, metaphors of potential within the incarnational process. The alchemical self in this process is the full capacity of the as-yet-unrealized soul potential, a capacity which is grounded in Spirit as the inexhaustible, limitless source of all manifesting selves. The self is an integrative metaphor, a representational ideogram of a developmental process that symbolizes our capacity to bring all aspects of experience and life into a single, harmonized identity. As a mandala of identity, the alchemical self is an evolving awareness that seeks to balance tensions, polarities, and divergence in soul life by drawing that life toward a more complete, complex, full manifestation. The self is not "one thing" but a central, organizing dynamic of processes by which the deepest soul potentials are actualized. Soul is the medium of interconnection and relationship that sustains identity in terms of a unique synthesis of awareness — in feelings, in mental life, in intuitive perceptions. Self is the organizing principle that assembles individual experience, potential, and intentionality in relationship to the All, to the whole of created being. Soul is specific, responsive and reactive, while self is reflective and transcendent. When mind reflects soul, it images the processes of incarnational relationships, perceives motivations, reactions and interactions; when mind reflects self, it contemplates the dynamic wholeness within which the incarnational being locates the deepest sources of meaning and life.

In this process, the healthy will plays a significant and central role. Will is the means by which soul creates relationships, either creatively through love, or self-destructively through hate or fear. The choice is there for each person, to choose a creative path of non-violence, love, and support or to will indiscriminately based on habit, conditioning, fear, frustration, dislike, or envy. In the alchemy of soul, the will is creatively attuned to maximize self-realization through positive, loving human relationships, and through a sustained commitment to personal development and relationships that support mutual growth and maturation. Knowledge of self requires an ever-deepening assemblage of individual capacities focused on the processes of transformation that lead to the highest spiritual realizations and to the maximum expression of those realizations in patterns consistent with individual ability. In the process of this quest for illumination, for direct knowledge or gnosis of the inner unity and depths of Spirit, the will is an intentional focal lens that brings that inner light to bear on the projects and desires of the healthy soul. We are not simply commanded or controlled by Spirit; it is the higher self that provides the context and meaning for Spirit's manifestation. As limited beings, we can reflect only a small portion of Spirit's capacity for realization; but as a mature self, we can organize and assemble our realizations into meaningful, motivating patterns helpful to others in their own alchemical quest.

By the phrase "bringing it all back home" I mean that we must not simply imagine the project of spiritual transformation as a quest for light and illumination, but as a process by which light and illumination are actualized in real relationships, in normative patterns of life like parenting and work (the fire of the hearth), which lead to new possibilities in living exemplary lives. What matters is not the intensity of the fire, but the use to which the fire is put; a single spark of experience and insight can create a great work, while a great fire and light can blind and overwhelm. The self, as an organizing principle by which Spirit becomes embodied, is a work of high art, an alchemical art that requires much training and practice. The will must be attuned to the needs and bindings of human relationships; it must seek to open and heal the concealed pain and sorrow and transform them into new life and rebirth. The alchemical stone is the magical substance that heals and opens the eyes, that teaches us to see where we were once blind and to hear where we once refused to listen. The fire of this stone is put to work in the processes of purifying the dross and accumulated layers of sedimentation that keep us from feeling and seeing anew. It is a fire that is directed and channeled for purposes of healing and creative work.

What is experienced and encountered must be integrated and interpreted. This requires effort, reflection, an engaged way of processing experience that allows glamour and ecstasy to fade and the substantive content to be shaped into meaningful perceptions that are sustained and amplified on a daily basis. As evolutionary co-participants, we are creating the very organs necessary for sustaining those higher perceptions of self. We are opening to Spirit and letting Spirit work in and through us so those organs can accommodate a more precise and penetrating awareness. But that work is conditional and relative to our own strengths and weaknesses; the instrumental aspect of this knowledge is inseparable from our self as a particular pattern of experience and integration. The will acts to guide the alchemical transformations along lines that best correspond to individual talents and learning. This learning may be very traditional and multigenerational, setting up its own boundaries and expectations, or it may be innovative and emergent. Even more significantly, such learning must draw directly on the self for its fullest and most complete expression. And that self is not predetermined, not a known entity or a specific form or structure as much as an emergent probability, a unique synthesis of Spirit facilitated through inner work and outer sensitivity.

The will must be attuned to both soul and self; through the self, Spirit is known and through soul, we know others as living partners in co-creation. Attuning the will to soul means that we respect the emotional and feeling basis of our relationships with others, that we cultivate empathy, and that we reflect on our feelings in ways that shed light on our motivations and behavior. Mind must reflect, think, and seek to understand the nature of feeling, sympathy, passion, desire, and aspiration. This is part of the soul work, to live in and through soul consciously, to develop a more soulful approach to living, a more deeply felt sense of interconnection and relationship. Soul, as the animate principle of individual identity, is a developmental quality that is capable of ongoing alchemical refinement, of more subtle perception and interactions. Will, in the life of soul, is the intentional, purposeful concern to seek an optimal way of life that meets others in soulful relationships, and that looks for expressive ways to enhance and to communicate soul life. The self, as the organizing totality, relates us to larger cosmic processes (and collective endeavors) through the unique assemblage of our full capacities, embracing the utmost expanse of our individual experiences. Soul, as the living, animate creature, seeks to realize those capacities through the alchemical work of inner transformation and outer correspondence. This outer correspondence is permeated by Spirit, by the world-soul, by the deepest psychic potentials that have yet to be actualized in humanity.

The will in relationship to self takes form through ideals, through spiritual goals and aspirations that represent the utmost possibility in individual development. Ideals of illumination or enlightenment, of mystical transformation or spiritual awakening to the many cross-currents of higher spiritual life, take form through will attuned to self. In this process, will can be informed by self through the medium of soul, to discipline the body, the mind, the heart, desires, or needs according to the ideals that self represents. As an emergent possibility, the self comes into expression through a variety of disciplines and symbolic processes directed toward the realization of a unique, luminous state. The process of will attuning to self is not simply conformity to an abstract notion of spiritual idealism; it is not a matter of becoming a Buddha or Christ, a Bodhisattva or a Saint. Those are only abstract notions of the ideal self-realization. In actual practice, the self is a unique synthesis that, in a realized individual, may be Christ-like or Buddha-like but is, in fact, more distinctive and less ideal. In the alchemy of soul, the goal is to acquire true, deep knowledge of self and to bring that soulful self, that harmonious and self-organizing wholeness, into complete expression through embodied, disciplined, compassionate living. It means to bring body, soul, and self into perfect harmony and integration through a living, alchemical practice that seeks to transform primal matter into multiple spiritual expressions.

The reality of Spirit in this process is the deep integrative presence, the primal source from which self acquires its potential for individuation. Spirit is the universal aspect, the dissolving medium of higher awareness, the luminous sea of the all-expansive presence that holds all souls, all selves, all bodies within the immeasurable embrace of its Mystery and Power. In Spirit I can sense and feel the process, the dynamics of the divine life, the currents that work through a multitude of energies to actualize self and soul in this world. I know that there is more, a greater mystery, beyond the traditional concept of God, in the inner directedness of these currents and in their ultimate origins and interactions. In the alchemy of soul, we are seeking the realization of individual capacity, the power and embodiment of the divine life in actual beings who are indeed, limited, partial, and only relatively illumined. The boundaries and possibilities of self are very great and we are evolving through stages to increasing awareness. In that process, soul is bound by its own self-conceptions and in the alchemy of soul, we seek to expand those boundaries continually without denying that there is knowledge which exceeds our grasp.

1. See Lee Irwin, 1994 for an overview of visionary modes among Native American vision seekers.

2. For an excellent psychological overview of the alchemical process, see Edward Edinger, 1996.

3. For the classic work on the occult hierarchies, see "The Celestial Hierarchy" in Colm Luibheid, 1987.

4. See James Ware, 1963: 2:95, p. 28.

5. The perennialist school has placed "transcendent unity" at the center of its religious ideology, see: James Cutsinger, 1997, and Huston Smith's earlier work, 1977.

CHAPTER FIVE
PRANIC SELF AS HIDDEN LOVE

The self as the ideal entity, as an illumined and fully aware identity that assimilates all life experiences into a single integrated harmony, is a being open to the cosmic aspects of incarnate life.[1] As a metonym, a part that symbolizes the whole, the self in the fully actualized sense is an image of creation, an archetypal being that surpasses the limits of ordinary sense perception and is open to the super-ordinate life. The goal of the alchemical transformation is to embody that archetypal being through a process of individual integration and existential commitment. It is not simply to imagine that ideal self, but to become that self through acts of committed and sustained living, to make the ideal real and to transform the ideal into a living practice, into a genuine way of life. The very concept of "ideal" is misleading if we think that it represents simply a mental construct, a noetic image, or an assemblage of characteristics removed from the actual struggle of embodied life, with all of its fractures, misalignments, and mistaken choices. The realization of self is a process of constant development that requires us to move step by step into an increasingly centered, responsible, and authentic spiritual life. The "higher self" as an image of this authentic life must continually shift, evolve, and grow out of the actual struggle for a realization of principles through embodied experience, learning, and practice. The image is not static but dynamic and must constantly undergo reevaluation and testing.

This development is not simply determined from within; it is not simply a matter of will or of emulating a particular ideal model. In the alchemy of soul, the individual must learn the principles and dynamics by which soul, self and Spirit unite with foundations of Being that exceed even the ideal integration of self. I call this intimate union of the soulful self with the transpersonal aspects of Spirit, the pranic-self, an expression of the universal aspects of identity that are transparent and open to the unbound dimensions of co-creation. The term *prana* comes from the classic, Sanskrit texts of India and is in many ways similar (though not identical) to the western esoteric concept of the "fifth essence" (quintessence), sometimes referred to as "aether" or pure "aer" (from the classic Greek and Pythagorean sources). Prana means "to breathe forth" or "vital breath, air"—just as aether means "very fine, very subtle air", often associated or correlated with heavenly fire or solar energy.[2] By "pranic self" I mean the fullness of self which is open to and aware of the subtle presence of Spirit, to the vaster transpersonal qualities that imbue life with awareness and which is yet the medium of a unique, personal identity. The pranic energy of Spirit, the quintessential air of life-giving breath, circulates in harmony with other elemental qualities to create a multitude of living beings, each aware and sentient. In reciprocity with that subtle awareness, the individual must seek to recover the primal relationship with Spirit by experiencing directly the transpersonal aspects of embodied life.

The pranic self is the illumined pearl of the heart, the psychic center by which the greater life is known and experienced. The distinction between self and pranic self is the difference between the full scope and ability of the individual self, as ideal spiritual knowledge and embodiment, and the universal self that unites the individual with the depths of Spirit, leading to the dissolution of self within the ecstasy of the All. More simply stated, the pranic self is the "higher" aspect of the embodied self, beyond which there is only the open expanse of truly transcendent qualities and awareness. The term "higher" here is conditional and relative, a metaphor, because the qualities of the pranic self are foundational, primal, and inseparable from the constituent elements of incarnate life. Just as there are "higher" aspects of self, there are also "lower" aspects in the images that we each hold of our identity as being particular, conditioned, and bound by social, historical, and cultural factors. For those in whom the self is conceived as no more than these conditional factors bound by genetics and biological determinism, there is only the limited alchemy of ordinary social processes. There is only the mundane fact of daily conditioned life enhanced or diminished by hereditary, cognitive skills, emotional responses, and varying degrees of education and opportunity, or by sheer chance and random consequence. In this sense, the "lower" aspect is based in the rational, cognitive, conditional immediacy of everyday learning and interaction. For these same persons, the "higher" aspects are seen as largely mythic (folk) paradigms whose illusionary contents reflect fictive ideas which, like other artistic expressions, are only imaginary and artificially speculative.

In the alchemy of soul, there is a fundamental affirmation that the "higher" aspects of self are neither speculative nor imaginary but utterly real and directly knowable. The pranic self in particular is a logogram, an esoteric verbal symbol, whose value and worth lies in its capacity to stimulate a participatory awareness that will affirm its transpersonal contents. A synthetic, solar-lunar metaphor of the pranic self is the image of the pearl, as a meditational image of the heart center, the center of breath, that leads the practitioner to discover an inner light, a lunar softness that can grow and expand into solar brilliance. This marriage or union of sun and moon, this Hieros Gamos (sacred union), is central to the work of alchemical-psychic transformation. Awakening to these perceptions requires the active use of the imagination; not as the work of fantasy or mere fiction, but as a focused, visual image that brings the full attention and capacity of mind to bear on the vitality of the pranic self. In breathing, we absorb the pure aer, the quintessential, pranic energy necessary to give and to sustain life. And in each breath, the pearl of the heart, envisioned at the center of breathing, becomes slowly illumined, its soft light expanding to fill the body. Breathe in slowly and evenly as you envision the pearl as a luminous object symbolizing the presence of the pranic energies of the heart. Each breath enhances the accumulation of its pranic qualities. It is not a physical point in the body, but a psychic concentration, a focal image able to dissolve into the actual energies that give the meditator life and vitality.

The energies of the pranic self are vast and far greater than the ordinary energies of daily awareness and normative action. As such, these energies cannot be reduced to a specific quality other than as an exercise in understanding various ways that those energies can be directed and experienced. But inherent in those qualitative experiences is a profound sense of unity, of interconnected Being, of multiple fields held within a vaster domain that far exceeds planetary consciousness and is inseparable from our local heliocosm (the sun and all its orbiting bodies). This unitary field extends throughout the subtle regions of UrSpace in which multiple energetic and conscious relationships are being enacted on a scope that utterly astounds and astonishes the contemplative soul. These are not simply imaginary spaces (though imagination can play a significant role here), but interactive domains that exceed any simple hierarchical analysis and which are complex and visionary beyond words. Spirit is the unifying medium of those domains, as it is also the life-giving presence that supports uncountable variations in life and incarnation. And it is Spirit that we breathe in and Spirit that we breathe out in every life-giving breath. It is Spirit that empowers our words, our thoughts, our feeling, our communications, our desires, dreams and hopes.

The pranic aspect of self symbolizes the deep center, the core of self that is a radiant presence that surpasses and encompasses the actualized self in a luminous manifestation of Spirit. But it is not literally a "center" other than as a symbol or practice for meditation. The pranic aspect pervades the entire energetic field, pervades the entire solar domain, and lends its animating qualities to the support of life in all its variations and variety. The pranic energy is a vital life-source, a subtle presence that fills UrSpace with its solar radiance, its astral energies, at a level far more subtle than physical organs can easily perceive. It permeates all elemental, atomic, and subatomic qualities and works in and through them to sustain life-presence. This pranic energy is a psychic life energy that constantly nourishes, stimulates growth, and fosters development in all species; in human beings, this biocosmic radiance energizes our thoughts, feelings, and awareness. Mostly it is perceived only very indirectly, as life and vitality and "good energy" (often as solar energy); but in the alchemy of soul, there is a progressive sensitivity to this energy as containing qualities of Spirit crucial to the transformation of human perceptions. If we choose to symbolize the process in an image, a logogram like the pearl of knowledge, at the center of breathing, we must also avoid the tendency to reduce it to a mere image. Prana and the pranic self are far more expansive and cosmological in nature than any symbol we may use to focus and enhance awareness.

Prana (or aether) is not an anthropomorphic idea—that is, an idea about the nature of our humanity cosmologized; it is a qualitative, energetic medium that supports all forms of life, not just human life. Like the sun that shines on all creatures, the pranic "aether" is a pervasive, subtle medium that supports sensory perception, mental and emotional awareness, and sensitivity to the life force in all living beings. As the ancient Indian Upanishads teach, prana is the basis of intuitive insight and self-knowledge, the ground of perception and sensory awareness, the source of life. And the ground of prana is UrSpace, the unbound spatiality of mind, imagination, and cosmic perception. This multidimensional space that incorporates the physical world into its extensive, multidimensional modes is itself permeated with prana, as life-energy, breath in a subtle, cosmological sense.[3] Prana is not "out there", but is an intermediary medium of Spirit that energizes sensory perception, animates mind, and penetrates soul at the deepest levels of the self. Like the energy of thought, it may be directed and intentionally shaped by emotional and mental tendencies through specific forms, images, and desires. As a very subtle energy, it is all-permeating, even to the level of the inmost self, and in fact, is an energizing vitality of that self that can be creatively shared with others. One of the primary forms of that sharing is through the energies of love, compassion, and healing relationships.

The pranic self references the mystical dimensions of human relationships and the sacred basis of our deepest cosmic identity as souls in search of wisdom. In the alchemy of soul, we seek to awaken our latent perceptions of this energy, to recognize its effects and influences, and to bring the will into a creative focus that can direct that energy toward healing and loving interactions. This requires a complete inner awakening, one that moves beyond the material and conditional life of habit and authority, and into the creative, open life of heart, soul, and Spirit. The penetrating depths of the pranic self may be known as the inmost center of soul and as an all-encompassing magnitude of incorporative space. The emergent self, the actual integrated, developing individual, must learn to accommodate to a variety of states and intuitions, to the lightning flash of Spirit as it manifests the expanding horizons of prana. The rhythms of this process are ones that oscillate between expansive openness to infinite horizons and the compressed, contracted states of individual, embodied being. The work of integration requires holding to the center in the midst of contractions and expansions that are archetypal for the birth of new awareness. Therefore, the personality, the discrete ego identity, must be balanced, healthy, emotionally stable, and mentally alert. This takes training and much practice.

AT THE HEART OF THE WORLD

Love is an energy of transformation. It is not static, nor simply responsive, but dynamic and interactive; a creative capacity whose power and effect can impact and transform the lives of others. As a heart centered expression of relationship, love is a power that unites us to the creative works of Spirit. As Spirit works to foster growth and development, to energize and expand capacity and creative engagement, so too, love works to foster similar growth and development. The correspondence between love and Spirit is, in the cosmological sense, that Spirit is a medium of multiple energies working creatively through all life forms, while love is the human expression of that energy personalized and shared cooperatively. In its biological expression, love and Spirit ground in the body as sexual and erotic energies. In emotional expression, they manifest in a harmony of will and intention. In mental life, they manifest as creative ideas and artistic images of wholeness, beauty, and interconnectedness. Love as a human expression of Spirit is a sense of empathy and compassion for all beings, a caring sense of co-relation that sustains itself through the world soul and makes life a joy, a current of emotional-mental-aesthetic and spiritual qualities. And love without Spirit is a contraction, a narrow circumscription that binds and blinds through self-serving passion and possessive desire.

At the heart of the world is Spirit and at the heart of Spirit is love. Not as an irreducible essence, but as an evolving quality of relationship that requires our assent and our inner determination to actualize. It is not simply given, but must be perfected and developed through human intentionality, through an ascent of the will to the loving, compassionate life. This requires transforming a narrow self-love into a more universalized, shared concern for the well-being and health of others. It does not mean denying self, but transforming self into the radiance of a loving heart whose emanations are truly a spontaneous expression of the inner qualities of Spirit. To reach this spontaneity is a Great Work, one that requires clearing out and unburdening the psychic life of the ego-self in order for the soul to be a medium of loving Spirit, free of the fearful and selfish tendencies that inhibit and bind us to an unenlightened austerity of emotional contraction and sorrow. We are free to choose. We can choose love as the medium of soul for co-creative life; or we can choose qualities less connective but more satisfying in terms of personal abilities or tendencies. In the alchemy of soul, love is a fundamental quality of the heart and the heart is the center of the Great Work, the place of the internal realization of the path.

Having heart, being a loving being, should in no way inhibit our capacities as thinking, creative individuals, as having a valid critical capacity to question and to seek alternative ways, paths, and practices. But imagine a world without love; a world that has lost the inner capacity for deep compassion. Such a world, restrained, compressed and contracted around individual concerns, is alienated from the cooperative life and from the creative energies of shared discovery, shared insights and satisfactions. It is therefore a world lacking genuine creative development because in such a world there is no real sharing, only competition, secrecy, constraint, and fear of betrayal. In a world that values love, placing it at the center of spiritual work and holding it as a central ethical value, intellectual freedom does not mean seeking to possess an idea or to claim ownership of processes or products of intellectual discovery. In a loving world, there is respect for the integrity of others and for their discoveries and efforts. There is an honoring that fully acknowledges and values the creative work and the contributions of each person. In a loving world there is balance that offers both the discoveries of Spirit and also honors those who discover; there is respect and reciprocity that does not violate either the individual or the collective.

We do not live in a deeply loving world. However, we can honor love and its power by choosing as individuals to make love and compassion a central value in our spiritual works. In the alchemy of soul, the heart has existential precedence over the everyday mind because that mind constantly succumbs to its own imperial sense of correctness and self-validating truth. But the heart is the center of relationships; it is the symbolic center of our capacity to care about others, to care about the world, to care enough to overcome our own tendencies toward inhabiting a closed mental universe. Mind should be cultivated, be capable of critical thought, aesthetic perception, imaginative, poetic appreciation and be informed and educated along a wide spectrum of subjects, cultures, and world views. But the heart must also be educated in order to weigh ideas and beliefs, our mental activities, in terms of the value and place they hold in a heart-centered, caring life. And the ethics of a spiritual life that flows forth from a heart centered love must determine which of those ideas, mental possibilities, or noetic forms best energize and foster a more loving world. In the translation of ideas into actions, the heart is the alchemical center that infuses those ideas with pranic energy, bringing those ideas into correspondence with Spirit, breathing life into them, and allowing will to act within the context of a loving, caring practice.

While the mind is active and stimulated in many, the heart often remains a closed and unopened vessel. This is true more for men, I believe, than for women. While mind and will can connect in the sense that ideas can motivate actions, these actions are all too often disconnected from ethical feelings, from compassionate concerns for the consequences of actions on others (particularly those who do not benefit from the action). In those whose hearts are closed, ideas take precedence over the more subtle and difficult issues of humanity, of valuing and caring about others, of concern for basic human or animal rights and needs, of taking the path that does not serve self-interest but serves to promote more compassionate ethical standards. Love is the center of that ethical concern. To be loving and truly effective in the application of ideas to communal needs and ideals requires an inner transformation, a true awakening to Spirit.[4] In the alchemy of soul, the heart has a greater existential claim than mind as the place of transformation and development because that is the place where we must relate our ideas and beliefs to others, to those we truly love and to the stranger, to all those for whom we care, and those in greater need than those we know. Mind-to-mind communication is a poor substitute and a poor imitation of heart-to-heart communion and sharing; but lacking experience, mind-to-mind becomes a substitute for intimacy and acts to fill a void in an over-mentalized way of life. True heart-to-heart communication requires compromise, sharing, and a suppleness of Spirit that promotes mutual insights by valuing the differences and uniqueness of each participant.

Just as the heart is the symbolic center of the pranic self, so too is the energy of love a heart centered manifestation. Love is the quality we choose, not a self-evident "essence" but a qualitative expression by which Spirit, acting through the heart center, infuses our relationships with loving presence. This does not require an act of will as much as an inner assent, a commitment to be a loving center of transformation, to manifest the loving capacities of Spirit. And the pranic energy nourishes this intention, just as it nourishes sensory perceptions and mental processes. Pranic energy cannot be reduced to a particular quality of Spirit, but it infuses all manifesting qualities, some more and some less, depending upon the will and intention of the individual. In the alchemy of soul, the practitioner must choose those qualities he or she wishes to actualize, must follow the natural gradient of their illumined potential in manifesting Spirit through the free-flowing energies of the evolving, pranic self. More than any other factor, this requires opening to the full field of the pranic domain, to the multidimensional universe of Spirit manifesting, to the heliocosm, to the mesocosmic totality through which individual capacities are energized and activated. And the will must be brought into assent and alignment with that activation, through the visionary processes of gradual (or sometimes rapid) inner awakening.

If we choose love as a quality we value, a quality that we hold as central to the process of self-knowledge, then the energies of Spirit manifest that quality through our practice of loving relationships. This is not an idea, it is a description of a developmental process by which certain qualities of being are actualized in real relationships with others. This practice is transformational because love is an energy of connection and relation that honors and sustains both the beloved and the lover. Compassion is an energy of Spirit, a pranic manifestation of life force, that stimulates an openness and receptivity to the inner life of others, to their sorrows, joys, and aspirations. It is also a healing power that provides stability and support for others through the positive, life-giving power of prana. Spirit sustains an uncountable multitude of processes and qualities, and prana as life force is a permeating solar dynamic whose qualitative capacity can be focused through acts of love and compassion. It can also be focused through mental activity, imaginative visualization, and action based upon a wide variety of motives and goals. So we must choose those qualities that best enhance our capacity for transformation. And one of the most valuable resources for that transformation is our creative, loving relationships with others. Such love and compassion comprises a sustaining power for further development through reciprocity and sharing of insights, practices, and goals.

At the heart of creation is a multitude of life-bearing worlds whose creatures are all valuable, and each one of them is a manifestation of Spirit. The life force flows through these worlds, energizing activity, reaction, sympathy, and choice. And the quality of life on a given world will certainly be a consequence of the choices made by a majority of its self-conscious inhabitants. Individual choice is also valuable and can be a radiant point of contact for others, through love and caring, to actualize latent qualities that best express shared spiritual ideals. In the alchemies of soul, there are many diverse ways, teachings, and practices, but these diversities converge in a deep ethic of loving kindness, in steadfast devotion to manifesting a more loving and intelligent world, and in the realizations of self as fully actualized, individuated potential. The ideal that is held, as the image or logogram of the heart, is to become an integral being whose unique abilities are manifest through expressive talents and creations. And the purpose of that expressive talent is to stimulate creative development in others, to enhance the nature of the world soul and to contribute to the ongoing spiritual transformation of humanity. Such contributions may be very gentle and subtle, diffused into a qualitative effect on others, as a wise and loving influence. The alchemy of soul is not a search for monumental effects, driven by egotistical needs for recognition or by a display of excessive accomplishment. Rather, it is a transformation into the subtle world, into affects and psychic influences that are attuned to the pranic heart of self and directed through qualitative relationships that stimulate growth and development at the level of each person's real needs.

The alchemy of soul is not an elite philosophy that proudly emphasizes its esotericism and occult knowledge, but an open and subtle art of deepening wisdom that expands into ever vaster and more profound horizons of meaning and contact with other beings. Like all art, it requires training, effort, and some knowledge of the craft and practice. It is not only an intellectual knowledge, but a loving and magical practice that is directed toward an exploration of the spiritual frontier, the expanding horizon of human possibility, and the deeper mysteries of creation. Not everything is known; much knowledge is truncated and partial, derived from conventional ideas or teachings rooted in static hierarchical thinking. Love directed toward others is a principle of growth that needs no doctrine or ideology; there is no single system of beliefs that can justify its power or value. But the practice of such love, and attunement to its pranic sources, can reveal a broad horizon of spiritual possibilities, all worthy of exploration. Each person must work according to his or her own degree of insight and maturity. This takes time and patience; it cannot be rushed or forced. The process is similar to the growth of an olive tree that takes many years to produce its first fruit, but then becoming fertile, is productive for many, many more years.

LISTENING WITH OPEN EARS

Each person must work on the personal development of heart, mind and will while also gaining experience and practice in love, sharing, and mutually reciprocal relationships. One without the other will create spiritual imbalance such that one may be loving but hold narrow views of the transformative process or very knowledgeable but weak in human relationships. Deeply grounded and rooted relationships require mastering the art of listening, of being able to hear others, regardless of how another's thoughts, words, and feelings may differ from one's own. Listening requires transparency and stability, receptivity and inner awareness of the differences that define our mutual perspectives. The ears must be open. The mind must be receptive and curious, not simply critical and defensive. The heart must be willing to love others in their differences, not just in their similarities. The body must be flexible and healthy, able to sustain dynamic transformations, and the senses must be opened to a higher continuum of perception. The aesthetic sense must be cultivated in order to feel and appreciate the harmonic resonances that manifest new forms and patterns in the co-creative energies of exploration. And there must be a firm ethical ground, a genuine sense of values that guide and direct the processes of shared discovery.

The pranic dimension of this listening is best expressed in a sensitivity for musical expression. The vibratory acoustics of prana are profoundly musical and sound is a medium of high art in the musical sense. Everything I write is supported by the music I listen to while writing; I choose the musical influences, those acoustic resonances that support and foster thinking in an alchemical sense. When I write, I always listen to music because it opens mind and heart to an additional dimension of influence that can flow into words, thoughts, and images. As in the Renaissance theory of magic and music, I find that music harmonizes my thoughts and brings my emotional and mental life into attunement with a certain etheric influence that is subtle and uplifting.[5] At this moment, I am listening to classical Indian *jugalbandhi* (by the Shringar brothers) where "one musical expression is played through two pair of hands" on sarod and violin. These artists are descended through twelve generations of musicians playing the complex and sacred music of Indian ragas in which sounds function to raise awareness through inner transformation and special yogic practices.

The training for this music is an alchemical art. For example, Sidhar Shringar writes that his musical teacher (*guru*) would require him to meditate in a large cave which had nine colorful paintings on the walls. Following the instructions of his guru, he would choose one painting and at night, on the full moon, he would meditate on that painting while playing an evening raga. Outside the cave, the guru would place another student who would listen to the music and try to identify which painting the musician was reflecting in his music.[6] This is a distinctly alchemical practice because it brings color, sound, imagination, mental clarity, and psychic perception into a single practice that necessitates a high degree of training and skill. And it centers on the sound, the resonance that evokes an increased sensitivity for acoustic phenomena and the ways in which music can facilitate imagination and responsiveness to the world and to others. In Hindu teachings, vibratory sound (*vak*) is a creative influence in the making of the world, particularly in the expressive aspects of human perception and feeling such that every time of day has its unique musical expressions. The primordial sound is the holy Vak, the harmonic energies

143

of creation, the feminine, divine resonance that becomes all words in all languages.[7]

Such music is part of the large, diverse collection of sacred music the world over. Much of this music is created through an inner development in which the performer or singer seeks to express, in music, spiritual values and perceptions. Or this music acts as a means for the facilitation of a more expansive awareness, as in drumming or chanting which acts to stimulate acoustic sensitivity. I have often experienced this with Sufi music, in the chanting and rhythmic energy of the *dhikr* (ritual invocatory chanting), in the poetry of the Sufi masters, and in drumming and flute that accompanies this art. The beautiful combination of these two traditions, Indian and Persian, is also part of the musical tradition (Ghazal) of northwest India, which excels in imparting to the listener a deep appreciation of both vocal and instrumental spirituality.[8] This too is a form of "two playing as one," while each maintains the integrity and grace of his unique instrumental abilities. Musical relationships, formed between performing instrumentalists or with vocalists, represent a potential spiritual synthesis in which the ears must be truly open to take in the rich and subtle harmonies that can act with immediacy and inspiration on the soul. Learning to hear the music is also an art, one that brings the listener into the performance and makes him or her a reflective center that can carry the impact and the acoustic formation into his or her speech and gesture.

The music we listen to shapes our responsiveness to the world. It opens us to the mastery of others whose musical talent and adept expression are truly joyful and enlivening. We carry the music with us, and the vibration sensitizes us to other types of acoustic expression. In an ordinary day, I listen to several hours or more of music, of many diverse types and kinds. This listening sensitizes my awareness when I listen to the voices of others or to sounds in nature. In the alchemy of soul, sound is a profound medium of perception, and the practitioner should learn to listen with joy and appreciation to the musical expressiveness of many cultures and times. The type of music we choose is a matter of individual sensitivity; there is no one best music, only better correspondences between various moods, needs, and stages of development. But without doubt, the music we listen to helps to shape our perceptions within the total world of sound and feeling. Music of a meditative and inner directed nature, gentle but highly artistic, subtle and specifically directed toward an expansion of soul in a nurturing and peaceful manner, is very supportive of opening the inner ears. But music of passion and joy, of celebration and energy, of wild and exploratory sound also has its place in the spiritual life, depending on the circumstances, place, time, and need.

Another indication of listening, of opening the ears, is the ability to hear the voice in another apart from the words she or he may speak, in the qualitative, acoustic sense that expresses (or fails to express) inner resonance. The quality of the voice, its naturalness, its rhythm, pace, and modulations, can communicate sometimes more than the actual words or implied meaning. Some voices are passionless, flat, angry, fearful; others are emotionally burdened, hesitant, nasal, echoing high in the head rather than resonant in the chest. With the ears open, one can clearly hear if the words are coming from the heart or head, are true or misleading, honest or dishonest, sincere or false. The qualities of the voice are like lines on the face; they reflect the life and struggle, the success and failure of the individual, the degree to which he or she has attained the spiritual perspective that brings true inner calm and peace. In the alchemy of soul, we can bring music into our speaking and writing, we can bring acoustic expansiveness into expression through harmonic development of voice and ear, mediated by an alchemy of speech and hearing. Therefore, choose carefully the music you take in as a guide to opening your ears; explore new dimensions of sound and music in order to find the spiritual harmonies that best express the awakening of inner sensitivity.

The ear is an organ of the soul through its capacity to sense the pranic energies of love in words spoken with compassion, kindness, and genuine concern for others. Loving sound, as an acoustic energy that fosters healing, is an artful synthesis of intention, and words, and actions that fully support those words and intentions. What brings resonance to words is the consistency between the words and the soul of the speaker. Soulful words come from the heart, absorb the intellective meanings, and transform those meanings into expressive qualities of sound. Just as a musician may play music with greater or lesser degrees of soul or technical skill, so too, words may be spoken or heard with varying degrees of sincerity or eloquence. Sometimes the speaker speaks with soulful intent but is not heard soulfully by others; sometimes the speaker is eloquent and gives an amazing technical display of verbal skill but demonstrates little or no soulfulness because those words have not been fully enlivened with the pranic energies of love. A mathematician may speak soulfully about his art and yet not be heard by those who claim to be spiritual practitioners of a soulful path. Opening the ears also means opening the mind to differences and other ways of thinking or seeing. It means becoming increasingly sensitive to the soulful quality of the speakers words while also taking in the meaning and intent which may, sometimes surprisingly, not always rise to the quality of the speaker's soul development.

Often, there are discontinuities between the soulful quality of the sound and the implied meaning of the words. The discontinuity is often twofold: first there is the discontinuity that may exist between the real perceptions or awareness and the inadequacy of words to convey those impressions; secondly, there are the discontinuities that exist between the speaker and the listener. Our words are not universal signs; they are instead relative verbal markers that suggest as much as they actually say. What they suggest is dependent upon the internal life of each person; what they say is a conventional sign, a meaning that can be read in several ways, depending on circumstance and intention. There is no language without these liminal qualities; they are the source of all poetry, metaphor, and suggestion in verbal form. Listening with open ears means hearing the full range, as in music, not simply to hear a conventional motif, but to sense the full capacity of the combinations of sound and sense. The meanings are like a river — we can stand on the shore and watch the current and attend to what we recognize or we can plunge in and become part of the stream of all sound and acoustic meaning. This plunge is a plunge into the pranic spaces of sound, into the density of multilayered sounds sounding harmonically on varying levels of resonance as a fractal river of possible correspondences and meaningful conjunctions.

The whole world is speaking, as is the very heliocosm, in the harmonics of an ancient language of soul. But it is a speaking that requires much listening and an increasing sensitivity for sound in a more interior sense. Soul must become the resonant matrix. Like a string vibrating in harmony with one that is plucked nearby, it must open to the soundings that fill the world with resonance. There also exists a great deal of disharmonious sound, of disconnected, techno-sound, strictly mechanical and electronic, that generates a confusing discontinuity within this ancient language of soul. Distractive, jarring, invasive, such sound grinds away the capacity to hear, deadens sensitivity, and creates an over layer of vibration that deafens the more subtle harmonics of soulful speech. Yet, in the midst of this cacophony of excessive war machines, roaring engines, screeching brakes, and screaming sirens is an emergent electronic artistry that is also seeking heart-centered expression to contribute to the language of soul. This language of soul is global and soulful through its capacity to find expression in any spoken tongue, living or dead, in the words of Swahili or ancient Egyptian, in Sanskrit, Chinese, English or Arabic. It is not a language of culture or history but a language of soul that speaks and is heard through the loving heart and finds expression in any tongue that speaks with compassion and care for others.

Opening the ears means opening the heart, caring about what others say, wanting to hear what is valuable and worthy in their lives, leading to a deepening of perception for the richness of incarnate experience. But it is not a matter of mere gossip or of talk for its own sake; it is intentional communication, however light or serious, however sober or comic, that leads toward new insights and a mutual sharing of perspectives that enriches all participants. Hearing with the ears open is a step into the unknown because what is possible in sound, in hearing, is far from fully realized in most people. There is a higher kind of hearing, an attunement to sound in a more subtle, emergent sense that extends into rich emotional and mental spheres whose contents are clairaudient and visionary. Such speaking may take on poetic forms that require a poetic ear, an ear attuned to the visionary verbal arts. In listening to the Psalms of David or those of the Zend Avesta, to the Sufi poems of Rumi or Hafiz, to the visionary words of William Blake or Robinson Jeffers, the ears must be opened and the mind receptive to the metaphoric word, to the poetic forms of inspiration that move soul toward new perception. It is a twofold listening: hearing the words in a context of new association and perception, and hearing the words as a transformation of language into soul work.

Soul development requires listening with genuine receptivity to poetic speech so that it can impact the heart and create an opening to the pranic energies that infuse the world through sound. Those energies seek embodiment in poetic expression to a degree that is richer and more aesthetically powerful than simple descriptive or explanatory language. This is because the pranic energies are very potent sources of creativity that cannot be contained by one-dimensional speech or "pure description" These energies go far beyond the conventional, jargon-laden speech of pragmatism and rational analysis. These energies can be embodied in expressive forms that are, like classical Chinese, highly layered, aesthetically rich, and able to express many image-ideas simultaneously.

This multi-speech is, like dreams, the true language of soul bringing into metaphoric verbal forms a richness of possible meanings that resonate with soulful ears and a loving heart. Love embraces the richness, the texture, the taste of words spoken or written with soul, because love opens us to multiple dimensions of meaning or hearing. To hear with the ears open is to hear with the heart, with the soul, with a deep loving desire to behold the world in a series of illuminating images that resonate with the hidden energies of creation. Listening with open ears means learning to hear the symphony that is sounding around and through us and to give voice to it in harmony with the voices of others. I call such harmony love.

SEEING WITH RECEPTIVE EYES

Like the ears, the eyes too must be opened, must become transparent to the pranic energies that enliven and animate the world. This requires seeing in a new sense, not simply observing in a detached or distracted fashion, disengaged from the energies that surround and sustain all living things. It means breaking through the visual stereotypes that flatten the world and suppress the perception that we are multidimensional beings and not simply technical images of machines or an assemblage of electronic, organic parts. The human body is a field of energies and these energies are living, life-giving sources of awareness sustained and nourished by prana and the solar-lunar subtleties of light. Ordinary sight is evolutionary insofar as we are able to learn new ways of perceiving by cultivating the latent qualities of our visionary potential. The light that animates the world is not simply energy, it is a vitality that animates and enlivens, and quickens life by illuminating a world rich in color, saturated with hues, tones, and shades of refracted light. The spectral lines of the sun reveal that this light carries the very signatures of creation that animate our bodies at the atomic level such that we are all creatures of stardust and light.[9]

The perception of the visible field is an on-going, expansive opening to ever more subtle energies, and to the interactions between those energies. In the alchemies of soul, there are many records of the opening of the visionary eyes to the physical world that results in a banishing of stereotypes for a more subtle, direct perception of these energies, to the color and auric dimensions of energetic relations. However, it is of little use to substitute one stereotype for another, as though such seeing were simply a matter of learning a new perceptual order or pattern. By stereotype I mean a conditioned way of seeing, a tendency to see only in terms of conventional attitudes toward the visible world, a convention that denies the capacity to see into the more energetic spectrum that surrounds and penetrates every living creature. For many years, I have been able to observe the multi-spectral energies that surround living beings, plants, animals, and even non-living substances. This happens in a very irregular and unpredictable way, spontaneously, and without any conscious effort to invoke such seeing. At one point in my life, over thirty years ago, these auric perceptions were so intense, so regular and fascinating, so absorbing and compelling that the energy, tremendously vibrant and colorful, was surrounding everyone and everything. Finally, I chose to suppress it, that is, to lower my threshold of sensitivity so that it now occurs in a more subtle and less dramatic manner. However, at unpredictable moments, it will suddenly manifest as though a light has been turned on and I see the person surrounded by a multi-spectral nimbus of color. Just as quickly, if I divert my attention, it will fade.

Learning to open our eyes means learning to see the spectral energies that actually surround and sustain physical life. However, such perceptions can themselves be easily stereotyped by assuming that there is a fixed description of these energies or of the order or nature of the colors, each with specific meanings. Such has not been my experience. The colors shift and change constantly, affected by mood, attitude, environment, health, and many other factors, including one's own state and presuppositions. What red may express for one person may be quite different for another person, as well as what red may mean for the observer. While some generic comments may be made about color, overall, color perception seems to be highly subjective once it is liberated from stereotyped templates or narrowly conceived schemas. Much of the color literature is theoretical and symbolic and is highly stereotyped by various esoteric conventions. But actual perception reveals that the phenomenon is highly complex and very sensitive to dynamic interactions that can change the appearance and energy quickly. Further, these energies mix and interact with the subtle vitality of others as well as with the surrounding environment, particularly through emotional reactions and unguarded receptivity. Some people are clearly influenced by subtle pranic influences (bright solar or softer lunar) in ways that constantly challenge them to integrate their perceptions in order to maintain stability and emotional health.

Learning to open the eyes means not stopping at external appearance, but becoming aware of the more subtle energetic nuances that inhabit the body, the mind, the emotions, and the perceptual organs. Eyes are a link to a visionary capacity; they symbolize the processes by which we can "see" into new worlds—actual, emergent, and imaginary. And color is a mode of perception that is by no means secondary (contra Aristotle), but a primary light phenomenon that is intrinsic to the photonic energies of suns and stars. The visible spectrum blends into the invisible spectrum, but both can be incorporated into an alchemy of seeing that embraces the full-spectrum capacity of our psycho-physical-noetic abilities. In developing this capacity, it is generally easier to see these energetic formations around others than around oneself. This is because we are conditioned to differentiate the world around us more carefully than when we regard say, our own hand or arm. Further, such perception is not focused on physical appearance as much as it is on local field perception, on the surrounding aura of the life force, its modes and expressive contours. And color acts to emphasize particular states, particular moods or attitudes, and specific physical conditions.

In perceiving such energies, there must be an inner opening of mind and heart that allows for the possibility of this perception through an increasing sensitivity to energetic states and interactions. Just as we feel emotional reactions, we can also feel these energies from a heart-centered, clear-minded openness to the world and to others. And we can also see these energies, learn to become more sensitive to their manifestations, both externally, in the incarnate world, and internally, through dreams and visionary states. At the same time that I have observed these energies surrounding others I have also experienced similar perceptions in my dreams. This distinction between inner and outer is only an artifact of stereotyped thinking; in a deeper sense, inner and outer blend into each other through the pranic energies of Spirit that harmonize and unify the world. The distinction between inner and outer is a "soft barrier," like the semi-permeable membranes of perception that surround each of us. Through an alchemy of soul, we can alter these perceptions, align our will, and become much more skillful in understanding the messages that these energies convey. Like a doctor reading the skin tone or pallor of another, it is possible to diagnose the energetic fields in ways that support therapeutic healing and positive loving relationships. Inner and outer must blend in a rich field of perceptions, unconditioned by stereotypical thinking, and open to exploration and deeper understanding.

Dream perceptions are also very important because they allow for more creative, energetic interactions. Through hundreds of dreams in which I have perceived auras and a multitude of other energies, I have come to realize that our psychic-visionary capacity is continually undergoing refinement and development in the dream state. Often these dreams manifest distinct psychic abilities and processes of experimentation that seek to extend or develop latent psychic capacities. Opening the eyes in dreams means learning to trust the dream experience as an exploratory ground for the testing of psychic abilities. This a powerful context for new kinds of seeing, for greater clairvoyant perceptions that allow a person to gaze into a distant past or future and to see with radical clarity a multitude of possible worlds and beings. And these dreams are colorful! Color is magnetic in such a dreaming context, vivid and luminous, indicating a wide variety of energetic states. Learning to see in the visionary mode is like dreaming while wide awake, developing a capacity to enter the energetic dimensions of full spectrum seeing, with the eyes wide open. As the "soft barrier" becomes more sensitive and transparent, the inner-outer dichotomy begins to dissolve into a new unity. The self begins to live in an interactive, energetic state of co-relation, learning to perceive directly the visionary reality. Color in this wakening context can be a cue for entering into a more psychically sensitive state, as it is in for many artists. Color is rich in emotional and soulful density, a reflection of varying degrees of energetic manifestation.

Alchemical seeing also requires imagination. The stereotype of hard boundaries between physical sensations and imaginative ideas, between objective and subjective, is an artifact of a divided self and a divided culture. A perception of the animate character of the world is not an illusion but an intimation, a sensory connection with the qualities of life that infuse nature. The function of the imagination is to provide a medium of synthesis in which ideas, images, and a felt sense of the enlivened world can blend and crystallize into new perceptions and psychic forms. The process of emergence is highly dependent upon our capacity to envision the full complexity of the world we inhabit. As science has shown, the world is far more energetic and interactive than what appears to conventional physical perception. We are surrounded by radiant energies, gravitational fields, electromagnetic phenomena, plasmic discharges, and solar-lunar influences of many subtle types. Envisioning those energies requires an active imagination, just as conceiving the nature and scope of the cosmos also requires imaginative thinking and visualizing.[10] In a similar manner, the perception of life as an energetic process can also be enhanced through an active use of imagination. For a moment, imagine that your body is surrounded by layered fields of energy and also imagine that you can feel and perceive those energies by allowing them to manifest through a heightened awareness This requires keen attention to peripheral vision, to liminal perceptions that may seem to be only fantastic but which are in fact emergent qualities of new perception.

Study the energy of your own hand and how it feels to touch another person. What can you tell by the quality of touch? Impressions are flowing constantly through the energetic media that surround our physical bodies. But the perception of those energies is not bound by a perceptual constant, or by a fixed system of meanings or appearances. This is because our own energies are always involved in the process; the lens that we peer through colors our vision of what we see. Therefore we must develop skills in interpreting what appears, in relationship to what we feel or think, and we must understand that the self-other relationship is reciprocal and interactive. While the light of the sun may be separated out into a fixed visible spectrum (as popularized by Newton), the energies of the body are interactive and constantly subject to change and modulation. Feeling and thought can alter the energies, such as when an idea strikes with force, catalyzing us to act, or when a mood qualifies our response or receptivity to others. We are not objects engaged in mechanical processes; we are living beings with many subtle energetic aspects, particularly concentrated in thought, feeling, and action. And these aspects can be made visible to a perceptive mind through an alchemy of soul that seeks to validate the energetic media through direct perception. This requires cultivating an imaginative approach to perception, to imaginatively "see" into the subtle energetic media that enliven us.

The power of mind in this process is linked to the power of higher perception as we seek to train our senses. This means we must take as a working premise that the senses are not strictly limited to physical perceptions, but may also become more psychically sensitive, more soulful, and thus more receptive to the pranic influences that truly support life. The reality of Spirit is found through such perceptions. Such an alchemy of perception is not a physical art, but a psychic and spiritual art that opens the doors of perception onto a much vaster, living cosmos in which Spirit is the underlying basis of all perception, thought, and feeling. Opening to the energetic manifestations of Spirit is to open to subtle realms of creative awareness, to the pranic and etheric order, which might well support a quantum view of the universe.[11] The medium of visual perception is not simply visible light, but is also a transformative medium, and metaphor, that supplements consciousness and mind. What we see in the imaginative, creative sense is an index of what is possible in the realms of direct perception. We can train the mind to sense the supplemental energies that help to nourish physical life; at the same time, we can enhance our soulful perceptions of a more complex subtle world. In the alchemy of soul, the eyes must be opened to the invisible realm of diverse energetic manifestations to a degree that those manifestations become visible through a developmental transformation of the senses.

HEALING WITH UNMOVING TOUCH

Healing is an act of love and care that works through an energetic relationship that is often spontaneous and a function of loving intent. The first time I experienced the power of healing, many years ago, was through a relationship with a very sick female cat that my wife brought into the house from the back woods. This cat was very grateful to have found a home but she was quite ill. I was sitting on the floor petting her one evening and feeling sympathy for her condition when quite suddenly and unexpectedly I felt an energy flow through me, through my arm and hand, into this little creature. Simultaneously, Ms. Katchemouskie (our name for her) also felt this energy and let out a low meow that was clearly one of approval. I knew she had been healed and in fact from that moment on, she began to act quite normally and was clearly much improved. After this initial healing, she would often come to me when not feeling well, and I would stroke her and she would always be grateful. Two aspects of this healing surprised me: first, there was no intention to heal, only a feeling of sympathy; second, the energy flow was quite vivid and felt explicitly through my body, down my arm, into the animal. Subsequently, I had dreams of healing that involved simply touching another person and letting the energies work through me without making any attempt to control or direct the process.

My perceptions of this healing energy, which I have felt often since then, is like a warmth similar to an emotional reaction that spreads throughout my body, a current of energies sometimes very subtle and at other times, very explicit. Later I discovered that certain people would draw this kind of energy response from me, even in a handshake or by

153

touching me. As I learned to moderate the flow of this energy, I was able to learn how to direct or retain it under circumstances that might otherwise exhaust me. I also learned from my dreams how to direct and control it with greater focus and attention. Though my abilities in this area are quite modest, I am on occasion able to affect others in ways that they can very clearly feel and I have helped people with a variety of illnesses or injuries. However, I believe these abilities, which are far more developed in others, are somewhat a secondary consequence of my overall alchemical soul work. As a natural phenomenon, I regard healing as a spontaneous event between two people who are able to establish a caring and genuine sympathy (friends or strangers). The sources of that healing energy are, I believe, pranic in nature—that is, they do not come from the individual but rather flow through the individual as a natural conduit of sympathetic resonances which are inherent to reciprocal field structures between incarnate life forms.

The healing energies are grounded through an inner capacity to open to the pranic influence, particularly through a willingness to be an instrument of healing. It is surprising to consider how many people resist the idea that healing is a function of loving intention. The tendency to depersonalize the healing act, to make it a matter of mechanical or systemic actions, reflects alienation from the body as an instrument of love and from the mind as a genuine source of healing compassion. It also reflects the tendency to deny the value of intention in the healing act, as though healing were a matter of technique, strictly manipulative, or constrained by a specific body of knowledge. But spiritual healing of the body or mind or soul is, in the deepest sense, spontaneous and a function of the loving intent and compassion of the healer. As a source of healing, the power of Spirit is without compare, but its manifestation requires appropriate intention and a willingness to act as a grounding source for healing energies. Healing, in this sense, is a matter of directed intention to instrumentalize the healing through one's own body, through loving hands, through a gentle touch that heals.[12]

Further, this healing works by soliciting healing energies from within the one who seeks healing, as an invocation and call to open to the pranic and spiritual capacities that surround and envelop each person. In healing I can call forth the latent healing energy within the other person. It is a "calling forth" that does not simply direct energy to another, but evokes energy from within the other; it is a process of sharing and mutual discovery. To tap the healing energy is to tap the capacity that we each have to realize our potential for self-healing through positive, supportive relationships. The deeper levels of self, in the process of emergence and manifestation, are filled with a capacity for transformation that is by no means limited to the individual, but which flows into every relationship, into every smile and tear. These energies are subtle and constantly at work in the body, sometimes blocked or cathected or misdirected, but always accessible to the well-intended mind. The condition and health of these energies within one person can act spontaneously on the well-being of another simply through contact or normal interactions. Like being around someone who is very happy and optimistic, it can change the mood and attitude quite naturally and without effort. This is particularly true if the effect results from deeply held intention and purposeful living, and not simply from mood or momentary passions.

In the alchemy of soul, the soulful person is one that seeks healing and the healing of others through motives of compassion and hope for a healthier, integrated way of life. This requires opening to the deepest possible energies of our being, to the natural qualities of our interactive exchanges, by making the work conscious through cultivating a healing and loving touch. It also means keeping the body flexible, healthy, and energized by practicing artful disciplines of bodily healthy, such as various types of Yoga, T'ai Chi, or other techniques grounded in deep energy work. These systems are ancient and have evolved directly through practice and application. They are quite profound and can help to cultivate the correct flow of the pranic vitality that sustains our psycho-physical life. As a practitioner of T'ai Chi, I have a deep respect for this form of martial art which has many applications to health and to healing. This work is highly alchemical because it leads to inner transformation and a much more conscious awareness of the ways in which energy (or chi) flows in and through the bodily structures. And mind is an integral part of deepening the practice through careful attention and clarity of thought and intent.[13]

For me, the energy of healing is a pervasive solar and pranic energy, an energy of subtle light that can be directed through intent and purity of mind and body. While the application of this living energy can be spontaneous and may require little or no effort on the part of some individuals, for most people it requires some training and practice. It also requires an appropriate attitude of mind, a mental receptivity to both physical and psychic transformations induced by a clear intent to heal.

And it requires an attitude of gracious humility insofar as such healing is, in fact, not an act of will as much as an ascent of will to a process that draws on resources greater and more encompassing than even the most illumined personality. There is a distinction in this process between the healer and the healing; the healer must work on his or her spiritual clarity of mind, heart, and intent so that the healing flows forth through the medium of Spirit as attuned to the healer. But the healer does not possess the healing power per se, even when it occurs through an act of will on the part of the healer. In the more narrowly defined act of healing, the healer's intent or will may create a link by which he or she takes on the other person's illness. But then, the healer must release that acquired energy or suffer the effects of the illness.

In the more expansive sense, the healer becomes simply a medium for energies to acquire focus and application, pass through the healer, and leave no impression or after-effects. This type of healing can be done by drawing the healing energies directly through the person being healed, not through one's self. Envision the healing as a process in which the healing light flows out of the depths of the body of the ill person as called by the healer. The healer does not transmit those energies through his or her body but, through an act of clarity and invocation, calls the energy through the other. This practice, which I follow, is a kind of encompassing of the other within the higher field of the self that observes the injury or illness and then invokes the presence of Spirit to heal the illness through the soul of the ill person. In either approach, the medium of Spirit conducts the healing energies in such a way that they do not cling to the healer — they simply flow in and do the work of healing, and then dissolve back into the normal vitality of the living body.

The energies of healing are adaptive and multidimensional; they are grounded in the unitary matrix of Spirit but, as Spirit, such energies can conform to the particular needs of the illness in ways that are far more subtle and immediate than can be envisioned by the healer. Thus, the healing is not a function of a particular visualization or a result of having a more medically precise knowledge of the body (though such knowledge may assist the accuracy of the healing process). The transformative work has a spontaneity that is germane to Spirit; as in Reiki, the energies do the work necessary while the intent of the healer is simply to solicit and transmit a healing flow. And, as noted, this solicitation is grounded in a loving concern for the other, in sympathetic and positive feelings that compassionately seek the good and welfare of the other. It requires more than mental intent; there must also be heart, a soul-centered willingness to be a source of healing for others. In the alchemy of soul, the healing arts are a natural feature of inner development and may have more or less acuity in a given individual based, I believe, in both the willingness to heal and the correct receptivity to the healing presence.

At times the healing presence can take the form of various entities. It is often recorded that healing may be a consequence of spiritual guidance received from a wide variety of beings, such as those in the afterworlds, various angelic and animal spirits, and a wide diversity of visionary and archetypal forms. For example, much healing is done in the name of the Christ or Sophia, just as there is an esoteric tradition of the Healing Buddha, or of the healing powers of various Hindu or Muslim or Christian saints. Many indigenous traditions in Africa, Australia, Asia, and the Americas use spirit helpers for healing. In the alchemy of soul, these entities become intermediary forms of Spirit that act to catalyze transformative abilities, but they are generally not literalized to a concrete form or *idée fixe*. Such forms and appearances are part of the greater work of inner transformation and become allies in the sense that they act to crystallize the regenerative powers of soul in forms that are recognizable and familiar enough to establish rapport with the power of the form. Yet, the form itself is still an intermediary of the healing and visionary potential. Rather than allow the form to become paramount, in the alchemy of soul it is the energies of the form that must be accessed and directed. Spirits are like persons seen in a dream—they may change, mutate, evolve or devolve, depending on the psychic disposition of the dreamer. In healing, they are not the goal or the desired end of healing, but are helpful media for the healing work. The intent is always to find the deeper energies, the fluid and flowing access to prana and chi, rather then to embody that energy in forms that limit its expression and creative work.

SCULPTED BODIES OF LIGHT

I want to address the lunar aspect of solar light as a reflected light that illumines the shadow realms of human awareness. Let us think of bodies of light as they stand in luminous forms on a natural ground of soft darkness. In your mind's eye, regard the human body as it stands in a quarter moon lunar world, radiant with its own inner light, with a gentle field of luminous energies surrounding its physical form. Imagine, further, that this light comes from within the individual and is a living, animate light. Now observe that the person is standing outside, in nature, and that this inner light is also in the trees, plants, bushes, grasses and weeds. In this lunar landscape, there is nothing that lives that is not filled with this animate, subtle dream light, including a very soft, almost invisible light that radiates from the ground, from the earth itself. The stars are the origin of this light, though in direct solar form it tends to overpower human perceptions of the other, closer and more subtle forms that seem to be absorbed and masked by the solar energies of our sun. Whatever lives has this light, these subtle energies of form and materialization that intersect and hold the physical structures.

This landscape of lunar lights and reflected solar influences is an alchemical image of the sculpted bodies that we see in visible, waking life. It is a dreaming image insofar as it refers to the reflected light as dampened and softened by exposure to a vaster darkness, to the open space of cosmic immensities. The moon in this landscape is an image of various degrees of illumination, moving though stages from dark to full to dark to full as emblematic of the cycles of transformation that move us into and out of varying degrees of lunar consciousness. Lunar consciousness is a dreaming place or a visionary place of encounter with that greater darkness, that as-yet unknown immensity, which represents the full human potential in a living cosmos of multiple dimensions and multiple temporal-spatial orders. This subtle realm is easily lost and overpowered by the direct solar light of the ordinary waking world where the subtle becomes invisible and the obvious inadequacies of human life stand forth in the blunt, stark brilliance of worldly inequalities, in fixed forms, in temporal preoccupation. The visible material world is also a symbol, a well-lit place of complex interactions that obscure the motives and desires that arise in the lunar world.

In the alchemy of soul, the lunar world, the landscape of subtle light and shadow is a creative ground of transformation, a place of alchemical work. The moon is the sign of the white sulfur, the wet, liquid, fluid quicksilver, milk, the pure Mercury, the *argent vive* (living silver), the supple feathered serpent whose power is to dissolve the fixed form. The Sun, as yellow sulfur, is the gold lion, the hot, dry power of fixation and coagulation, that which gives form to the fluid substance, the genetic seed. Night, as a shadow of the sun, is the dream time whose moonlight is the fluid, free associations of interconnection and metaphor, the moon being a soul image of the Philosopher's Stone.[14] Journeys into the lunar landscape, into the numinous shadows of night, lit by the inner luminosity of Spirit, are a necessary aspect of the alchemical work. Some say that this "going down" into night's shadow is a journey into a place of fear and trembling, and indeed, shadowed life can be fearsome and disturbing. But the opposition between sun and moon, the polarity of the "solar male above" and the "lunar female below" is a false image. It is a creation of hierarchic male thought, a polarity that values rational logic and social power over the dismantling influence of the non-rational, fluid imagination.

The image of the subtle body of light is an image of the imagination, an image of the lunar landscape of earth, not of the moon, but under the lunar influence of possibility discovered by dissolving form. Let us dissolve the body, dissolve its hard, defined boundaries, its material mass and structural organic parts into a softer image, an image infused with vital, fluid light. Let us observe the body through the lamp of the illumined eye that no longer stops at the organic boundary, but envisions a more complex field of sustaining energies, such that "inner and outer" become more metaphoric than actual. In the lunar light, boundaries dissolve, fade into shadows, blend into the surrounding energetic fields, creating a more resonant, interactive milieu of rich perception, a chiaroscuro of light, shadow, and muted forms. Descending into this rich field of lunar imagery, we can begin to see the multiple, subtle energies of body that are not bound to its strict material outline or form. And we can begin to see the interconnections between the subtle field and the energies of other forms, beings, and living presences.

Going into the fluid lunar realm is a work of poetic discovery, a way to open into dream time that can result in a new aesthetic of expression. But we must also be prepared to experience varying degrees of dismantlement, varying tendencies toward plurality and disconjunctive tension. This is the place of feeling and passion activated through the imagination, through a dreaming space in which all things are possible. The infinite ocean of night is the great container of possibility, of unknown places, forms, beings, appearances and of sudden and unexpected images, feelings, worries, and fears. It is a place of mystery and possibility, of vaster horizons and great territories of unexplored potential. And it is a place of experimentation, trial and error, encounter, struggle, conflict, and of powerful, moving forces. Far from being "empty," it is full beyond imagining; layered and interactive with strange attractors and forbidden

159

pleasures, it acts on the soul as the domain of psychic creativity uninhibited by rational or social values. But it is far more than a domain of irrational passion or libidinous desires; it is also the dwelling place of the primal energies of creation. It is the place of visionary transformations no longer bound by the narrow confines of solar logic. It is a place of dreaming that allows the soul a fuller and more complete access to its own inner creative potential, a place where the inner dramas of soul life can be enacted and explored.

This lunar landscape is also the dwelling place of the Midnight Sun, a fundamental symbol of the transformative power of deep night, of the Hour of Hermes (3:00 AM), in which the soul experiences the presence of Spirit. For Spirit dwells in the dark as well as in the light; it dwells wherever beings enact the dramas of soul, especially in the places of passion, desire, and aspiration. Bodies of light are sometimes most easily seen in this place of lunar dreams. Consider a flying dream. In this dream, the dreamer is lucid and knows that she or he is in the dreaming state, in the fluid lunar condition where a thought can actualize an event and a feeling hypostatize an action in symbolic form. In that state, the dreamer can create a remarkable variety of possible events or happenings and is not bound by the solar logic of everyday. Free to fly, to explore not just this world but any possible world, the dreamer can ascend or descend at will. In every direction there is something to be learned, or someone to be encountered who can offer insight into the very nature of soul life. Here it is possible to meet the Christ or the Buddha, to encounter an illumined being, to hold concourse with an angel, or to dissolve the dream form and travel between whole worlds of perception and experience. And Spirit is the indwelling presence of each world and being encountered, luminous in lunar guise as yet another dreaming soul. This is the place of the Midnight Sun that illumines the visionary dream.

The dream body is but one manifestation of the sculpted body of light; in its dematerialized lunar form, the body is capable of profound transformations. Dreamers may change gender, become animals, mythic creatures, angels or demons. And the infused energy of these dreaming states can carry into waking perception such that the solar world becomes increasingly animated by the dreaming power of mind and soul. Such alchemical work takes discipline and careful movement into the intersections between lunar and solar consciousness. The Great Work requires inner stability, a self-development that can handle the infusion of

160

the imaginative and rational without abandoning inner poise and balance. The converse movement is also desirable, the bringing of light into the realm of lunar shadows, not as a Prometheus who steals the light of the gods, but as a torch carrier of the Lesser and Greater Mysteries, as one who honors the gods and goddesses and yet seeks to know them through vision and inner transformation. The unveiling of the sculpted bodies of light is a greater mystery than is presently realized because that unveiling is part of an emergent revelation—an unveiling of the evolving form, of the yet unfinished work of humanity seeking to realize its potential in a balanced and integrated image. There is no one image, only a series of percepts that support diversity in a holistic fashion that honors both Spirit and matter.

Fragmentary aspects of the self must be acknowledged and reintegrated, even while we seek greater coherence through our relationships and encounters in both the lunar and solar worlds. The journey into the lunar marks a process by which we recover those fragments of self and soul that we may have abandoned in conformity to the solar mandates of social, cultural, and family life. One such fragment is the capacity to know and perceive magically; to retain the alchemical vision of the animate universe. The magical perceptions of childhood need not be abandoned; they need to be fostered and brought to maturity as part of the human heritage. The dreaming self is also the real self, not a poor cousin of the waking ego, but a masterful teacher and psychopomp, a guide to the hidden world of human possibilities. In this context, the alchemical self cannot be known without embracing the full equality of the lunar and solar consciousness. And it is not just the waking and sleeping mind or soul, but all those states of perception, half-waking or half-sleeping, meditative or visionary, intuitive or empathic, artistic or technological, that sustain an expanding frontier of human capacity.

Every fragment needs to be reclaimed, not censured because it does not adapt, but nurtured because it offers a nuance unseen in the solar state. The bodies of lights are many; they layer the individual in ways that make the physical a ground or holding space for a rainbow body of energies. We are surrounded by these energies, these light bodies layered by psychic soul stratum. But these energies are not fully healthy or balanced; many are contracted and repressed, shadowed, fragmented, dislocated, and divided. There is a natural tendency toward plurality at the heart of soul that represents the diversity of possible directions or soul capacities as-yet undeveloped, nascent, or simply repressed.[15] Full flowering of the sculpted bodies of light requires a complete development of soul that illumines the entire interior landscape. This is a work of many lifetimes. It is in many ways a multigenerational work, a global process of co-evolution, not a realization of a predetermined goal, or of a single individual, but the co-discovery of what might be and is yet unrealized within us. Every step we take towards integration and wholeness contributes to this process of co-evolution. Clarity of insight, a power to heal or to create, an inspiration that creates joy, all contribute to the inner revelation of human potential just as every act of violence, degradation, and harm limits that potential and bends it toward a narrower, more controlled horizon.

The discovery of soul is also a process by which we heal the injury, the wound, the "one-eyed seeing" that only knows a single path as valid. There are innumerable alchemies of soul. What we share in this process is a determination to find strategic means to heal the past, present, and future in order to fully realize our capacity as co-creators and visionary explorers of human potential. I do not seek to overthrow any worldview or to deny the value that others may find in a particular path. The alchemy of soul that I propose is one rooted in non-violence, individual responsibility, and creative love that seek partnership and community as a means for future transformation. The sculpted bodies of light are part of us; they are the inner forms made manifest, the lucid power of illumination made visible. They are not a finished work, but images of emergence and awakening that will require great stability and patience to comprehend and to utilize for creative, peaceful ends. And these bodies are directly able to absorb and apprehend the pranic basis of life; they are not mere illusions, but a new frontier of human identity.

We are beings of flesh, beings of bone and molecules, beings of energy and light, beings of dream and imagination, beings of soul and Spirit. We are living embodiments of a living cosmos whose dimensionality we barely know and hardly comprehend. Far from being masters of our destiny, we are much more the product of species conflict and competition. At the level of the individual, the real work is a work of love and integrity. The path of inner stability must not be a closure of potential; instead we must open our perceptions and open our hearts and souls to the energies of life that surround and inhabit us in all directions. We must have the courage to live as embodied beings of light and color that inhabit both the solar and lunar worlds of creation. As we advance into the depths of human

162

potential, the forms will inevitably change, the structures will dissolve, again and again, as we absorb the energetic possibilities and seek new expression and creation. The work is to discipline ourselves to a standard of freedom that seeks to harm none but to utilize the gifts of each for the betterment of all. The work is one of body, soul, and mind; not of one or of the other, but each in its place with its appropriate powers and capacities, each balanced by the other, not bound, but free to express the inner vision that illumines each stage of the path. In this way, we can each become a sculpted body whose light is one of many in a luminous, expanding world.

1. Marcus Chown (2001: 2) writes, "Each and every one of us is stardust made flesh."

2. For more on aether/aer, see Peter Kingsley, 1996: 15-29.

3. Kaushiitaki Upanishad 3.2; Brihadaaranyaka Upanishad 4.1.3; see Robert Hume, 1971: 128, 308, 321.

4. See Lee Irwin, 1999.

5. For a summary of the Renaissance theory of magic influence of sound, see Marsilo Ficino, 1980, specifically chapter three: *De vita Coelitus Comparanda* (1489) and D. P. Walker, 2000.

6. CD Disk Liner notes, RealWorld: K. Sridhan and K. Shivakumar Shringar, 1989.

7. For more on sacred music of India and its spiritual philosophy of sound, see Guy Beck, 1993; the idea of the holy Vak is similar to the later Logos ideas of Christianity but with a strong aesthetic emphasis as well as philosophical interpretations.

8. For example listen to the music of Kayhan Kalhor and Shujaat Husain Khan, in *Moonrise Over the Silk Road* (1998) or *Lost Sounds of the Silk Road* (1999).

9. See Chown, 2001.

10. Ken Croswell, 1997.

11. For more on reclaiming the concept of ether in contemporary quantum physics, see Sid Deutsch, 1999.

12. My thanks to David Spangler for our discussions on healing and the power of "loving hands" which he explains so well; see David Spangler, 2001.

13. My thanks to Sifu Loretta Celeste for her many years of patient instruction and guidance in the work of T'ai Chi; for a good introduction to the practice see, Paul Dong & Aristes Esser, 1990, and Liang Shou-Yu & Wu Wei-Ching, 1993.

14. Lyndy Abraham, 1998: 119-120.

15. James Hillman, 1991:38-45.

CHAPTER SIX
THE SOPHIA-CHRIST WORK

There is a distinction between Christ and what I call the Sophianic Christ work. The figure of the Sophia-Christ in the alchemy of soul is an image of the integrated self, the realized self that has undergone a synthesis and union of the solar-lunar consciousness. The incarnate Christ is the male Logos potential within each individual; the act of incarnation is an ongoing creative process and the Christ potential is a presence that teaches love, compassion, and healing. It is also an image of union that recognizes the importance of an illumined, shared wisdom, the Mary-Sophia of spiritual wisdom, erotic love, and co-creative partnership. It is not Christ alone, but Christ in relationship to the feminine Sophia principle, the holy wisdom of Spirit as embodied by the female Eros through the work of sacred marriage. From the perspective of the alchemy of soul, the Christ-work manifests through the integration of the masculine-feminine contrasts, in the union of Logos and Eros, through co-equal partnership and mutuality. The Christ potential is within all, male or female, but its manifestations come through the work of incarnation in forms consistent with gender differences and gender nuances. The Christ potential, as I understand it, is not in fact simply "transcendental" or other-worldly, but very much this-worldly and immanent to a degree that is inseparable from the actuality of physical, incarnate life. The very purpose of the Sophianic Christ incarnation is redemptive world transformation, not world transcendence.

Alchemical work is a work of transmutation that emphasizes the value and importance of the creation, not as confinement or limitation, but as an evolutionary ground for embodied life that must meet those limitations in a spirit of joy and reverence. The concept of the "fall" is a symbol of human abasement that is rooted in the struggles of life, in its passions and desires, and in the harmful conflicts that proceed from desires unchecked by moral or spiritual guidelines. At the heart of the alchemy of soul is a deep and reverent affirmation of incarnate life; not human life as a trial, or as "fallen", but as deep-seated embodiment in a place of beauty and power that challenges us to rise to our full capacities and potential. We are "fallen" only when we deny the wonder of the creative process and fail to recognize our obligation to embrace the gift of life through positive loving relationships. The fall in this sense is a fall into materialism without Spirit or a fall into Spirit without valuing incarnation. And pride is the source of these denials—that human beings are either without spiritual perception or that material life has no value. Spirit is the very source of material life and only through physical, incarnate life can we actually realize our full potential, including the full realization of our inherent spiritual capacities.

The Christ image is one of human spiritual realization, an image of inner potential actualized through the "descent of Spirit" into the human heart. It is not the only image, nor is it the highest image. There is no "highest" image, only a concordance of images from all traditions, East or West. The Christ presence is an image actualized in the heart of the individual through an awakening to Spirit, in the esoteric context of Christianity, which inspires each individual to lead a better, more compassionate and intelligent life. If we hold to the Christ presence in living a better life, then we will find a more loving touch, a more loving reception of the other, a more loving wisdom that holds similarity and difference as two bright lights on the path. Exclusivity is part of the fall, a darkness; denial of the paths of others is a pride that seeks to justify its faith through condemnation rather than through a witnessing Christ presence that affirms the freedom of human diversity. The Christ light can be contracted to a narrow beam that lights only a known pathway rather than shedding its greater light on the unknown and unseen. A Sophianic light can stimulate discovery and new vision and not simply light a closed cell that is barren and barred against difference.

The radiant Sophia is not a subordinate image but is a brilliance that arouses and fills the Christ with understanding and insight. It is an abundance of images that reflect the creative possibilities of illumined understanding and true gnosis. But this wisdom, this gnosis or divine knowledge, does not lie outside of the incarnate world in some etheric realm or as a goal that requires a denial of incarnational life. It is a wisdom that inhabits every human soul and gives inspiration to each individual according to his or her gifts and capacities. An external view of the Sophia may result in artificial proclamations about her "lower and higher" degrees, exalting a type of "transcendental gnosis" that is seen as superior to all other types. I regard this as mostly a mark of spiritual pride, a demonstration of a lack of inner experience in which ideology becomes a substitute for the tremendous variety and range of gnostic illuminations as they reflect the exact needs and capacities of the individual. In the alchemy of soul, illumination is an individual work that adapts and shifts and evolves through the unique stages of each person's growth and development. The incarnational principle, in the Christ work, is to develop just those gifts that are most expressive of individual capacity and to hold an ideal of illumination that supports the alchemical work without denying that there is always more work to be done, more to see, and more to comprehend.

Transcendent experiences are only one dimension of the process, not its goal nor its ultimate ideal. As incarnate beings, our task is to bring those moments of vision and transformation, those ecstatic self-transcending unions with the All, into form and content that teaches us more about the process of being incarnate. In the alchemy of soul, we seek not to transcend, but to bring the transcendent into incarnate expression through respect for the human body, the human social order, and for the created worlds. The Great Work is the making and remaking of the soul, through processes of inner illumination and ecstasy, through moral life and creative application, through loving human relationships, and a careful stewardship of the earth and all its creatures. We do not turn our back on the world for the joy of personal ecstasy; we do not deny the value of creation because of a difficult and challenging life. We accept this incarnate state, this sense of being more than body or mind, of being Spirit-filled and soulful beings with a destiny that is inscribed in flesh and written on the face of our world. The image of the Incarnate Christ is one that does not seek to overthrow or deny the world, but in harmony with the divine Sophia, to be a birth-father and a birth-mother in bringing this world to perfection, to create through the Sophianic Christ potential a great reservoir of healing love with lasting commitment to social harmony and a balanced, co-equal way of life.

The Christ image is mutable and changes according to the understanding of the individual practitioner. There is no one image, no correct form. And in the alchemical process, there must be a union of male and female aspects, an integration of the innocence of the Adamic Christ with the wisdom of the Sophianic Eve. The spiritual marriage comes about because each person can recognize, within him or her self, the presence of the other, the value and good of the other as a spiritual principle and not just as a sexual or gender difference. The distinction is not between male and female, but between principles of distinct incarnation. Spirit incarnates through the polarity of flesh for the creation of the sacred triad of mother-father-child, which is the path of species generation. The distinction is not superficial but rooted in a deep causality of Spirit—to create through difference, to engender through distinctiveness which must not be erased or ignored in the process of spiritual maturation. We do not grow out of our gender but into our gender, we become the spiritual principle of our particular gendered being. Our gender differences are a manifestation of Spirit, of fundamental creative expression in our own polarized nature, which works to create uniqueness by investing gender with creative differences. Such diversity reflects the full range of gender expression in a global culture of wide-ranging gender types and kinds. Stereotyped gender polarity is more than social, though it is certainly socially informed. It often carries all the emotional and psychic injustices of gender bias and cultural discrimination. This is not a minor point, but a major teaching insofar as it illustrates the human capacity for gender dominance and manipulation within a single species, even between partners bound by children and family relationships.

The Christ teaching is not to bring a sword that severs the family or denies sexuality and gender differences. The deeper teaching is to bring a mantle that is placed over the shoulders of the male and the female as equals in spiritual power and social relevance. There is no subordination, no "obedience" of female to male. A co-equal partnership is a relationship which seeks to enhance and value the differences each person brings to that partnership. Thus the Sophia is not subordinate to Christ; together, they represent an integration of the lunar and solar principles. Each has its own unique power and capacities; they are by no means identical, and the differences are of great importance. Failure to value these differences will only result in a masking of the spiritual process that is already inscribed into our bodies and minds. In the Hermetic path, the above and the below, the male and the female, each has a unique power and each brings unique energies to the many processes by which the whole is assimilated without masking diversity. Otherwise there is no distinctiveness, no edge with which excess and superficiality can be cut away, no means for bringing out the hidden form within the stone. Such integration is not a matter of polish and perfection, but of having a seeing eye that can recognize the value of what is unique and can affirm the contribution of each that fosters a healthy diversity.

The Christ work is a work of inner and outer transformation carried out in accordance with the natural character of the individual, enhanced through training and spiritual practice. There is a kind of natural spirituality; a fluid and generous nature that seeks to help others without seeking personal benefits that, with deep compassion, can hold open a possibility for emergence. But these tendencies can be developed far beyond the natural type through a powerful alchemy that seeks to actualize in the fullest sense the Sophianic Christ work, the illumination of heart and mind that can act ever more directly in service of the spiritual needs of others. The work is not always dramatic or obvious; sometimes it is very subtle and hardly visible to others. The Sophianic-Christ can be a source of great comfort and a sustaining presence that fully supports individual development without any expectation of conformity to a particular doctrine or a single teaching. The Sophianic wisdom is very broad and inclusive; it manifests as a depth of intelligence that can illumine any subject or problem if held with receptivity to its creative influx. It is a wisdom that seeks to manifest in and through the world for its transformation, not drawing the individual away from the world but illuminating its energies as they work to sustain the ongoing creation process. The Christ presence is a masculine stability of love whose aim is healing, truthfulness, and sincerity in holding to spiritual principles. The Sophianic presence is a wisdom that holds diversity and difference with great respect, nurturing individual development.

The Sophianic Christ work is not a particular set of actions or a series of goals. It is a spontaneous and freely responsive care, a concern for the well being of others, a compassionate interest in sustaining personal development and growth, to nurture the sick and to inspire the healthy. In the alchemy of soul, the Sophia-Christ work is a transformational opening to new depths of perception, to seeing the sculpted bodies of light, to enacting the healing of the world through an energy of will that is non-violent and non-exclusive. The will is directed toward self-transformation as the primary ground of spiritual life, to teach through example, to illustrate a path through its full embodiment in one's own alchemy of transformation. It is not a work of proselytizing a teaching, but of applying a teaching to inner awakening that then becomes a sign of the worth and value of the path. No two lives are identical and no two realizations of the path are the same. Thus, in the alchemy of soul, the Sophianic Christ work must differentiate according to the differences that make us distinct as individuals, and yet it is a work that holds love and human relationships at the center of its development. The power is turned inward to promote growth and outward to illustrate values and teachings through example.

The real alchemy of soul is a spontaneous teaching through presence, a Sophianic Christ presence that adapts to and expresses the unique incarnational value of the person. The incarnational being is not secondary in this process but primary and central to the entire purpose of human life.

FROM WINE INTO WATER

The movement within the alchemy of soul is from unknowing to knowing, through processes of ecstasy and sobriety, through visions, to simplicity and pure living. In such a movement, the wine is the sweet taste of the Christ presence, the joy of the Sophianic wisdom, as they unite and dawn in the illumination of the heart, mind, and soul. We do not proceed from sobriety to sobriety but through love, joy and wonder to purposeful living, with clear intent directed toward the manifestations of self in creative action and relations. And there is a miraculous aspect to this process, a wonder that comes only from true transformation. Such transformation is not merely a concept or an intellectual construct. It requires liberation of energies that are all too often bound by narrow expectations and limited thoughts or beliefs. It requires a willingness to die to an older, less aware self and to discover a new, emergent self that moves and acts with capacities far greater than those based simply in ideas or thoughts. The key here is willingness—not just belief or thought, but thought guided by a will that moves beyond faith into direct, personal knowledge. It is a will directed toward inner awakening of potential that is realized in actual experience and given clear expression in human relationships. It is a will disposed to love with humility, and to knowledge that is grounded in direct illumination without fear or pride.

The miracle of this process is in the ways by which the individual is transformed in stages to an ever-opening horizon of insight. The further we advance into the miracle of spiritual illumination, the more we connect with the interwoven causalities that direct life toward a positive and fruitful maturation. These causal principles are not based in a strict psychology of human needs or desires, but extend beyond both the instinctual and archetypal forms that we presently recognize as defining our species evolution. We are moving beyond those forms, not simply into an affirmation of their past virtue or beauty or power. We are moving into the yet-to-be, into the emergence of new metapsychologies that will redefine our human capacities in terms of shared inner potential. The causal principles are an intrinsic feature of this emergence, a host of energies and relationships that extend far beyond an overtly material view of the world. At the heart of this causality is the miracle of Spirit, diverse with energies of creation, laden with capacity to transform, a profound stimulus of inner opening.

Working through the medium of a vast spectrum of energetic forms, Spirit inheres within all creation down to the minutest sub-atomic particle to the greatest macro-forms of the heavens, encompassing an uncountable multitude of cosmoi and creatures. As an inner presence, Spirit holds the totality of creation within an embrace that is all containing and yet freely indeterminate. As it seeks to enhance awareness, to stimulate the evolution of species toward true self-awakening, it supports all manner of diversity as it also seeks to sustain collective coherence and wisdom with regard to an enduring and lasting maturity. There is freedom in individual choice and realization, but there is also an inner stability that supports that diversity in moving toward deeper interior connections This deeper unity is an expression of Spirit-in-depth, not only in the acts of incarnation, but also as an inner, abiding unity that is not bound by any forms, species ideas, or spiritual teachings. This inner unity is the sweetest wine; it is the breath of God, the fire that lies at the heart of creation, luminous and effervescent with life and creative potential. It is the wine of the holy marriage, an ecstasy that requires balance and stability to absorb and integrate.

The causal principles are brought into focus and given creative intention through a deep compassion that wells out of inner unity as nurturing desire, as a primal concern to give shelter and comfort to others. In Sophianic wisdom, this nurturing desire takes the form of spiritual teachings that encourage tolerance, openness to new ideas, receptivity to the values and beliefs of others, and a radiant manifestation of nurturing love. Yet, this nurturing love comes out of the fires of divine love, out of the ecstasy of the pure wine of unity and oneness. The depth of this living unity is immeasurable and its potential for expression exceeds all human acts of communication; it overflows into the living hearts of beings on uncounted worlds, in all dimensions, visible, transparent, and invisible. It is the wisdom that holds all knowledge and all human understanding within a deep potential that can be known only through incarnating its actuality in specific forms and expressions. The ecstatic union, the true gnosis of the spiritual marriage, is a joy so intense and a love so strong that it cannot be communicated in words, though songs may be sung, poems written, dances danced, and its beauty may shimmer in the space between each letter. The holding space of that unity is limitless, but the actual realization of the potential is specific and aligned with the real capacities of each individual, each community.

In the Christ, this love takes the form of a healing touch, an invocation of ecstasy in a sober smile whose touch is more than words and promises. The actuality of Spirit is to turn the wine of ecstasy into the healing water of revivification, to the *aqua vita* (water of life) that blesses and heals. The Christ gnosis, the Christ knowledge, is the miracle of attaining the divine life, acquiring holy vision, tasting the sweetest wine of the divine presence, and then transmuting it into healing, loving compassion of a nurturing Sophianic wisdom. This is a miracle. It moves beyond the mystical into the magical; it takes the vision as the source of its inspiration, the unity of the immeasurable presence as the healing spring from which all may drink. In the gospel, Christ says, "Come all of you who are thirsty, believe and springs of living water will flow forth from you."[1] And these living waters, these inner springs are the presence of the Holy Mother Spirit within each heart, within the depths of a knowledge that can experience directly the healing power and presence. And the origin of that healing water is the wine of the true gnosis, the fire at the heart of creation that gives life and awareness, that unites us with all created life, dissolves our differences, and immerses us in direct illumination. But then, we come out of that inner baptism, out of the fire transformed, out into the world, bringing with us the water of life, the healing presence.

This union of fire and water is an alchemical sign, another indication of the genuine inner marriage, of the union of opposites now reconciled and made whole in each other. How can these waters flow through the living heart if it remains closed to the greater mysteries of inner transformation and illumination? Illumination is necessary; faith alone can only carry so much of the burden, but the transformation of wounds, of injuries and suffering, of old habits and displaced energies, requires more than faith. It requires knowledge and then, action. So all three are necessary: faith that seeks to understand, knowledge that attains illumination, and action that applies both faith and knowledge to the suffering and needs of a grieving world. The transformation of wine into water is the movement from Spirit, the soul's union with Spirit, into the world where soul, heart, mind, and body must be a temple of Spirit for the greater healing. The living water is the animate presence of Spirit transferred through touch, through a kiss, through a look, a prayer, or a presence. For that water to live, we must taste the wine of presence. Christ is one such example of that presence and in Christ, that presence is animate with Sophianic compassion, with the gifts of Theotokos (Divine Mother) that nurtures all life, human, animal, or plant.

The self transformed by ecstasy seeks to bless every living creature and no longer lives as a master or ruler or king. Now the transformed self lives as brother, sister and relative to all the ancestral spirits and to the unbroken heritage of every generation that must be healed. This water is not only for the living, but also for those who no longer inhabit flesh but continue to live in the worlds between. It is not simply healing for those we love, but healing for all the earth, for all generations, for all beings. The great work of healing has hardly begun, and much damage, pain, and suffering has been caused in the name of Christ. Therefore we must each take responsibility for the sorrow and share the cup of ecstasy by filling it with living water—with compassion, nurturing love, peace, non-violence and genuine respect and co-regard. Let the Sophianic wisdom guide you. In the Christ, we find an example of healing love and generative transformation; in the Sophia, an intuitive wisdom that guides and reveals the hidden sorrows, the suffering that must be healed, the work that gives back and does not demand or take or condemn. The Mary-Sophia is a profound sign, she is the living wisdom that unites the compassion of motherhood with the wisdom of divine mysteries. She gives birth to a holy child, her healing capacity, her healing love.

We can drink lightly from the wine of inner unity and the fire of dissolved merging. Even a single sip can regenerate an entire life of suffering, can affirm the value of seeking no matter how long the journey or how grievous the pain or injury. As we drink more deeply, we face the challenge of sustaining inner balance as the creative energies unlock, of not drowning in the immeasurable depths. We may plunge in—such is the nature of certain souls; we may utterly give over to that dissolving fire and experience the loss of all specific identity. But we will come back to the rudiments of incarnate life, back to the presence of the distinctive personality, back to the individual configuration that desires, reacts, evaluates, thinks, speaks, and makes promises. What matters, what truly matters, is not the depth of the immersion nor the degree of the death and rebirth, but the wisdom that is brought back that heals, that is truly wise and understanding, that is part of the quiet revolution, of the overturning of impeded thought whose selfish roots still choke the vineyard. Wise and humble workers are not in search of the affirmations of others; they carry out the work of transformation quietly, with great integrity and power, because they do not place themselves above, but below. In the alchemy of soul, there is no need for self-proclaiming, we need to sustain only the obvious work of healing and wisdom.

The Christ presence, in this work, is a continual sense of a healing power, a constant awareness that Spirit is at work, moving through each person, activating the latent powers of Being through an open expression of love and compassion. The wine is transformed into water; the water heals and satisfies the spiritual thirst because it opens the heart to a new depth, to an inner capacity of light, to the dynamic work of soul resuscitation. The souls of many are asleep; they are not awake to the inner potential, to the capacity of self that allows for new perception and insight. These higher powers of perception are brought into play as the soul becomes more attuned to the inner light, to the Christ presence, to the power of Spirit working through the medium of dreams, visions, and developing psychic perceptions. Jesus exemplified these kinds of psychic perceptions and abilities, just as he exemplifies the higher gnosis in his transfiguration on Mount Tabor when "his face shone like the sun, and his clothes became as white as the light."[2] And such abilities are inherent to human soul capacity; they need only be encouraged and developed through clear intention and receptive practice. The working of Spirit through our embodied life gives us many abilities, at first unseen; but if we follow the threads of the teaching into the depths of the heart where Spirit itself becomes the way, the teachings, the true life will manifest. We must awaken the soul from its sleeping state, from the strictly physical, unconscious life, and learn an alchemy that will liberate the deeper energies, the deeper love and healing.

THE MANIFEST MIRACLES OF EVERYDAY

There are three great miracles of everyday life: miracles of love, miracles of healing, and miracles of creative vision. These three together reflect a great cycle of transformation and spiritual awakening. When love, healing, and spiritual vision work together, they reflect the depths of our true human capacities, even in a simple touch, or glance, or smile. By the term miracle, I mean a visible consequence, a manifestation of Spirit that in its visible form may seem extraordinary but which is often only a natural ability amplified and brought forward through a deep spiritual intention. This intention is not itself the miracle, but it is the inner key to any miraculous event. Intentions of the heart, mind, or will create a focal attention that is then amplified by Spirit according to the soul's capacity and inner receptivity. In the alchemy of soul, the soul's intent, the deep incarnational purpose, is the causal root of an individual's capacity to act in a miraculous, manifest way. To know this purpose, this causal root, this deep identity of the self, as it spans all life experience, lifetime after lifetime, is to acquire the recognition of deep intentions. We can go into Spirit, into Mystery, into the sacred depths of creation, but not simply to experience that which is greater than self, of that which IS self in a deep, immanent, cosmic sense. We go into that depth so we may fully know the root cause, the incarnational intention of our specific human capacities. We go into the incarnations of Spirit in order to find the causal center of our own miraculous abilities.

Self-knowledge in this sense is not simply psychological, but meta-psychological. Our individual psychology is informed by our incarnational intent, and the degree of clarity which informs this intent is the very source of our inmost miraculous capacity. Coming into this life, we may well forget and be blind to our deep self-intent, to the incarnational purpose that underlies our immediate, conditioned states, that lies deeper than the normative or collective values that would claim to represent human life. But human life is a mystery whose contents we barely recognize because of collective sentiments, in-group and out-group conflicts, and conservative tendencies that hold to patterns of dominance and a willful denial of the value of other ways of life. The metapsychology of soul refers to life tendencies and aspirations both before and after a particular incarnation. Soul life is intrinsic to all self-knowledge, and the discovery of spiritual power and ability is a direct acknowledgment of the soul's deep intentions. Those intentions form the appropriate attitudes and disciplines that carry over from this life into other lives. Often, such knowledge requires breaking through the collective mindset, disengaging from the normative beliefs and ideologies, in search of a deeper self-awareness and soul intent.

The full knowledge of self is not simply a fusion of conscious ideas and thoughts with an arbitrarily defined "unconscious." True self-knowledge must break through the collective impasse of the reified unconscious and ascend into the heights and descend into the depths of

Being in order to discover the true luminosity of soul and self-capacity. Soul-knowledge is more than an encounter with archetypal imagery and collective contents; it is also an emergent knowledge infused with Spirit that is in the process of fulfilling root intentions carried though many lifetimes and not simply motivated by immediate circumstances. Opening to the luminous body, receiving the inspirations of love, knowing the sources of illumination within Spirit, the visionary gnosis, is only part of the journey into a full metapsychology of soul intent. Through dreams, visions, expanded seeing and hearing, through the opening of clairvoyant capacities and paranormal perceptions, we enter into the intentional thought-worlds of soul. In this process, we can penetrate through the conditional boundaries or collective life and touch the root causal states that motivate soul in the processes of incarnation. We must expand our creative visionary capacity to embrace a full cosmos of living spiritual powers whose work and energy is connected to our own intentional purposes or goals.

The miracle of creative vision is a capacity to expand the intentional thought-world—through imaginative work, through a visualization of full human potential in a living cosmos of multiple others, and through an embrace that expands into UrSpace as the primal visionary ground from which all dreams, imaginative work, and visionary miracles arise. The everyday miracle of creative vision must arise from the soul's intention to see and to understand the interconnected relationships that animate and enliven the full spectrum of spiritual life. We must imagine the soul as working through multiple lives, through greater cycles of creative transformation whose purpose is to bring to full expression the latent spiritual capacities in each and every species, and not just in human capacity. This creative vision is grounded in the animate quality of life as valuable and miraculous—the birth of the eagle is no less a miracle than the birth of any child or of any other life form. In the creative vision, life is a miracle, all life, every tree, plant, animal, mineral, sun, star or moon. We are surrounded with the Greatest Miracle—Life, an orb or planet of tremendous beauty in which the pairing of species is an ongoing miracle; that life is abundant, overflows, spills forth its fruitfulness, and multiplies. And this miracle is a soul miracle because it is through soul and through an opening to its depths that we can feel and know the everyday miracle of life as sacred and holy.

The miracle of life is held through a power of soul that is greater

175

than the soul of any individual and greater than collective humanity. Spirit holds and infuses life. The animate wholeness of a world is held in the sacred space of all its animate aspects, from a crystal-iron core of volcanic heat through rocks and minerals, through plants, animals, birds, terrestrial elementals, and the animate spirits of all nature and archetypal creation to the transcendent forms of the highest spiritual visions, expressed in its wholeness as the feminine World Soul, the Anima Mundi. The primal symbol of incarnation is the earth as webbed and energized by life-force and held in the World Soul as the most precious of all miracles, a living planet, a green, blue, and sepia-toned world of billions of creatures. This is perhaps the greatest of all miracles. And the power of soul must expand to incorporate the totality of the living being that is the earth soul, the complete synthesis and interconnected wholeness of nature held in the embrace of all souls whose care and intention will determine the quality of life possible in such a miraculous world. True self-knowledge begins when we feel and recognize the intention to hold the living earth as sacred, as a holy work of creation, and when we choose it as an incarnational ground for our highest spiritual intentions.

As we grow into soul awareness, our knowledge of self expands to incorporate not only our world but the heavens and the infinite creation processes of the mesocosmic and macrocosmic becoming. And this too is an everyday miracle. To look into heaven, at the moon, the planets, the stars, the galactic formations; to see through instruments the radio waves, invisible energies and X-rays, the microcosmic background, the mysteries of stellar formations and the eccentricities of cosmic life, is a visionary miracle. Soul life seeks to encompass, to expand, and to absorb the possibilities of visionary space and time, in order to know itself in the fullest sense of all creation. Self-knowledge includes this awareness of an infinite universe, of branching probabilities that can bend time as well as space into new forms and dimensions. It is this vaster creative vision that is the natural home of soul. The visionary capacity, its dreaming power, is evoked through the vastness of interstellar potential, complexity and the great cycles of cosmic formation, dissolution, and reformation. And soul moves through these great cycles with profound attachments to its incarnational root purposes, to enliven the world with a profound knowledge of deep, creative potential. Awakening to both mysteries within and mysteries without, we find our selves returning to an open state of developing perception in which knowledge continues to expand and

176

incorporate ever more complex and miraculous possibilities.

We live amidst the miracle of continually deepening, multidimensional life and this deepening challenges us to greater soul work. And one of the most central and necessary miracles is healing work, the restoration of soul balance, the capacity to intend healing as a redress for imbalance and excess. When the visionary miracle of life contracts to the bound horizon of selfish needs, to the shrunken space of fear and shame and guilt, the power of soul is diminished. To liberate the soul from these negative states of anxiety and despair is a great healing work.[3] Healing inner anxiety is often a long and difficult task, because the soul has lost connection with its sense of purpose and intention and no healing method can simply instill such an intention as an act of therapy. The miracle of the healing work is when we find the way into depths of soul through the transformation of perception and memory, so we can overcome the traumas of past repression and habitual living. These two movements—one to heal memory and the other to open perception—represent the twin movements of soul toward inner purification and outer incorporation. The healing of memory also includes the recovery of deep incarnational intention that instills purpose and direction for life affirmation. We are not simply driven by habit and conditioning; we can choose and make active, meaningful decisions that help to determine our self direction and relations to others.

Self-healing begins with the recovery of soul depth, an opening inward to the possibilities of human potential, an opening outward to new perceptions based in a creative vision, an expansion into a fully animate, living cosmos. Christ work is a healing work and the Christ image is a healing image, as is the nurturing image of the Holy Sophia. Our capacity to heal is based in our capacity to open to those depths that are the very sources of life within Spirit. We must fully feel and embrace the animate qualities of Spirit as transformational knowing that Spirit can heal our deepest injury, soothe our greatest fears, and transform our bound condition into one of freedom through creative inspiration. Through clear intention, a healing intention that is born out of our incarnational purpose, we can bring light into the most negative circumstance or memory. The Christ work is that incarnational work of healing; Sophia is the wisdom that informs that work and gives it an intelligible content. Sophia is the illumined wisdom, guided by a clear intent to heal through intelligible means, through insights into the human heart, mind, and soul. Sophianic wisdom is the light that guides our understanding in fathoming the human being as a carrier of creative purpose, a purpose that may well be lost, confused, distorted, or undeveloped in souls bound by collective and conservative thought or belief. To liberate the soul from the terrible binding of violent history, from oppression and personal denial, from the confusion of contradictory, self-serving authority, is part of the Great Work of the illumined soul.

In the alchemy of soul, we seek self-healing and we seek to heal others, because both are necessary aspects of a single creative process. The Christ work is a healing miracle in loving touch, the Sophianic wisdom instills insights and understanding of how the process of healing, the loving touch, actually works. The Sophianic Christ is a therapeutic image of the soul awakening to its full potential, being healed and healing, attuned with an incarnational intention to represent Spirit as animate and alive in all human relationships within a visionary universe of multiple healing sources. The Christ does not work alone, nor is he the only soul image of transformation or healing; the Sophia is only one image of the feminine power of such work. The soul will move toward those images and powers that best represent its incarnational intentions, and in that process, there will be emergence and new expressions of healing capacity and power. All human beings have a capacity to heal both themselves and others; we need only affirm and recognize our natural capacities for such work. Self-knowledge affirms this deep intention to live in a healthy and vibrant world of purposeful, co-creative work. The miracle of healing is simply allowing Spirit to work through the healing process until a hug or a touch can instill confidence and affirmation in the other, can support the opening of the other to his or her inner potential.

The essence of this process is the miracle of love as a spontaneous gift, a free giving that does not seek recompense or recognition, but simply affirms the other in affirming the miracle of life. When we open to the visionary world, becoming aware of our incarnational intentions, developing a clear spiritual affirmation in living respectful and caring lives, then love is the natural medium of miraculous transformation. It requires no special technique and no particular visionary training because it flows forth spontaneously, from the inner work of alchemical transformations. What is required is the cultivation of a loving heart, of love as a medium of healing that is non-possessive and non-compelling for the other. The Sophianic Christ love is spontaneous and yet directed and focused through clear intentions to heal and to share the gift. It flows forth most fully where it is called by affinity to a need that corresponds with incarnational intent. What we intend deeply will inevitably manifest as a work between self and another; we heal most effectively where we are in correspondence with the intentions of others. Often, this degree of correspondence is missed due to outward manifestation of thoughts, beliefs, or mental-emotive attitudes. But beneath this surface of conditioned attitudes lie deeper soul intentions which can and will respond to the work of others, regardless of the external beliefs of the incarnate personality. The great miracle of love penetrates the surface and through an aware and clear intention, it can heal even those who are completely unaware of their inmost soul desires and their incarnational purpose.

FAMILY, CHILDREN, FRIENDS

Our relationships are neither arbitrary nor determined, but a consequence of inner connections in a shared intentional meta-psychology. Often, we may not know why another attracts us or why we might give birth to those who are so distinctively other or uniquely motivated in a particular social or family circumstance. Our relationships with others are correspondent with the intentional purposes of soul; the depths of self hold powerful desires and aspirations that subtly act to attract and repel others. These deeper purposes are woven from the multiple strands of experience gathered over many lifetimes. Often they are unclear and unintegrated, creating inner tensions and confusion in personal relationships because we do not read correctly the nature of those deeper intentions, in ourselves or in others. This is particularly true in familial relationships when the collective attitude is to regard children as subordinate to parents who are "possessors," who demand or expect obedience, loyalty, or like-mindedness. Nothing so distorts the psychic life as a parent who fails to honor the unique and individual quality of mind and soul that each new child incarnates. Through the developmental processes of childhood, each soul explores its potential to be a unique being with specific gifts, talents, and predispositions—which may be quite different and challenging to the parents. And the more gifted or impaired the child, the greater the parental challenge to recognize and hold a quality of love that best supports an emergence that avoids the malformations of selfish impositions.

Children are a great spiritual gift, a challenge to hold in loving space that allows for differences while instilling a respect for life and diversity through example and deeply centered support. Many children today are emotionally and mentally confused by the often broken lives of parents, either by their anxieties, repressive measures, or by an undefined permissiveness that only gives examples of self-indulgence or harried and sporadic affection, superficially supportive. There is a profound lack of understanding on the part of adults for the value and worth of children as part of and intrinsic to the creative spiritual processes of life affirmation. Children come to us through the inner working of soul's metapsychology. It is neither an arbitrary process nor a random, material event; it is not a matter of genetic determination, but of soul intention working through Spirit. Spirit is itself a genetic medium, and every chromosome, every DNA helix, every genetic molecule is a vehicle for Spirit and the medium of biochemical interaction is nurtured by Spirit at the level of its most minute processes. But beyond that miracle of life-generating biology is an even more astonishing metapsychology that binds intention and soul within the subtle materials of physical transformation. This mystery is not understood or recognized by many parents; consequently, there is no appreciation for the most profound miracle of soul's transformation into an incarnate, embodied personality.

The meta-psychology of family relationships is complex; its motivational structures are usually multigenerational, ranging over historic interactions that completely invert or reverse normative role relations in any given incarnation. The causal relations between souls cannot be summarized or reduced to a single model — this is because the complexity of soul relationships reflects the total life of the collective. Each soul, as the poet John Donne once noted, is "not an island but a piece of the main," and this means that the metapsychology of any individual is an index of both the familial and the collective, and embodies in certain ways the tensions and complexity of his or her time and place of incarnation. There are no simple "karmic laws" here; the actual metapsychology is far more complex than any simple causal dynamics of past relationships can represent accurately. And deeper yet is the incarnational intent, the inner determination that best characterizes the purpose and value of a particular lifetime. Insofar as this intent is known and conscious, the life can be shaped accordingly; but insofar as it is unrecognized or obscure, the individual is subject to all the fluxuations and uncertainties of an unanchored life. There is no one intent, but the intentions of incarnation are primal and they act to give form and content to our relationships with others, even when we do not recognize the exact nature of that intent. Central to the alchemy of soul is the process of clarifying this incarnational intent, bringing it clearly to mind as the purpose and meaning of a given lifetime.

When this intent is clear, we can choose our family, our parents, and even, under special circumstances, our children. This is a mysterious learning process. Partly, it is a matter of creating an intent for children that corresponds to the life goals of the parent, seeking to embody a soul that resonates with the aspirations and deeper purposes of the parents' developed self-knowledge. However, this does not mean that the intent is to birth a child who serves the parent or who embodies the parent's own goals and aspirations. The alchemical intent is to birth a child whose own work, whose own creative abilities, will correspond and compliment the spiritual goals of the parents—even while that child follows his or her own unique path. Thus, one cannot simply choose the soul that is attracted; that soul carries lessons and embodies unique perspectives that may profoundly challenge the parents to move beyond their expected desires or wants. The parental goal is to provide a supportive context for the creative unfolding of each child that nurtures unique aspects of self awareness. The miracle of birth, of childhood and maturation, reflects complex processes of interaction that are not only biological and familial, but also cultural and historical. The clarity of intent, its realized actualization through existential commitment and embodied practice, is a lifetime challenge. Parents must hold the responsibility of nurturing deep intentional life by honoring the soul realizations of their children. And a child holds a responsibility for honoring the intentional lives of the parents while still recognizing his or her own incarnational purpose.

How can we honor soul expression in others if we do not perceive its workings within our own lives? This is why, in the alchemy of soul, the individual strives to bring into full realization the inner potential that reflects the unique gifts and abilities of expressive soul awareness. We must turn toward the deeper core of values and intentions that motivate positive spiritual transformation, embodying those values in real actions and real relationships with others. Integrity in this case is a matter of honoring the soul's aspiration by living according to principles of Spirit and not just according to collective beliefs and unexamined attitudes that may be self-serving and destructive. These principles can only be known by delving into the depths of soul, into the visionary heart of our capacities for transformation of self and of the world. The family is the inner circle of this process, the place where the alchemy of soul is first fostered or repressed, cultivated or ignored, nurtured or forgotten. We have a spiritual obligation to honor our children as incarnate souls in search of their highest potential. We have an obligation to protect them from the personal violence and miasma of collective thought and action that would condemn them to a fragmented, isolated life of confusion and frustration. The true depths of frustration arise out of the discontinuity between our soul intent and the substitute intent that is formed in response to a superficial way of life, in response to strictly material concerns, or pragmatic adaptation to values lacking spiritual content or purpose.

In the alchemy of soul, there is a spiritual obligation to model the values we hold as most consistent with true soul life. The dulling artifice and obscuring stereotypes of collective behavior must be stripped away for a brighter expression of inner purpose and individual ability. Children are the most precious expression of cosmos and creation; the health of our children is the most significant sign of the health and vitality of our cultures and our shared historical era. In order to bring into focus the deeper potential of soul, children need very strong, very clear examples of others who live according to deep inner commitments to the realization of soul potential. Without such examples, soul becomes an abstract idea, a logos sign that has no real emotional or somatic content. But soul life is a highly emotive, visionary, sensitive response to the energies and actions of a living cosmos. Greatness of soul is rare because too many adults hold only a vague abstract notion of soul which they do not live or embody. Instead they think about soul or discuss it, but it remains a pale construct and not a reality of living based in spiritual intention and responsiveness. True greatness of soul feels the suffering of the world; it feels and knows the incomplete development, clearly recognizes the pain and bound condition of others, and offers from its own depths a healing intent, a loving relation of support, and a willingness to engage others at the soul level.

Our friends come to us in accord with our own inner dispositions, in accord with the psychic life of soul desires (positively and negatively). And we come to our friends based upon their soul life, more or less consciously, more or less guided by the processes of intuition and empathy, by the correspondent resonance between soul intentions. Even as children, our intentions are an attractive medium that brings us into relationship with others, requiring us to cut through the stereotypes of collective thought and behavior in order to find the unique and precious gift of true friendship. In young children, these intentions are less specific and less determined by the cultural present, but in adults these intentions can easily be overlaid with acquired and learned ideas or beliefs that constantly push against the inner life of the individual, thus obscuring soul relations. The friend we value is the one who lives according to the soul's life, whose authenticity is a reflection of an inner commitment to a way of life highly valued and embodied. For some, this may be more practical than aesthetic or intellectual, more emotional and relational than transcendent or ecstatic. But the deeper intent is to live not according to a single model or example, but according to the inspirations of Spirit as soul seeks to realize inner goals that promote life, peace, and well-being.

Our true friends are those who support and encourage our growth and development, who can act as examples of centered life, of compassionate care and warmth for others. To be a "friend of Christ" means to live as one who fully supports the healing and awakening of the world to love and genuine healing wisdom. The Sophia-inspired Christ in me loves and supports the Christ in you, just as the Christ in you loves and supports the Christ in me. This is not because we each embody the Christ Spirit in the same way, but because the Christ Spirit is broad and adaptive, inclusive, not exclusive, and does not discriminate based on identity in belief or thought. Sophianic wisdom is a creative presence that illumines the heart of every creature and seeks to bring that creature to the utmost realization of its inner potential. If we truly love our children and honor and support our friends, we will be equally supported and loved, even though we may think differently and seek to realize our soul intentions in unique and individual ways. Love does not equalize, it differentiates. Love honors the differences but nurtures the humanity and passion and concern of the aspiring soul. To be a great soul is to love humanity with a deep healing intent, like the Sophianic Christ, for the good of all and not just for the good of the elect or chosen. Love differentiates because it is a means for Spirit to express its inner potential, not by conformity, but through diverse, rich complexity.

If we can honor the children, regard them with the true reverence and respect they deserve because as adults we are dedicated to alchemical transformation, then our children will be our closest friends. Not through conformity in thought or belief or behavior, but through the power of love that honors the differences in expressing deep soul intentions. The significant child-parent bond is the soul relationship, the way in which the inner being of each person reflects and opens to the inner being of the other. When we can do this gently, with honor, respect and detachment from the immediate outcome of our efforts, then we can cultivate the soul process in others. The growth and development of soul is a multigenerational process, a deep incarnational project of multiple lifetimes, and requires great patience and inner clarity of purpose, lifetime after lifetime. Too often, we are caught in the immediacy of passion and desires that are only consequential in the moment, but which in perspective are seen to be shallow or superficial. This is why we must descend to deeper soul awareness in order to overcome the tendencies to remain caught on the surface of life. Through loving friendships, through respectful sharing of soul, through an honoring of all life and all spirits, we can support each other in cultivating new ideals of intentional purpose. These ideals are inseparable from our responsibilities as friends, parents, teachers, or students of the works and teachings of others.

WORK, PLAY, AND INNER DISCIPLINE

In the alchemy of soul, there is an expansive sense of joy, and one who lacks this joy has not yet discovered the true depths of Spirit. While there is sorrow and suffering in the world, there is also beauty, happiness, and wonder. In the spiritual life, there is a complementarity and balance that allows for positive, negative, and intermediary emotions and reactions to conditional life. The alchemical goal is to hold the balance, hold the center, while expanding the boundaries and directing the process to ever more inclusive understanding. Joy includes the physical life—the emotions of shared happiness, positive sexual relations, beautifully prepared food, a hot shower, a warm bed, a comfortable chair, a cold glass of iced tea. The spiritual life is a celebration of the sensory beauty of creation—the multicolored spectrum of garden flowers, the magic of the rainbow, the startling green of the forest after spring rain, the smell of cedar and pine, the blue sky and majesty of mountain heights, the rough exhilaration of ocean waves or a thunder storm, or the turbulence of a windy, cold, cloud-filled twilight. There is joy in beholding the processes of life at every level of complexity, from the very small to the very great.

The sorrow is a direct effect of our capacity to see the joy and beauty that is denied or disfigured through a more grasping and controlling mentality. Because we can see and feel the joy and wonder, we can also feel the horror and terror of its denial or destruction by those who are closed to soul and who live according to appetites based on indifferent or selfish satisfactions. Nothing is more destructive than a loss of empathy and indifference toward principles of reciprocity—but we know this because we can experience the joy of what is shared and held through mutual respect and love. It is important to embrace the joy and the pleasure of life, to experience fully the satisfaction of physical, incarnate embodiment. This is a spiritual teaching. Creation is the place of Spirit manifesting; it is the place of joy in which harmony of soul can resonate with the joy of others in sharing the good of natural, embodied life. In the alchemy of soul, we work with the body as a divine ground of revelation through increasing sensory awareness. The physical life is a miracle of joy when lived through healthy, loving relationships that honor the physical as a means through which the spiritual is given form and content. As we expand sensory awareness into the subtle realms of perception, we can still honor the physical means through which those senses distinguish discrete aspects of the full sensorium. We can honor the beauty and joy of sensations which open the world to our full perception and awareness.

The basis of play is not simply giving up work, but opening the senses and relaxing the body, giving attention to exercising our capacity for alternative perceptions. Play involves shifting the sensory field, placing attention in a different arena of action, and allowing spontaneity and resourcefulness to motivate freer, more imaginative behavior. Play involves breaking down the routines and habits that tend toward pragmatic and necessary actions for the maintenance of ordinary life. But more, play involves creative exploration, having fun through exploring new situations and new modes of self-expression. Perhaps it is energetic and involves exercise or play in a focused and intentional practice that is truly enjoyable and gives a sense of pleasure in bodily health, flexibility, a general sense of well-being. Perhaps it is a matter of just resting, sinking down into a quiet and calm that opens mind and heart to a more inner, reflective awareness. And perhaps it is experimental, a seeking out of experience that is new and unusual to give new perspective and nuance to habitual attitudes of mind or emotion. Play is a creative opportunity to explore as well as to rest or to exercise or to reflect.

Another aspect of play in the alchemy of soul is the exploration of mood, insight, and self-expression in experimental forms—for example, through ritual, body paints, mask making, music, dance, games, and many other creative arts. The alchemical aspect of such play is the way in which it enhances self-knowledge through enjoyable and pleasurable interactions and activities often, but not always, with others—sometimes friends, sometimes strangers. Play in this sense refers to activities that challenge us to find greater spontaneity and interactions with others outside the context of normative role expectations. It concerns opening to the possibility of a more enhanced way of perceiving, experimenting within group relations, participating in communal events, attending rituals that open awareness to the underlying dynamics of soul, providing opportunities for growth without demands or expectations. There is a Sophianic Christ work that is playful and filled with joy through interactions with others in a loving context of group relations that can be deeply restful and at the same time expansive and spiritually stimulating. It is play in a more active and engaged sense, not in the passive mode of a spectator, but in the mode of a full participant. The spectator mode is the weakest form of play because it requires only a minimal engagement and does not activate the will or the creative abilities. The participant mode of play is far better as a means to encourage or provoke personal development.

When work is routine, it can drain the participant of any real sense of accomplishment because his or her actions flow from a habitual pattern that limits creative exploration and alternatives. Further, a worker may well be subordinate to a structural hierarchy that has very low concern for the creative, developmental life of the employee. Even those higher in the structural pattern may be forced to conform to norms or work patterns that in no way serve their soul intentions but in fact, suppress and override them. The challenge is to find, or to develop, a work pattern that also includes some sense of play and creative expression. A high degree of polarity between work and play is a cultural sign of widespread dysfunctional economic and political structures. Such a polarity reflects a denial of human creativity and happiness and instead offers wealth or power as more fundamental to material human aspiration. But this is a false attribution. The deep intentions of soul are rarely motivated by desire for either wealth or power. But, in not knowing these truly deep intentions, wealth and power become a substitute for a lack of depth and insight into soul. Life becomes motivated by external collective norms that rise from the immediacy of personal desires for recognition, influence, or privileges that serve the individual at the cost of minimizing the rights and pleasures of others. Thus, corporations can justify the exploitation of underpaid workers because they produce goods that are less expensive for a wealthier

186

class of people than those who actually manufacture the goods. This form of common exploitation reflects the soulless depths of those who most benefit, including the harm wrought to the unconscious buyer caught in the corporate miasma of profit and exploitation.

Work should have an ethical core that sustains a sense of joy in life and supports the value of all beings; work should spring from a soulful concern to support the right of every human being to live a positive, creative life. Life is not about wealth or power but about shared, empathic living; it is about kindness and soulful relationships that seek the good of others, not their exploitation or enslavement. In the alchemy of soul, work is a means for spiritual development, not a form of unthinking support or exploitation based in accumulating benefits at the cost of depriving others of their livelihood or well-being. We must think about the form of work we choose — work that is not bracketed and closed from playfulness and creative expression, work that is not oppressive but rewarding in a deep, soulful sense. The alchemy of work requires courage and inner strength to choose those forms of work that will enhance and not diminish self-knowledge and self-expression. Work is not a matter of serving impersonal interests that benefit the few, but of choosing conscious activities that will allow for continued development. And where those forms of work are not immediately available, we must create them, bringing our souls to bear on the problem and thus generating the work that keeps us whole and gives us the satisfaction of enjoying life because we do not choose to exploit or deny the creative needs of others.

The inner discipline of the Christ-Sophia work is to take joy and pleasure in one's work because it is a soul work and a work that, no matter what the difficulties or challenges, gives a sense of soul fulfillment. All work requires some degree of discipline, even in those circumstances where spontaneity is most required. Work as improvisation requires a learned flexibility and adaptivity, and work as structure requires adaptation and learning. The Christ work is not about teaching or studying as much as it is about following an inner discipline that brings the Sophia-Christ presence into every circumstance, however spontaneous or however structured. This can be accomplished through three means: the first is through cultivating a genuine of love for others, not determined by role or social position. The second is to cultivate the Sophia-Christ presence as a living reality in accordance with spiritual values that are part of our everyday decisions and actions. The third is to bring Sophia Christ presence through the gifts of Spirit that come to us when we are grounded in deep soul intentions. We must intend, from the depths of soul, to be Lamps of Spirit through purity of motivation and commitment to the realization of our full spiritual potential. Like the wise virgins at the wedding feast who kept their lamps filled with pure oil so that even when the bride and groom arrived late they were prepared, so too the soul must hold pure motivations that light the way toward the coming of that presence.[4] The motivation is to manifest Spirit in thought, word, and deed, and to live according to the life intentions of soul incarnation.

This discipline is not simply a form of external action, but an interaction, a relational development between the outer structures of the world and the inner processes of Spirit. Both are crucial because the world outwardly manifests our thoughts, ideas, and beliefs, but inwardly, what we think and contemplate becomes the reality in which we live. This relationship between the deep interior and the materialization of world forms is a spiritual process of profound significance. It includes both work and play, relaxation and the joyful exploration of potential in a multitude of dynamic circumstances. The spiritual path is not simply work, work, work. Such a construct has lost the joy and the pleasure of embodied life. Creative spiritual development is also playful, experimental, and expansive through overturning restrictive and binding forms. Discipline, in the alchemical sense, needs redefinition as a joyful exploration of potential, as an increasing ability to bring your full attention and will to whatever you do — be it play, relaxation, work, or spiritual practices. When discipline is only work, then it has not tapped the central current of Spirit that gives joy and timelessness to its unfolding. When Spirit infuses the discipline, it ceases to be simply a routine task of will and becomes an interactive unfolding, an inner opening as Spirit directs the action through an effortless attunement.

I have experienced this many times, in many different practices, in work, play, T'ai Chi, meditation, prayer and community rituals. There is an opening, an inner release that allows for an enhancing presence that flows with perfect continuity and gentle urging in the midst of the practice or work. The urging is an inner prompting that draws the soul, often through images and signs, to adapt the work or practice toward an often unpredictable expression. There is an inner guidance that flows out of the work that grounds it in a joyful feeling of freedom and openness to Spirit, such that the moment is expansive and effortless. I have often noticed that this happens after the basic discipline of learning the practice, thoug "beginner's luck" is exactly this kind of thing—the first time, withou knowledge or expectation, sometimes allows Spirit to joyfully enter the activity before an individual learns habits or ideas concerning a more developed doing. In spiritual discipline, we work toward just this kind of spontaneity and inner joy so the work moves beyond an act of will and becomes an expression of soul intent guided by Spirit. In the alchemy of soul, the individual work springs not simply from personal effort, but also from an inner affirmation of intention that invokes Spirit, liberates the bound will, and opens the heart and mind to inspiration and joy. When joy is present in the work, then play and innovation can also find expression. In this way, discipline leads to healing and new energy, and work becomes simply another aspect of the path.

MYSTERIES OF INITIATION

Sophianic Christ work is a mystery which cannot be controlled or predetermined in its expressions or outcome. The depths of this work arise from soul intentions that aim at world transformation through co-operative, co-creative respect and appreciation for the great diversity that is held in the wholeness of Spirit. Every individual must find the unique and particular ways in which the united energies of the Christ and the Sophia can manifests in and through him or her. But such manifestation does not come simply in the form of an autonomous gift from "outside" directing the subordinate personality toward a particular task. In a mature spirituality, the Christ and Sophia work is integral to the personality, and identity is neither splintered off into discrete subordinate fragments nor subservient to some "higher power". As mature beings, we must learn to stand on our own feet, to embrace our spiritual potentials as gifts of Spirit that require us to undergo the necessary initiations to fully claim and integrate those gifts as inseparable from our deep soul intentions. We are not subordinate to the Christ or the Sophia but are the very means by which the Sophianic wisdom and Christ love is given mature definition and substance in actual lives. Knowing this work as a part of ourselves, as an intrinsic aspect of soul intention, places upon us the responsibility of claiming those gifts as thoroughly part of our deep identity.

We do not subordinate ourselves to Christ or Sophia but stand with each as brothers and sisters in the great work of world transformation; we fully honor the gifts of Spirit without subordination or submission to any archetypal forms or patterns. We do not place ourselves above, but in the middle, and below when necessary, in the face of presence that is greater and more profound than our own realized integration. We hold to the value and task of individual responsibility in relationship to other powers—spirits, angels, devas, or any beings—that might seem to claim our allegiance or submission. It is thoroughly possible to honor those whose abilities exceed our own, without surrendering our will or intention to them and without denying the value of each person's individual accomplishments, however simple or profound. The Sophia-Christ work is one of honoring all forms of spiritual accomplishment without assuming a subordinate role simply because a spiritual other manifests more wisdom or power or love than that attained in our own practices. From these spiritual others we can learn to grow, and develop—but the Christ-Sophia work must act in each person according to his or her ability and this does not requires subordinating one's will to the demands of others who may claim a superior spiritual understanding. True spiritual understanding, in the alchemy of soul, will support individual differences, however great or small, and will constantly act to cultivate spiritual responsibility in each person.

In the process of seeking to actualize the Christ work and the Sophia wisdom, there are many initiations. These initiations lead, sometimes step by step, sometimes in great leaps forward and sudden slips backwards, to an ever-deepening awareness of how this work and wisdom must be realized through the unique gifts of the individual and not through artificial ideals, goals, or preconceived patterns. The alchemy of soul requires us to seek self-knowledge, expanded awareness, openness to the subtle body of light, and clarity of thought in order to enter the Lunar-Solar depths of Spirit and to attain the realization of soul intentions that are unique to each individual. This takes a lifetime of effort, even in the midst of ongoing visionary awakenings, experiences of illumination, or joyful insights. It is not a matter of realizing a predetermined end. True initiation involves inner discovery of power and capacity that is shaped by soul desire and the development of self-knowledge, a recognition of personal strengths and abilities as well as weaknesses and limitations. Initiations occur at exactly that moment when we face a crisis and choose to overcome a boundary or move into a new space of relationship to ways of life we might once have rejected or failed to understand or recognize. Initiation is a process, not simply an event; it is a process of opening to new understanding or insights that may come long after the actual awakening experience. Initiation sets up a possibility for understanding that can change individual perspectives and facilitate growth and maturation.

Initiations can also fail. Sometimes they fail because they are sought prematurely and undertaken while the soul is still unready to accept or utilize the full impact of the experience. The Sophianic Christ work can remain superficial and external in the sense that one claims to embrace the Christ or Sophia ideal but only grasps an outer aspect—a particular behavior, a unique image, a certain habit of mind or practice—that lacks the inner prompting toward personal development and unique self-expression. True initiation challenges the heart and soul to deepen and to transform the mental and emotional universe of collective thought into an individuated, integrated visionary world. Such a world, in the initiatory sense, is uniquely configured while it also participates in a shared wholeness of higher values and attitudes toward spiritual development. The actual path and practice for every alchemy of soul is unique, but those paths converge in cultivating a shared reality of positive spiritual values and perceptions. Love is such a value, as is kindness, care for the well being of others, hope for world peace, a nurturing sense of support for all living creatures, a healing concern for those who are struggling or abused or denied equal access to the basic goods and necessities of practical life. Many other such values converge through the multitude of paths and practices that reflect a mature spiritual worldview.

In the Christ-Sophia work, each person must seek to form those values in a way that is expressed in the daily round through ever deepening initiation into soul work and self transformation. But these values are best discovered in the process of the opening of the heart, in the discovery of the deeper self that guides the transformations of soul toward a full flowering of inner potential. These values are not imposed from without but flourish from within; they come into clarity of expression by experiencing directly the work of Spirit in the human heart. Through an alchemy of soul, we become more loving, more concerned for the healing of others and of the world, more committed to a way of life that becomes increasingly altruistic as the transformation deepens and we open into a living cosmos of interconnected beings. Through purity of mind and heart, we can see directly the reality of the Sophianic Christ work as it manifests through wise and loving relationships, a more open and receptive mind and freer depths of feeling and subtle perception. To attain this knowledge it is necessary to undergo the initiations that life offers us in all circumstances, even through crisis and trauma. Love and passion are both initiatory, as is childbirth and the death of loved ones. Changes in work, relationships, community membership, the loss or gain of friends, can all be initiatory.

What is necessary is to relate these changes to the process of self-development, to the rudiments of inner soul intention such that those intentions are not deflected but instead are strengthened in their purpose and aim. Initiations come in dreams and visions, in the encounter with the strange and mysterious, through confrontation and through radically shifting perceptions. We must be prepared to drop our preoccupation with a comfortable lifestyle or be willing to abandon routines that cushion or buffer us from overcoming our own weaknesses and fears. If we are too buffered, too sheltered, then we will not make the inner changes necessary. Initiation involves risk and challenge—to shift perspectives we must be willing to experience our own vulnerabilities. But we must also have the inner confidence to not be paralyzed by those vulnerabilities in order to move forward toward greater integration. Accidents, sudden reversals of fortune, unpredicted events, startling changes in collective life, communal disruption or family conflicts can all be initiatory if treated in the appropriate manner. How does the event serve the purposes of soul intention? What is the soulful response? What is the obligation of the soul purpose we carry within us in these dramatic and challenging circumstances? Insofar as we hold to soul intention and act with integrity, the experience will carry us to a deep level of realization of our inner potential for growth and development.

Dreams are a primary source for initiation, as the complex depths of the psyche are more accessible for the work of ongoing transformation. Dreams can carry the dreamer into any number of alternative worlds and states of perception, all of which are relevant to the processes of the Great Work. But not all dreams are initiatory, and the dreamer must distinguish between dream types. The higher value dreams are those that open the dreamer to new perceptions and a greater world of convergence and interaction. In visions, there is also initiation, although the danger is that the visionary form will be literalized and taken to be an autonomous entity or as an end in itself, when in fact, it is only a means to a higher realization, the full discovery of the pranic self. Waking imagination can act as initiation when the seer guides the imaginative process toward deeper evocation of soul, allowing imagination to work as a means for soliciting imagery and feeling that is instructive for self-development. Body work of many types is also initiatic. It allows for the deep release of held energies and opens to an increasing flow of psychic intensity, supporting the development of much more responsive and sensitive energies in relationship to others and for the development of intrinsic psychic capacities. Yoga, T'ai Chi, Shiatsu, Nia, Reiki, Polarity Therapy, Healing Touch, and various types of kundalini work can all be initiatic if handled in the correct manner and applied to the overall processes of self-development.

The Sophia-Christ work is non-exclusive, integrative, and part of a life path of healing and service to others. Initiation begins when the work flows spontaneously, without effort or willfulness, into a loving touch, a compassionate concern, and a heartfelt empathy for the suffering and needs of others. The Christ work can be very great, as well as very subtle, in holding within the chalice of our life an intention to heal through love, compassion, as well as a deep Sophianic wisdom that gives insight and clarity to the purposes of healing. Initiation proceeds further when we learn that empathy and healing love do not require us to suffer with others as they suffer, nor to descend into the hell worlds of horror and abuse as they are experienced by others. The task is not to hold the wound, not to suffer the pain for others, but to bring healing to that pain and to close the wound with love and wholeness that is not diminished by the presence of suffering in others. Empathy is not identifying with the pain and suffering of others. Empathy means standing fully in the presence of sorrow and pain while remaining centered, calm, and compassionate; it mean to fully offer healing for that sorrow without diminishing one's personal stance in Spirit. In an even higher sense, empathy means manifesting the Sophianic Christ presence as a luminous source of transformation that overcomes the pain, closes the wound, and completely heals the sorrow.

The Christ-Sophia work is a great work of heart and soul. It stems from the depths of self-knowledge and flourishes through the expanded capacities of deep soul intention to live as a healer who nurtures the spiritual potential in others. Integrating the Christ mystery into one's life as a source of inspiration can lead to miraculous work based not on technique or analysis, but on a free and deep love that sustains the wisdom of the Sophianic logos. It is a highly mindful love, a love that is an expression of Spirit flowing through the unique gifts and abilities of the individual brought to perfection through years of practice, devotion, and dedication to the task of self transformation. We are all capable of healing others and of healing ourselves to the degree to which we deem possible. In some this is a narrow horizon, but in others such a horizon is infinite and indefinable. In the Christ-Sophia work we must each seek to find the expansive boundaries of our own potential for love and wisdom. This is not a matter of abstract theory or mental speculation, but one of continual self-examination, of cultivating deep intentions of the heart, and of acquiring a direct and personal knowledge of inner potential in order to direct and shape its expressions. This potential is profoundly powerful, and only through great stability and inner work can any individual successfully manifest its full development. Every life is unique, every form a blossoming forth of possibility. The soulful opening of the heart allows for a wisdom that can only bring increasing maturity as a powerful, expressive love in all our relations with others.

1. John 7:37-38; Revelations 21:6.
2. Matthew 17:1-2.
3. See Robert Sardello, 1999 and 2001; also see Lee Irwin, 2001.
4. Matthew 25:1-13.

CHAPTER SEVEN
COMMUNAL WILL AND ACTS OF CREATION

The alchemical aspect of community is expressed in the creative interactions of many individuals working to coordinate their idea-beliefs for the purposes of transformation. Community, in this alchemical sense, is not a matter of collective merging or submergence of the individual perspective, nor does it mean a subordination of the individual to a collective identity. There is a significant difference between the alchemical community and any from of mass consciousness that functions through authoritarian social structures and inherited processes of mental or emotional sublimation. The foundation of lasting spiritual community does not rise on principles of identity with mass consciousness, but on principles of individuation and personal development that serve to enhance communal processes of growth and development. Drawing on this principle of differentiation, it is possible to distinguish varying degrees of leadership and influence within a given community. Spiritual leadership is a function of personal development and communal participation, in the alchemical sense, and requires teaching the value of balancing service with creative innovation and independence of thought gained through processes of maturation. The role of the individual in the community is to find the unique balance that serves both the needs of the community and the needs of the individual. The role of leadership should grow out of this balance, based on an ever-deepening insight into communal and individual developmental processes.

A minimal relationship for community is the dyad, two persons in relationship that each value the other's insights and commitments to a process of realizing shared and individual goals. But shared goals may not mean identical goals, and this difference in goals between individuals is significant. In an authoritarian social structure, there is little or no room for individual differences that do not directly serve the interests of the social or institutional hierarchy. Thus, conformity requires self-denial insofar as it might challenge the authority of the structure. But authority is not the binding principle of spiritual community in the alchemical sense. In a dyad, there may also be self-denial in the sense that one sacrifices or makes compromises in order to sustain the creative aspects of the relationship. But this compromise is not a result of one person dominating another; such domination is antithetical to the alchemical process and leads to stagnation, inner resistance, and dissolution without refinement or transformation. In the healthy, loving, dyad two people learn to share, to respect the individual needs of each partner, and to acquire a willingness to bend, adapt, and adjudicate differences, thus allowing for divergence in order that the relationship may grow and develop. This is not a matter of marked boundaries as much as a willingness to enter into another life with empathy and love while maintaining integrity and inner conviction.

In larger group processes, these same principles of adaptation and adjustment are necessary in order that each person be heard and respected. However, in forming spiritual community, there are shared values and teachings that may also require adaptations in order to foster insights and new attitudes that are often unknown and poorly understood by those attracted to communal ideals or goals. In this process, the embodiment or incarnation of those communal ideals is not a matter of external authority, but of inner integrity and the actualization of principled living. Unlike a personal, one-to-one relationship where goals may be evolved through mutual desires and needs, in spiritual community the goals reflect standards of behavior and thought which are regarded as necessary and preliminary to the realization of the spiritual ideals of the community. In order to practice the alchemy of soul in a communal setting, there are standards, or principles of behavior and thought, that must be internalized in order for the goals of the communal process to be actualized. And yet, because the alchemy of soul requires individuation, each person is encouraged to seek the unique synthesis and resonance that best reflects his or her interpretation of the communal ideals. Rather than mandated forms of belief or specific behavior, the alchemy of soul follows an inner path of adaptation to spiritual ideals that must be personalized.

What, then, is the purpose of community if it is not simply conformity to shared goals or obedience to behavioral norms? The purpose of community is to foster love and support, to create an environment in which an alchemy of soul may flourish through a supportive and nurturing context of human relationships. This is not a matter of conformity to hierarchical structures but of developing a horizontal web of co-creative, supportive relations that interconnect and which also sustain a vertical axis by affirming the power and presence of Spirit in communal life. The esoteric image here is the spindle; the center pole is the continuous presence and affirmation of Spirit and the thread is the basis of our interwoven connection that leads us back to the center but that does not bind us in the pattern. The thread allows us to move out and back freely, based on our ability to sustain reciprocity with others and to not violate the internal realization of shared spiritual principles. The turning of the spindle reflects the dynamics of the interactions that promote and foster growth in all members. The weaving is a constant interplay between moving out from the vertical axis (but always being connected) and then moving back towards the axis in activities that promote a direct awareness of spiritual presence. Sometimes we expand and sometimes we contract, and both directions are good and necessary.

At the still center of the alchemical community is that presence, that Inmost Being of the heart and body of each individual, shared with others. It is an incarnate presence, not outside the individual and not outside of the body, but within the body and brain and heart and will. Spirit is universal or omnipresent, but the vehicle for the realization of that universal presence is the body and the incarnational soul, now animate and living through the senses and physical miracle of embodied life. What creates connective relationships between community members is soulfulness as a feeling center of living relationships, as a heart-centered, psychic resonance fostered and developed through alchemical practices. In this process, self is the unifying integration of all feeling, perception, awareness, and soul-centered action; it is the higher aspect that expands into Spirit as it reverently perceives past-present-future activities as a part of a Great Work among a vast multitude of beings. In a metaphorical way, all beings participate in the alchemy of growth and development. Spirit, as an animating presence, works for the elevation of all souls, but these diverse paths and teachings take a multitude of forms, many unrelated to the specifics of alchemical practice. In the alchemy of soul, we undergo constant rediscovery of this process as we deepen into our most authentic work, our true calling to express and embody selfhood through soul development.

The self is an evolving entity, not a fixed and timeless reality, one that exceeds present personality and present soulful incarnation. This self in a community context can be brought to fuller expressiveness through an affirmation of embodiment rather than through a denial of body or ego or soul. The alchemical transformation works in stages to bring about a synthesis, a unity of self-knowledge that recognizes the transpersonal aspect of divinity as integral to soul's identity. But such knowledge is by no means the goal of incarnate life. We are not simply here to marvel and passively unite with a transpersonal horizon, to be "one with the infinite;"

we are here to actualize that very knowledge into viable living forms of life, culture, and historical embodiment. For, in fact, this is exactly what has happened in all spiritual traditions. Many communities have mystical teachers and living embodiments of the transcendent presence, but those beings are only incarnate, individual examples of what is possible. As enlightened beings, they embody particular forms of spiritual realization not as ideals for imitation, but as examples of possibility. In the alchemy of soul, the challenge is to embody the knowledge (gnosis) of the transpersonal horizon in actual, committed living and real beingness through responsible human relationships, not in detachment from the world as illusion, but in passionate commitment to the world as the primal ground of creation.

I do not hold the goal of the direct experience of the transcendent as the "highest manifestation," but I do honor such experience as crucial and invaluable in the processes of human evolution. In the alchemy of soul, there is no "highest manifestation" — there is only the work of each individual seeking to realize his or her full potential, his or her inner capacity that may serve the processes of shared spiritual development. When the direct experience of the transcendent or transpersonal flows into creative work, great change and development can occur. However, such experience can also block and impede development if the individual emphasizes those features of transcendence that seem unrelated to embodiment and the processes of incarnation in ongoing worldly life. The recovery of soul in this process proceeds better from love and empathy than it does from detached observation, world-denial, and a poor understanding of embodied, incarnational life. What is the purpose of humanity in creation? It is not simply to serve a remote god and it is not simply to realize the inadequacy of physical or social life. Creation is more than just play or illusion. The purpose of human life is to revere, celebrate, and to be co-creators in incarnational evolution It is to fully recognize and celebrate the miracle of creation, the beauty of the world, the wonder of nature and cosmos, and to contribute our own energies and passions to co-creating a more mature, empowered sense of intra-species joy in transforming the world. Such transformation is not illusory but a divine calling.

The formation of spiritual community also takes courage and discipline. This means that the power of inner transformation is not simply a discarding of ego or the "lower personality" but a perfection of self through simplicity, purity of motives, generosity and a developed compassion and wisdom. This does not come simply because of transpersonal or mystical experiences. I have had many such experiences and in the process I have realized that the wisdom of incarnation and of embodied worldly life is learned not simply through mystical experience but also through inner discipline and a principled way of life and thought. The mature spiritual life is not simply a consequence of mystical illumination; it may also emphasize intelligence, inner discipline, study, good habits, a compassionate attitude, a clear moral life, and great skill in understanding human psychology, society, and cultural processes of historical identity formation. All of these are important aspects, but above all the mature spiritual life requires a high degree of self-knowledge, compassion, and insight into soul-life as it relates to the processes of creation and human development. It also includes an informed awareness of the world and the struggle of people everywhere to realize a more just and beneficial way of life without straining or destroying the very fabric of the natural world upon which we depend as embodied, incarnate souls.

The value of spiritual community is that it can be a container, a basket, a holder of multiple human aspirations that can be fostered through shared ideals and teachings. The teachings are never closed; always, Spirit is acting to foster growth and development. In community we can reach out to those of like-minded interests and values, and find the harmony of intent that best expresses the goals of the community. Those goals are found through processes of inner realization of our human potential; they are not simply a fixed set of ideals but an open-ended process, a dynamic of inner and outer work that must be shaped according to the leadership of its most mature members. As the processes of inner realization become manifest, in the life and integrity and beauty of soul of each individual, the means for the formation of such community are born. They are then fostered through a committed union of intentions whose purposes are to foster a similar growth in others, with humility and flexible efforts to continue the alchemical realization. The basis is always love first, then knowledge or skills; the most significant leadership will always come from those whose capacity for love, whose depth of loving presence, is a model to others and a felt reality to every member of the community. Such a love is not created, but a gift of Spirit born through many years of compassionate care and work for the spiritual good of others.

THE HALLOWS AS RIGHT RELATIONS

In the Grail story, certain symbols with strong alchemical associations represent the quest for spiritual knowledge. These symbols, known as the "hallows," are sacred objects which hold a numinous presence that can only be accessed by the dedicated Grail seeker. To the non-seeker, these symbols are only abstract notions and archaic signs of a lost language of soul. To the seeker, they are resonant symbols whose language moves beyond symbolism into sacrament, so that they no longer simply represent but actually carry the sacred contents as they manifest in the mind and heart of the seeker. In the communal setting, these hallows are a means for establishing communal norms that can be held by each individual in ways unique to his or her development. They must be approached in a sacramental sense, not as simple representations, but as carriers of the specific values and beliefs of the community. Just as the cup in the Eucharist is a Grail object, one that carries the blood and water of the Christ transformation, and just as the bread is a sacrament that is more than a symbol or metaphor, one that becomes the body of the Christ, so too are the hallows.[1] Each hallow is a sacrament that carries meaning and presence. The traditional hallows I want to discuss are five: the stone, the staff, the sword, the cup and the candle.[2]

The context for understanding these hallows in the alchemy of soul is to understand how they hold a certain energy of transformation in a communal as well as individual sense. There is a three-sided relationship here, as in a triangle: the top point is Spirit which radiates downward in two rays. The ray to the left descends to the individual psyche and the ray to the right descends to the spiritual community. Thus, the relationship between the individual and the community is mediated by Spirit. Each of the hallows can be imaged in the place of Spirit, as also mediating between the individual and the community. In the center of this triangle, we must envision the inscription of the Sign of Infinity, as a figure eight lying on its side. This sign is a reminder that the hallow images are relative, archetypal signs whose contents are sustained by a greater wholeness that is immeasurable and without limits. A line connects the Sign of Infinity with the hallow at the top of the triangle. Three in this case is really four, that is, the identifiable hallow, plus the individual and the community, plus the unifying wholeness of the Infinite, written (1+2+1) as the correct notation for its sacramental value. In a scriptural sense, this mathematical formula translates into language as "I AM I" (1+2+1, Ex 3:14), where this Name is a communal name, as well as an individual name.

The hallow of the stone is the first hallow. This is the hallow of stability and embodiment, the *prima materia* for the work of transformation, and is the body that holds the precious minerals of life and vital awareness. Envision a stone that sparkles with distinctive precious mineral contents; the stone must be broken down, the mineral extracted, refined and purified, and then recombined with the stone to become the Philosopher's Stone, the tincture of which renews life and breath in others. Any and every stone could be the basis for the transformational work, but not every stone is willing to be broken and refined; instead, a stone may hold fiercely to its fixed form and contents, fearing to be destroyed in the processes of transformation. This is the hallow of humility, or gracious surrender to the stages of death and rebirth, even to the point at which the stone is ground to dust and blown away into the wind. I once had a vivid, inner vision of Anubis, as a boatman who brought me back from Sarras, the Isle of Transformation, and to whom I offered a small handful of precious stones. He took them and, saying nothing, he crushed them to powder in his right hand and then blew the dust into my eyes as I stared at him in awe. When the dust blew into my eyes, my soul opened into a multilevel reality, a vision of UrSpace—that was the gift of the dream dust, vision dust, the power of the stone to carry a soul to higher awareness through a gift honoring this power, even as the stone was ground to powder.

The stone is a hallow of humility in community as well, a stability in the face of differences that can mediate through Spirit, the power of individual transformation. What the stone gives to community is its willingness to be dissolved in the heat of difference while also giving a powerful capacity to resist arbitrary, ungrounded fluxuation. The stability is holding a place of power that is your own. The humility is a willingness not to assert your strength, to resist tendencies toward dominance or submission, and yet to sit firmly with that strength in the place that is uniquely you. This "you" is a transformative center undergoing constant annihilation and rebirth, continual purification, which can hold increasingly vaster energies with complete calm and stability. The stone holds within itself the precious metals that can be forged into any number of instruments of will or love or knowledge, but the secret of the stone is its capacity to reclaim that precious ore by dissolving our instrumentality in order to hold potential in readiness for each and every arising situation. The sacramental value of the stone is found in the ways Spirit can animate the stone, making it a touchstone that can transform others. Without humility, there can be no deep flowing forth and back. Without humility, the stone will exhaust its power of renewal, its strength, lose its precious ore, and become only a lump of unenlightened matter.

The second hallow is the staff, a masculine symbol of the creative will that can put forth a new branch or shoot even after many years of simply supporting the efforts of discipline and adherence to external order. Alchemically, the staff is the living wood, the organic world of the green, vibrant, living vegetative world. The stone reflects the mineral and metal of nature, the staff, the living wood, the tree and plant that is neither cut for the fire nor discarded as waste or impediment. This is the support that gives intention to the journey; it is the hazelwood wand and the briar rose, the oak and the mistletoe, the phallic rod of springtime that flowers and sends its sap into the root and branch and limb. It is not the dry or rotten wood, but the moist wood, the green wood of new growth, flexible and capable of bending, not rigid or brittle. This is the hallow of sincere honesty that allows for open exchange, an expression of will that is moderated by mutuality and shared adventure. It is also the honesty that holds to a truth even in resisting the truths of others. It is the emergent will that follows an inner inspiration and does not fear going against the grain or setting out in quest of the fulfillment of an inner inspiration. It is an honesty that recognizes its own limits and determines to overcome them through creative exploration and a lifelong quest for wisdom and insight.

As a communal hallow, the staff is the implement of will by which we intervene to prevent harm or violence to self or others. It is also the implement with which we can probe into uncertain areas, a dark crevasse, a delicate sensitivity, in order to bring healing where a wound may otherwise fester in shadows and self-denial. In community, many may join together to work creatively for solutions to larger problems where the staff is used as an exercise in contesting ideas without injuring a fellow contestant. A conflict of staffs can be an exercise in differences whose purpose is to sharpen and enhance ideographic reflexes and improve clarity of mind and purpose. A misuse of the staff is an abusive will, one that simply knocks down the other without concern for improving mutual relations. It is a dishonesty that conceals a desire for power, or which seeks to manipulate others for purposes incongruent with higher value transformation. Honesty in communal life is a matter of standing forth by giving a genuine account of one's own motives and goals without subterfuge or misdirection. It is also sacramental in the sense that an honest, creative will seeks to embody its creativity in forms that do not dishonor or deny the differences between individuals. The sacrament of the staff is found in its capacity to embody a creative vitality that does no harm and that inspires and arouses others to act creatively. In the shaman's tree, one can climb to a higher limb and narrate the soul's journey because one accepts the honest limits set by the spirit of place, time, and circumstances.

The third hallow is the sword, forged from the metal extracted from the stone. The symbolism of the "sword in the stone" reflects the ingrained ore of the stone that has been extracted, smelted and forged by the creative will into an implement capable of expressing the committed passions of the heart. Learning to handle a sword is an art that requires great focus and adaptability. It also requires genuine courage, an inner strength that can act in accordance with a commitment to meet the injustice and imbalance of the world with mature spiritual values. The heart is the place of the sword, while will is centered in the stomach and solar plexus; the tongue can be a sword, thought can be a sword. But the sword of the heart is what motivates the word of the tongue, so that courage in this sense is a hallow that speaks according to the passionate truths of the heart. This courage is a reflection of the continuity between thought, word, and deed, such that what I think, or say and do, creates a unified, double-edged image. When humility and creative will combine with a passionate dedication to defend against injustice or social disequilibrium and excess, then the sword (which contains "word") becomes a true hallow, a true speaking-out. It requires strength to meet strength, a flexible, responsive, centered strength, one that seeks an extension meant to deflect and disarm a threat or attack.

In the communal sense, the hallow of the sword is pointed downward, toward the earth, as a sign of its presence, a sharpness of mind, a clarity of purpose that combines with others to resist violence and unrest in all its various collective forms. This is the sword that blesses, that transmits valor and courage, that honors the skills and abilities of each person and grants mastery to those who learn the necessary control and quickness. Its use flows best in spontaneity, a fluid mindfulness that adapts and that knows the value of an unpredictable response. This requires communal work to develop a practice that can inspire but not bind, one that raises the necessary energy but also results in a free expressiveness ever respectful of the value and worth of others. The fellowship of the sword is an occult mystery; like the mystery of each of the hallows, it creates a sacrament by having been

203

forged and re-forged, brought to an edge and then hammered back to bluntness, never harming or causing injury to another. Such a sword is never drawn from its sheath except with utmost focus and concentration, but the body is relaxed and supple, the staging ground well suited to the action. Whoever advances in the sword must also advance in the stone; if they are separated, then the mastery will be lost. The sword of community is differentiated will able to adapt according to the diverse talents of each developed member.

The fourth hallow is the cup, the feminine receptacle, the normative symbol of the Grail as a holy vessel filled with the Aqua Vita, the pure waters of life. The function of the cup is to hold a precious liquid, but the cup itself is precious because it is a symbol of the womb, just as the staff is a symbol of the phallus; united, they form the mortar and pestle. The cup is also the Hermetic vessel, the place within which the alchemical transformation occurs, a symbol of the noetic chalice, the image of the Christ cup. This is the cup of love and purity, the willing connection with the heart and soul of others through empathy and compassion. How much compassion does our cup hold, how able are we to offer others a drink when they thirst? What is the quality of the love we offer? Is it restrained, conditional, minimal? Or are we able to hold a true Grail cup, an overflowing abundance of pure love and compassion that nurtures freely those whose thirst is a thirst of soul. This is the hallow of soul-love, of a soul to soul relationship, that is nourished by an inner purity of motive and non-attachment, by warmth and caring that does not demand or seek a measured response. The cup is polished by our efforts to develop a non-clinging mind, an unperturbed heart, and an inner stability of intent with regard to others. To love another in the spiritual work of world transformation is an agape love, a deep caring for humanity, one that works for the highest good of each relationship in the name of the quest for true spiritual mutuality. It is a search for the embodiment of that good in the heart and mind and will of the other, to hold that love as creative presence, as living water.

In the communal sense, the cup is a symbol of shared dedication to principles of communal life that foster Spirit (the living water) and make it available to every member through loving relationships. In a ritual image, the cup is passed from member to member as they stand in a circle facing inward, at the center of which is a candle whose flame signifies true gnosis. As the cup, with purest water and a sprig of mint, is passed, each person in turn takes a sip, wiping the rim after each drink with a pure white linen cloth. This symbolizes the holding power of love and the fluid life of Spirit, where the sprig of mint is the symbol of incarnation and the white linen cloth, a sign of the need for purity of motive and intent. The hallow of the cup is not something that can be simply found or made; it must be sought through inner work, through an alchemy of soul that results in a free, open, non-possessive love and compassion that springs forth from joy and presence. It is not an outward seeking, nor can it be acquired simply through imitation. Only through embracing and undertaking the quest, can the cup be found. The question is primordial: "Who does the Grail serve"? Unless this question is answered at the soul level, no cup will suffice to hold the energies and powers of Spirit in the deep alchemical soul sense. This is the cup also offered to Christ in the garden, which he could not refuse, the cup of the surrendered will.[3]

The fifth hallow is the candle, the sacred flame of the divine presence in the heart and mind and soul, as an illuminating gift of Spirit. This candle, or this flame, is in the center of the circle of the four hallows and is the direct link to the light that makes each hallow a sacred sign of inner awakening. This is the light of gnosis, true knowledge of Spirit, true opening to the light, true encounter with the magnifying power of the seed-light, the divine spark planted in the soul of every living creature. The body of the candle is a pure vegetative wax, the stuff of organic life, shaped to sustain a light that is a beacon to the light within others. From one candle, many such candles can be lit; from one light, the one can be known to others. This flame is in the heart-mind where it must be sheltered and guarded from the excess and distraction that would deny it a place at the center. The crystal globe that surrounds it is the polished orb of our entire understanding, the flame, a radiant mind that is transparent to the light, sustained by the luminous oil of a sacred tree whose purity makes it almost invisible. Such a light is always both individual and communal. There is no real distinction between its manifestations as one or as many at the level of its inward unity. In its outer manifestations, the alchemy of soul creates the unique touchstone that is illumined from within by the work of individual soul awakening. Thus, like a ray of light split by a pure prism of glass, the many colors become distinct while the energy only shifts its wave length and frequency.

ENTERING RITUAL SPACE UNADORNED

There are three kinds of ritual space I want to discuss: the ritual space of the home, that is a semi-private space; the public space of communal rituals; and the intrapersonal ritual space of communal relationships. By "ritual space", I mean the place within which the dual acts of reverence and invocation are performed. This might be quite simple, a gesture or a nod of the head, or it might be more complex, for example, a space within which a ceremony is performed, or a place of communal activity that expresses reverence. There is also a more magical interpretation of ritual space as a place where power is invoked, or, more alchemically, the place of the retort (Vas Hermeticum), the alchemical vessel of the heart, wherein the Great Work is carried out. The creation of such a space begins with intention, a clear purpose to invoke presence, while the symbolization of that intention is carried out by creating a relational space, a place within which Spirit can manifest, a *temenos*, or place of sacred manifestation. The intention is not to create presence but to invoke presence through an action of solicitation whose effectiveness depends on the purity and inner development of the individuals who make the invocation. In the alchemy of soul, this is largely a matter of the internal realization of potential and of the magnitude and potency of soul that is brought to the invocation.

The key concept for ritual work is refinement of purpose and a skillful means by which simple acts are made into sacred invocations. In the ritual space of the home or one's private living space, however small, the action begins with a clear intention to perform a gesture of reverence and invocation. For example, it might be expressed in lighting a candle and recognizing the symbolic and sacramental meaning of the flame of the candle. It is not the action, but the intention that matters. In the alchemy of soul, it is very important to shape intentions to the processes of self-development. Introspection is one method, where the intent is to analyze or observe carefully the activities of mind and heart. But cultivating spiritual presence is not simply a matter of intelligent thought or self awareness. It is also a matter of cultivating a practice that solicits and invokes presence on a daily basis. What you bring into the ritual space is your work, your inner development, and also your desire to be a Grail vessel, to hold the presence of Spirit as a life gift for others. Alchemical rites are the rites and mysteries of opening to Spirit and receiving the clarity of true gnosis and genuine illuminations of heart and mind, as symbolized in the candle flame. To enter ritual space in this sense is to stand or kneel in the presence of holiness whose temple is the human form.

In the home, the ritual space is any space where you can practice solicitation and inner prayer without disturbance or interruptions. It is very important that all members of the family respect and honor such a practice, even if they do not practice it. In the alchemy of soul, prayer is an important aspect of self-development, and privacy for this practice is essential. Part of the alchemical practice is to focus inwardly and to call upon inner presence, using images which can act to focalize attention.[4] To harness awareness in order to guide development, it is necessary to take time on a daily basis to center the heart in opening to the greater wholeness, to the totality of a soul embracing a love for all creation. And in that love, we allow ourselves to be embraced and to sustain an inner acknowledgement of the gifts of Spirit as they are given, day by day, hour by hour, minute by minute. The guiding presence can be imaged in many ways, as a Christ presence, as the Divine Sophia, as a living light or sacred power that guides the soul toward greater maturity and responsible living. Part of the task of the alchemy of soul is for each person to find that image which best acts to solicit presence, and then to take the time, on a daily basis, to practice the invocation of that image as a means for greater self-development.

The space in which this practice is carried out should be a place of rest and quiet, a place where the individual can truly relax and open to Spirit without fear of distraction or interruption. The actual entry into the ritual practice should be done with great attention to the purpose or goal of the practice; simplicity and humility are required. This simplicity is an inner quality, a simplicity of heart that is not burdened by distracting thoughts or doubts or demands and expectations. It should be a naked simplicity of intent to open the heart to Spirit through an inner focus on breathing, quieting the mind, and cultivating the image that represents the goal of the practice. This image might be nothing more than a seed of light or a pure, golden white lotus of the heart or a gnostic ember whose glow and warmth is cultivated by breath and inner focus. We sink into the primordial waters of Nun, the ancient Egyptian Aeon whose dark creation waters hold all life and energy. We invoke the life power to create the seed of light from which the soul is animated and vitalized, nourishing body, mind, and awareness. It is very helpful, but not always necessary, to have a teacher to assist one in this practice.

Another kind of ritual space is the intrapersonal space of human

207

relationships which can be sacralized through a cultivation of love and concern for others. This practice is also essential to the alchemy of soul. The ritual aspect of this space is to honor the sacred within others, to recognize that the alchemy of soul is an art of transformation at work in everyone. Thus, in greeting another, we acknowledge the potential in each person for gnosis and illumination, by honoring him or her as a vessel of the Grail. As a practice, it is necessary to cultivate reverence for others regardless of their degree of internal work. Even if a person fully denies and dismisses such work, nevertheless, the practice is to honor the presence of Spirit within that person as a potential for higher awareness. This means not judging others but simply accepting them as implicit carriers of the Grail light, which one's own light may spark to greater brilliance. Such a spark must be lit within and then be transmitted in the spontaneity of love and care we give to others. It is this heart-to-heart connection that allows Spirit to flow between individuals without words, or teachings, or explicit actions. The ritual space created is based on the depths of an individual's capacity to revere each relationship as one that can or may contribute to a quickening of soulfulness and an open sharing of concerns and ideals. This is not a matter of a shared worldview or conformity to a particular teaching, but rather a function of the illumined heart able to offer the cup whether or not it is received.

The development of intrapersonal ritual space requires an intention to hold open a possibility for deeper relationships based on processes of self-development. But more than holding open, the practice is also an invocation that calls forth a guiding intention to shape the relationship in terms of a soul-centered approach to living. This is best accomplished by exemplifying a soul-centered concern in all human relationships and working through those relationships in ways that sustain the inner continuity of higher values. These values are part of the structure of the alchemy of soul; they are practiced, not simply held or believed. The practicing of these values means exemplifying them in the daily round of human interactions from the most cursory exchange to those more demanding. When we interact only briefly with strangers, for example in service work, we should treat them with a ritual concern that honors their humanity and potential as carriers of the Grail light. This includes every person, from the most humble to the most exalted, each treated as equals, each requiring us to honor their spiritual capacities. We honor their individuality, their work, and their capacity for transformation as a basis for acknowledging the continuing work of Spirit in every person.

In the communal sense, ritual space is created whenever persons work together in harmony and with a cooperative will, even when they may disagree or contest a pattern of action or a communal norm. The basis of this harmony is rooted in a grounding sense of the sacred as present in everyday work and interaction. Again, simplicity of intention is crucial, so we can enter into the work unadorned, requiring nothing special or distinguishing in terms of our role or place within the community. Every person brings a potential for communal enhancement, but real relationships between people struggling to realize this potential may require great effort and concentration to bring about a possible synthesis between individual's whose paths are diverse and only partially developed. This is why the creation of ritual space is important—it gives a context for reframing actions as invocations of Spirit rather than as simply work or play. The sacralizing of communal work is an important step in the alchemy of soul because the work does not supplant the inner development but seeks to foster and enhance such development. Communal work is a sacrament insofar as each individual can connect the work with appropriate states of mind and heart that reflect inner values. Bringing good will or love into the work is highly important, and it ritualizes communal interaction because it is reveres and invokes spiritual potential.

What each person brings to a community is based on the depth of his or her inner work and how successful that work is in actually transforming awareness into a more illumined consciousness. Many people have spent years doing "inner work" but with poor results because they are hampered by emotional and mental problems that do not allow them to experience a genuinely lucid, compassionate integration. Familiarity with various techniques and a preoccupation with personal experience can result in very little development and in a great deal of inflation or misapprehension concerning the spiritual basis of communal work. Put as simply as possible, in the alchemy of soul, the goal is to bring forth the unique gifts of each individual while also contributing to the lasting development of others. To sacralize this work, it is only a matter of acting with a loving heart that seeks neither to deny the gifts of others nor to put oneself forward as more significant or aware in terms of personal maturity. The greatest teacher is the one who truly knows and holds the Grail light to such a degree that it is clearly seen by others. It is not a matter of words or promises or intellectual abilities, but of presence and a living compassion whose

209

wisdom is adaptive and grounded in offering insights into the real problems of daily life.

In the larger context of actual communal ceremonies, the practice of invocation is a crucial feature for calling forth that potential that resides not only in each individual but also in nature and in all creatures. The celebration of presence has innumerable forms and manifestations; there is no one form or practice that best summarizes the communal work. It is the task of each community to fathom the purpose of its membership and to design those rites that are most in keeping with communal alchemy and the search for true gnosis. As a general principle, I honor the tradition of the Celtic year in its eightfold division into the spring and autumn equinox, the summer and winter solstices and the four cross-points of the year between each equinox and solstice. Thus, roughly every six weeks, I celebrate the turning of the year in terms of communal rites marked by cosmological and agricultural celebrations. Moon phases may also be integrated into the core practice; additional rites can be added based on individual needs and communal circumstances.[5] Each point has its own unique meanings and practices but overall, this practice is based on "magic circle" work whose archetypal symbolism reflect the alchemy of inner transformation. Such a practice is very helpful in supporting soul development by tying the rituals to a seasonal round in which special days are appointed as times for honoring stages of development. These communal days are a time for building solidarity and for honoring the natural seasons as they reflect the cosmic year and the life cycle.

FOLLOWING A PATH LESS KNOWN

When I use the term "community" I am not referring to a specific organization, an esoteric order, or a specific institution. I am referring instead to the informal community of alchemical and Hermetic practitioners whose work brings them into meaningful relationships with others who are also practitioners of the inner arts of development. The nature of this community is fluid and ever changing, but it is built around enduring relationships between practitioners committed to a lifelong pattern of alchemical transformation. It is a community of souls dedicated to spiritual principles that seek to foster an enhanced awareness and participation in the spiritual mysteries of the illumined heart. This is not a matter of membership in an organization, nor is it necessary to institutionalize either the practice or the philosophy. The practice of inner alchemy and the Hermetic sciences is by no means routinized or reducible to a programmed application. The history of Western esoteric thought and practice is highly individualized and the teachings are variable and diverse, subject to the adaptive efforts of each practitioner. To routinize the practice through a strict institutionalization would in effect stultify the learning process by overriding the individuation that is necessary for a successful accomplishment of the work. The community of which I am speaking is based on a compassionate heart able to recognize, in others, a similarity of disposition and application.

This does not mean that esoteric communities do not exist; traditional esotericism is often structured into many diverse orders, lodges, sisterhoods, occult groups, and organizations. However, the alchemical community of those on a path of inner development, on any path that might foster a compassionate, loving intelligence attuned to cosmic reality, is an invisible community An actual visible order, organization, or fellowship is only an outer expression of this invisible community. To mistake the outer form for the real community is to misunderstand the nature of the work, and to lose its mystery. In the alchemy of soul, the opening of the heart, its soulful development, is a progressive expansion of awareness into a subtle universe of multiple beings, souls, energies, and cosmic dimensionality. It is not simply the human organization, which is in fact an imitation of this greater order, but also the emergence of human awareness into a more expansive horizon of relationships within the World Soul and beyond. The "invisible community" is not a particular structure of guides or spirit or masters (as within so many esoteric, theosophic schools), but is instead a very complex multidimensional, spectral consciousness. This consciousness is born through an "inversion" and expansion of ordinary introspective self-reflection.

At an early stage, the alchemy of soul tends toward an analysis of inner mental and emotional events, an enhanced awareness of the "streams of consciousness" that lead us, through visions, dreams, and meditative, self-reflective states, to an increasing understanding of our own soulful life. But at a more advanced stage, this self-reflection gives way to a more contemplative focus based on selective images that come to represent the inner work. As these images unfold potential and open the heart and soul to more expansive states, the mental life is transformed into a more mystical, gnostic sensitivity to happenings within the subtle worlds or "inner planes." As practice deepens, the self experience becomes more comprehensive and incorporative, opening into the depths of UrSpace, and revealing inner alchemy as a reflexive image that mirrors cosmological processes. At an even more advanced stage, there is an inversion by which the soul is suddenly opened to the full dimensionality of cosmic life and thus is seen as a focal containment within the Whole rather than as a being seeking wholeness. After such an expansive opening, the soul becomes increasingly sensitive to the "invisible community" such that, after a time, that community becomes a complex network within the World Soul. Not an organization per se, but an inner, energetic, luminous community of awakening souls whose connections are more than conventional or casual.

The outer esoteric organization, its structure, leadership, members and participants may be quite unaware of the full complexity of the invisible community, a community without name, irreducible to a particular image or order. This more global and multi-planed community is part of the evolving involutions of the World Soul and it cannot be held in a single form or a single image. A single image might represent it, as say a mandala or geometric form, but that image is, like the visible community, only a simple image of a much more complex reality. Often, a cosmological hierarchy is taught within the esoteric orders, but all of these hierarchies (which are highly diverse and reflect an older way of thinking) are simply the working mandalas of that community, more or less skillful ways of organizing a cosmological view. In the alchemy of soul, there is no "fixed order" which attempts to summarize the goal other than those which are heuristically designated for the purposes of illustration and reflection. They are relative maps, not the actual multi-dimensional reality. The invisible community extends far beyond the images and cannot easily accommodate a limited human, incarnational perspective.

Another aspect of this greater and less visible community is found in all the afterworld planes where it is possible to interact with those who have died. Persons who undergo out-of-body experiences and "astral projection" of various types, all have stories to tell about the invisible community of those who continue to live in alternate world planes.[6] Visionaries from every religious tradition have offered cosmological descriptions of the subtle worlds of psychic soul perception. None of these descriptions can be taken as absolute, yet every one of them has a certain validity and materialization within the World Soul, if only in the psychic sense. As noted throughout this book, it is that "psychic sense" which is the prime material of the transformation of self, and the greater the work, the more open the practitioner to probable psychic formations, the more likely he or she is to accept these multiplicities as partial expressions of a greater and more transpersonal wholeness Those worlds may well be "collective projections" which have a lasting impact on self-development insofar as an individual holds to any one of them as authoritative (or even centers on one as most significant). But from a more pluralistic, dynamic perspective, all these worlds simply reflect the continuing involutions of human psychic life as we seek to fathom the immense complexity of the World Soul and its full cosmic dimensionality.

The issue here is not the structure of the psychic cosmology, or of a particular image or construct of that cosmology. By "psychic cosmology," I refer to a human capacity to experience depths and heights of cosmic life not bound by strictly physical, emotional, or mental ideas. Opening to that greater dimensionality is part of the alchemy of soul. The invisible community is not an order or a structure, nor is it a hierarchy or "order of initiates". It is much greater than any single order or structure. The invisible community includes ALL psychic cosmologies—ancient, classical, modern, esoteric or futuristic. It has no boundaries and no particular valuation of the component dimensionality. The emphasis falls neither on structure nor on constructed organization (as a form of psychic materialization), but on the qualitative relationships between beings within those diverse orders or dimensions. The question is not "What is the structure?" but rather "What is the relationship between members of these structures to the as-yet unstructured?". This question is approached through the individual task of self-development in an expanding incorporation of ever greater complexity and dimensionality, a complexity which collapses entirely in the face of genuine illumination. Such a collapse does not negate the value of those structures, but points beyond them to a greater wholeness, a nurturing containment that has no outer limits and no boundaries but is infinite and as immeasurable as the universe itself.

The path less known is the path that does not seek structure as an end in itself and does not seek to impose a premature order on an endless variety of psychic states or perceptions. The incarnational aspect of the Great Work is in the embodiment of self as multidimensional being, one not bound by the strict order of a projected, possible structure. The fluidity of the alchemy of soul is found in being able to move between the worlds, to sustain loving relationships between a multitude of orders and beings without feeling a need to schematize those relationships. I do not deny that there are indeed more powerful and aware beings—the invisible community is one that leads to encounters that challenge our most fundamental assumptions about the nature of cosmos and incarnation. But the task is one of receptivity to the teachings and wisdom of others without denying the wisdom that comes from within, from a deeper gnosis that dissolves the invisible community into the holo-movement of ongoing involution and self-realization on a cosmic scale far greater than any local, esoteric configuration. A seeker may choose a particular order as a useful means to organize perception, but that order should never supplant the expansive complexity of actual psychic development. Otherwise, such an order becomes a bar to development because it freezes the evolutionary process in an image that only reflects a particular moment in the cultural and social life of the evolving community.

On a global scale, the psychic life is layered through time and culture to produce inner contents of experience that can manifest any of those layers or images as means for soul and self development. But more than the global aspect is also accessible to us if we accept the fundamental premise that psychic life has resonance with life throughout the cosmos, a basic Hermetic teaching. What we experience of the invisible community can extend beyond our present knowledge of this world or other worlds and open the soul to a vast continuum that includes as-yet unrecognized influences throughout the stellar or astral spaces. The internalization of modern scientific cosmology prepares the way for just such an influence, opening, as it does, a far vaster picture of galactic and trans-galactic life. We are in the very process of expanding our awareness into a continuum of psychic life that is immeasurably beyond all local and contingent cosmologies of past traditional societies or pre-modern cosmological thought. However, many of those older cosmologies have sustained a multidimensional view by describing a trans-physical universe of multiple beings and powers beyond normal human perception. Thus, the invisible community is a metaphor for the conjoint life we share with all incarnate life on every world throughout all cosmological space.

In the more immediate sense, we do not need to concern ourselves with either the scope or the multi-structures of the psychic worlds. We need only hold to the inner processes of psychic development and not cling to what may come to us through psychic perception, suprarational encounters, or inner visions. Every vision needs to be refined and subjected to the process of alchemical alignment in terms of the qualitative values

214

that nurture and sustain community life: love, compassion, kindness, gentleness, creativity, courage that seeks healing, and an inner wisdom capable of dissolving all differences into a unity of Spirit that promotes mutual growth and wholeness. The vision is secondary to this qualitative development. It is not a matter of communal structure or cosmological thought but of individual values that seek to enhance the creative and exploratory aspects of communal life. With inner development comes also an inner freedom that does not cling to form or order as the necessary predicate for spiritual maturation. The invisible community is knit by building loving relationships, being open to encounters, and having an inner stability that can sustain all the necessary transformative stages of self-realization. External community or organization is a choice that can promote or retard this process; what matters is clarity of intent not to allow structure to become a substitute for real gnosis and illumination.

BLESSINGS AND ANGELIC BEINGS

The invisible community is not simply populated by its human or post-mortem souls, but by a host of psychic entities whose variety and description surpasses any easy or convenient summary. The psychic cosmology of the invisible community has innumerable structures and inhabitants whose access is acquired through dreams, visions, and various cognitive and surpracognitive states. The fundamental basis of this encounter with the "angelic" other, with devas or spirits (animal or trans-human), with archetypal aeons or elementals, is an experience of a numinous entity whose identity is experienced as distinct from the identity of the perceiver. The basic paradigm is an I-Thou relationship between discrete beings, be it Moses at the burning bush or any other mystical encounter, that induces in the perceiver a sense of the uncanny, the holy, the numinous as rooted in a living relationship. Because these encounters tend toward the visionary, the numinous other is often experienced in terms of a being that corresponds to the worldview of the visionary. For example, an angel, djinn, deva, fravashi, or dakini are all meaningful spiritual entities in the traditions to which they correspond. In a post-traditional sense, such an encounter may even take the form of aliens or strange spirits that have no recognizable traditional identity or that may appear as manifestations from a wide range of mythological archetypes.

In the alchemy of soul, such encounters are part of the normative processes of an expanding self development. Some practitioners are more

215

receptive and responsive to these encounters and others are less so, but most individuals will experience some degree of numinous encounter. The distinctive quality of the encounter is the autonomous nature of the numinous other—it comes unannounced, manifests autonomy, presents itself as representing an alternative authority within the psychic world, and evokes intuitive insights normally inaccessible to the waking personality. In the expansive process of the encounter, the entity is part of the I-Thou relationship in which the numinous quality acts to enhance psychic perceptions. As perception develops, the individual is stimulated to develop supracognitive perceptions that support an increasing awareness of other such beings or entities. The psychic world becomes increasingly more visible within the framework of the supporting I-Thou relationship. The relationship may serve only a transitional function, facilitating a development in awareness and then allowing the individual to move into more enhanced overall psychic perception. In many ways, such relationships are markers on the path to greater individuation and maturity that no longer depends on a specific, usually predetermined, archetypal relationship.

The question of autonomy within the invisible community is a matter of relative maturity in being spiritually centered and grounded in the incarnational state. The question is not simply one concerning the autonomy of spirit, but the autonomy of self and the degree to which relationships play a more or less significant part in spiritual development. All spirits, entities, and luminous beings can be assimilated into higher orders of perception where self as a universal matrix contains all diverse entities. In the transpersonal sense, all that is "Self" is also "All that Is," thus reflecting the Hermetic saying, *Hen to Pan*, the One that is All. However, on the planes of diversity, there are innumerable distinctions that characterize the ways in which that psychic unity is differentiated into a multitude of diverse beings. The issue is thus a matter of perception and visionary capacity, not one of objectivity or permanence within a particular cosmic structure. Relationships are crucial in the formative and developmental process because they challenge us to grow beyond our normative boundaries and to accept alternative visions of life and creation. As incarnate beings, we are immersed in relational processes of development and these relations extend into the psychic world, into numinous encounters that reflect our stage of development and our capacity for higher illumination.

As we move between the One and the Many, the goal is not to dismiss or dissolve those relationships into the One, but to foster those relationships as intrinsic to the creative processes of mutual coexistence. What evolves within the psychic worlds is not illusory nor is it simply a matter of projection or human creation. There is an interplay between the human imagination, the latent psychic potential, the collective psychic life, and cosmological processes that connect us with other worlds and beings. Further, the capacity to project is itself profoundly creative. The formative nature of psychic life is based in a capacity to imagine and then, to make what we imagine real, even by granting it a mediated autonomy. This is why so many esoteric orders, east and west, have discussed the power of "thought forms" (or elementals) as created beings, such as found in various types of Tibetan or Hindu Tantra. There is a link between the generative power of thought and the substructures of cosmological imagination, such that an envisioned world takes on an autonomous function within the collective mindset. However, those imagined worlds also provide a psychic context for possible inhabitation by yet other psychic entities that are by no means simply projected by human beings. These numinous others are part of the greater invisible community that connects us to other worlds and realities as yet veiled by the conventional separation between mind and cosmos.

It is possible, in the alchemy of soul, to establish relationships with a variety of visionary beings. These relationships have many diverse functions, and overall they can provide a means for empowering actions that lead to greater efficacy in self-awareness. The primary function is the connection to numinous insights and abilities, an empowerment of self that acts in the world in a visible, qualitative sense. Thus, we may work with invisible helpers, guides, teachers, or Spirit friends and co-workers. Such guides may take many forms and extend from the animal (or even vegetable or mineral worlds) to post-mortem humans, higher spirits, angelic beings, devas, archetypal guides, and mythic or divine beings. They may manifest varying degrees of autonomy, from those easily solicited to those who come unsolicited and who are not responsive to the will or desire of the solicitor. Inevitably, the most potent entities are those least controlled and most autonomous, representing the unrealized aspects of the I-Thou relationship still marginal to, or in a necessary stage of, soul awakening. The key to healthy self-development is to establish a working relationship that is neither subordinate nor dependent. No entity, however autonomous, luminous, powerful, or overwhelming, requires in any way our submission or obedience for personal development. The quality of the relationship is configured through the I-Thou pattern as one of mutual respect, receptivity, and acknowledgement of the value and importance of individual autonomy and the special qualities that emerge through the relationship.

In the alchemy of soul, the individual is never required to abandon or renounce identity; in fact, the evolution of individual identity is central to the Great Work. What is required is a purification, refinement, distillation, and sublimation of diverse energies into an integrated, autonomous, respectful, loving being. In relating to the numinous other, these requirements are not changed. In meeting any other being, human or otherwise, we hold our grounded incarnation as an inviolable spiritual trust, to be a center of luminous consciousness standing fully in the divine presence, in Spirit, as a discrete, reverent being. How can we be less in relationship to any other being, however august or archetypal? Thus we do not submit to the power or autonomy of the other, nor do we attempt to become that power through false or inflated identification. The alchemy of soul requires standing in our own body, being ourselves, acknowledging our obligations and relationships, not surrendering our will to others, however psychic or subtle. Then, standing with humility, we open ears, heart and mind, to the wisdom, teaching, and instructions of the other and in taking in that guidance, we subject it to the alchemical processes of individual assimilation. Thus, every instruction must be tested in light of the integral realizations of the practitioner and not simply adopted because it comes from a numinous source. This is a fundamental principle of Hermetic alchemy.

Blessings can flow from this relationship, as the numinous source is able to attract a deeper order of resonance with psychic intentions. When we think of the numinous source as an aspect of higher self, we create a series of "identity intersects" where the present personality intersects with a psychical active identity, itself linked or intersecting with deeper psychic potentials which are passed on to the present personality as knowledge or unique abilities. But, if we think of the higher self as ultimately identical with the Whole, as a universal nexus, then the unique aspects of these intersections lose their specific value as they are absorbed into a unified, transpersonal identity. In the alchemy of soul, there is no need to diminish or disavow the distinctive aspects of identity that lead to encounters with other autonomous beings. What is sought is participation in the invisible community. The complexity of these relationships exceeds all self aspects in the direct personal sense; in the universal sense, all is absorbed but, even then, there is distinctiveness in identity. The blessing flows from the capacity to act as a recipient of diverse energies through diverse beings.

It is possible to direct healing energies in a universal sense, but often those energies will work through a multilayered process. The value of the discrete psychic relationship is that it modulates intrapsychic energies into specific forms, such that the presence of a certain being will qualify the type of healing or its more precise consequences. Spirit is a multitude of energies whose unity is suprasensual, but on the sensual plane those energies become discrete and have specific applications. The invisible community is an expression of the diversity of those energies that work alchemically through the stages of personal development to produce particular abilities and skills. Some may become great healers, others not; some may become cosmologists or ritual experts or visionary artists, others not. This is a consequence of inner development brought into resonance with those energies which are most attuned to the psychic gifts of the developing individual. Forming alliance with numinous helpers, allies, astral co-workers, is part of the process by which we embrace our wholeness. We do not seek to surpass or deny the value of these appearing and dissolving others, but we do acknowledge the diversity within the psychic cosmos, within UrSpace, and meet that diversity with humility and a sense of our own limits.

The blessing of the numinous other may come unasked and without any expectations, or it may come because it is invoked with certain requirements or prohibitions. The boundaries on these relationships are part of the internal dialogue which we establish within the self, as a meeting ground for interaction and relationship with all types of beings or entities. The goal is a "concord of spirit" that is integrative, supporting the free will and autonomy of the individual while also acknowledging the assistance and help of discrete energies and powers within Spirit. The blessings that flow from this concord in term of self-development are a greater sense of empowerment to work within the World Soul as an effective member of the invisible community. The blessings that are given arise from the degree of resonance and correspondence between the individual work being done and the primal energies that a numinous Spirit can contribute to that work. This is a matter of love and will, where mind and heart can shape the intention of the action so that it does indeed correspond to a loving connection with others—both with those who give and with those who receive. Self becomes, in this sense, an intermediary, a representative of a unique combination of abilities and skills whose synergy surpasses the ordinary personality and opens into the vaster but differentiated space of mutual creative work. In that work of blessing, the numinous other may take many forms, but each form is an intersection within self that opens to yet deeper inner possibility and potential.

THE EVOLUTIONARY SPIRIT OF CHANGE

We are in the process of awakening to our human potential on a global scale that is unique to the twenty-first century. In this process, there will be continual experimentation and a perhaps too casual dismissal of more traditional ways of thinking. I say this not because I wish to glorify a past age or to support a particular traditional worldview, but because within the various traditions there are many valuable writings, teachings, and practices that can contribute to the evolution of the human spirit. The movement into the trans-historical horizon is one that does not simply discard the past but seeks to assimilate the knowledge of the past into its contemporary and emergent forms.[7] In this process, the role of community is essential. As we move away from undifferentiated mass consciousness and national identities into a global future, the emergent role of community will be its function to differentiate itself according to the unique orientation of its members. Furthermore, membership in community need not be exclusive or sharply defined in terms of an insider-outsider dialectic. Community in the alchemical sense should have open boundaries in order to encourage diversity and ease of movement between communities. Individuals may be members of any number of communities without feeling a need for self-definition through membership in any exclusive community. Communities that lack this flexibility and receptivity to diversity in views or teachings are pursuing a visionary reality quite different than the one articulated here

The model of a given alchemical community can be articulated in three primary aspects. First, there is an outer membership that is open to diverse individuals with common goals which converge around shared concerns for personal development, responsible ethical life, and the maintenance of loving and creative human relationships. This general membership is part of the visible community of those interested and motivated to develop an increasing understanding of human potential and its actualization according to an internalized practice with practical applications. Resources for such development may extend well beyond any specific community and reflect a network of communities whose general organization offers advanced training in various areas. The general emphasis here is on personal spiritual growth and positive, loving human relationships. Emphasis must also fall on education, specifically on a variety of core Hermetic alchemical themes along with their various physical and psychic practices aimed at enhancing awareness, focus, flexibility, and intellectual and emotional clarity. This educational development should be comparative, historical, and applicable to personal daily life. The esoteric aspects of the alchemical practice should be graduated in relationship to the background and understanding of each individual.

Secondly, there is an inner membership of the alchemical community that constitutes its more advanced practitioners. This group is represented by long-term commitment to Hermetic alchemy, its practices and various degrees of expertise that link this inner membership to the invisible community (as mentioned above). The correspondence of the inner membership to the general alchemical practice must be differentiated according to the temperament and abilities of each individual. These members act as mediators between the practices of the outer membership and the larger invisible community as experienced by each of them in terms of their personal development. The "skill in means" (*upaya*) for more developed members must arise through the processes of inner individuation, spiritual awakening, and varying degrees of illuminative experience (as evidenced through contact with the invisible community). The true alchemy of soul is a pattern of development that seeks to maximize human relationships in terms of specific personal skills, real abilities, and self-selected areas of expertise. But there must also be an inner reality to such development, it cannot be simply a matter of service to the community, nor can such development be vital unless there is a real awakening of the heart to spiritual presence as an inner directive for mutually beneficial actions and positive communal growth.

The third aspect of the alchemical community is the real presence of Spirit as it manifests through both inner and outer members. There is no exclusivity within Spirit. Neither are the distinctions between "inner and outer" based on a superficial "esotericism" which is non-vital insofar as it remains simply intellectual or theoretical. The distinction is one of commitment to the particular goals and practices of the specific community and its particular leadership. However, it is always possible and highly likely that some members of the general community have exceptional gifts or psychic abilities that surpass those of the core community or even its most experienced members. The work of Spirit cannot be limited to the structural divisions that might exist in any such community. The goal of the alchemical community is not simply to preserve its own vision of the alchemical practice, but to provide access and a place of intersection with other individuals whose gifts can contribute to the qualitative excellence of communal life and practice. Thus, persons of many diverse backgrounds, with expertise in a wide range of areas and with highly developed specializations may each contribute to communal life in ways that meet the highest standards of excellence by its most developed members.

One criterion stands forth in this process, the capacity to evoke and to sustain a genuinely loving and compassionate heart and mind. The greater the coherence between thoughts, words, and deeds as directed by nurturing spiritual intentions and a clear ethics of respect and appreciation for incarnate diversity, the greater the contribution to all members of the community. A second criterion is the depth and completeness of inner illumination of the individual and his or her full integration of that experience into a visionary worldview that truly contributes to the alchemical work without dogmatism, self-inflation, or authoritarian expectations. An advanced practitioner can be very humble and not easily identifiable, and the most advanced practitioners are often the most invisible. This is because, in the Great Work, the greater the degree of refinement and pulverization, the greater the sublimation of all diverse shadow aspects, and the greater is the shedding of external identity. There is a transparency that begins to dawn, a simplicity that does not seek to magnify the inner realization or attainment. There is a loss of self in the external sense and a deepening that moves beyond the need for individuation. The integral dissolution of distinctions between inner and outer leads to a new relativism—the oneness of the many is gradually revealed as a manyness in which each individual is also truly one.

The presence of Spirit may also come unbidden and work through completely unrecognized members of the community (or even non-members). This means that Spirit can be an operative presence, moving and shaping communal events in ways entirely unpredictable and with unexpected consequences. This is good and necessary. There must be flexibility and adaptive power, a capacity to bend without breaking, whose grounded energy cannot be uprooted even as it redirects and re-channels the unexpected. In the evolutionary process, the emergent spiritual community will not hold its members nor bind them in any way. It will seek to give birth to individuals who can move and flourish beyond the community without dependency or a grasping need for its birthing fellowship. Overall, this means the emergence of a network of communities, not based in similar teachings but in sharing similar meta-goals—to nurture human development by providing a context for inner growth leading to applicable skills in the most outward sense, without losing or diminishing the source of that development.

There are many kinds of spiritual communities. Some communities may be transitional and primarily educational, with a more permanent resident staff, in which temporary members enter for a brief time to learn certain teachings and practices they can take into their daily lives. Such communities are really "Hermetic Schools" in which the basic practices and philosophies of internal alchemy can be learned and put into practice. These schools are not so much part of a general, collective educational system as they are places for more esoteric studies and personal development. The value of such schools is that they can offer direct personal guidance based on the skills and capacities of the individual while also offering a community experience with group practices and cooperative projects aimed an communal integration. The goals of such a community are primarily developmental, with a fivefold synaesthetic approach of teaching and practices: body-sensory work, emotional development, comparative intellectual training, intuitive-meditative practice, and ritual-symbolic work. All of these are necessary components of a holistic, Hermetic training. The pentagram symbolizes this process where each of the points of the star represents an area and the center is representative of illumined, soulful self-knowledge. The incarnational emphasis is on the fluid integration of body-will-heart-mind-imagination for a greater soul development that seeks to bring these five into harmonious union within Spirit.

Another kind of community, more permanent, is one dedicated to practices in which members live together and form solidarity through a way of life dedicated to full and complete spiritual actualization. It is a community whose members have made the choice to live in a communal setting as optimal for spiritual development. Such alchemical communities would not be based on a strict policy of conformity to a specific practice, other than the general shared responsibilities necessary for the maintenance of appropriate physical and social needs. An important feature of such a community is the extension of its membership capacity to those who may dwell apart from it in nearby locals, including some forms of hermitage for persons in need of periodic solitude. Solitude is a central feature of the Hermetic process and no amount of communal activity can offer the same benefits and insights that such solitude engenders. The structure of these communities must moderate the tensions between communal activity, group interaction, and individual periods of solitude and quiet. Solitude and privacy are paramount for inner, alchemical development. The constant demands of externalized work and communal relationships can easily exhaust the necessary energy required for such development.

A third kind of community is the service community. In the alchemical sense, it is necessary to recognize that for some persons an active service can be the best way for them to bring forward their inner gifts. Such a community is oriented by its membership to dedicate its primary creative energy toward specific social and collective needs. Here the alchemical work is through relationships of service to others who may not in any way share the goals or practices of the community. Yet, even in such a community there must be a place for both Mary and Martha, that is, for active commitment and for contemplative reflection.[8] A strict outwardly directed action is more often driven by will than by inner insight and intuitive knowledge. The goals of a service community in the alchemical sense require an inner transformation that acknowledges the mystery of Spirit as primary in the working out of external service tasks. This mystery moves in unpredictable ways in charging its members with diverse roles, not all of which are outer directed and some of which have to do with internal guidance for community members. Action is not simply responsive to outer needs but able to draw on the still center within for the energy and guidance required for the realization of spiritual goals. Inward and outward must be balanced and harmonized.

All of these types of community are evolutionary because they grapple with the problem of ongoing developmental change and emergence. The alchemy of soul is dynamic and has no final goals beyond the continuing maturation and insights of its practitioners. In solitude or in community, in love relations or in public service, the alchemy of soul seeks to establish a coherent center of integration that is continually seeking to enhance and to acknowledge the presence and value of Spirit in all aspects of life. As a spiritual practice, alchemies of soul are diverse and individually interpreted, each with its own unique qualitative synthesis, and each offering variation and diversity while fostering an inner unity of illumination. The forms that alchemical communities might take are beyond counting, and the diversity of its members must reflect the diversity of our human capacity for living a genuinely creative spiritual life. The task of each individual within such an alchemical community, and within the invisible community, is to fully actualize the unique gifts and abilities latent within. What must be brought forward is a loving heart that knows its own capacities (or limits), offering its gifts with humility and a promise to continue this inner work throughout a lifetime of dedicated practice.

The scope of the invisible community is beyond imagining. Our contributions, on a person by person basis, only enhance the wonders of creative diversity. In carrying out this work we are preparing a place for future generations to also emerge and to carry forward the works and gifts of the heart. In the context of the World Soul, many such communities are now emerging and will continue to emerge even in the face of greater social chaos. Regardless of the overt impulses of the collective, the alchemical transformation is well underway and each person has an opportunity to find his or her path that leads to an opening into the greater community of souls who have already dedicated themselves to the work of world transformation. The greater community is the global community, the network of spiral communications that links us psychically and soulfully to the works of others in the maturation of the World Soul. We are not alone; there are many at work with us both visibly and invisibly. Only when we break down the inner barriers, dissolve the tensions that blind us to our own and to others' potential, can we truly see the scope of the evolutionary transformation. It is an amazing, mind-expanding perception to know and to feel the whole of the collective as its merges with the cosmological and transpersonal multiverse of all beings. In such a perception we can only rejoice and offer, with reverence, a heartfelt thanks for all the work and aid we receive every day and every hour. May our minds and hearts be open to that Mystery, now and always. Amen.

1. Sergius Bulgakov, 1997.

2. See Lee Irwin, 2005 for more on the hallows and the elements.

3. Mark 14:36.

4. Matthew 6:6: "But when you pray, go into your room, close the door and pray to your Father, who is unseen. Then your Father, who sees what is done in secret, will reward you."

5. For a general introduction to the Celtic year, see: John Robert King, 1996.

6. See: Robert Monroe, 1994; Waldo Vieira, 1995; Robert Bruce, 1999.

7. On the trans-historical horizon, see: Lee Irwin, 1996: 147ff..

8. Luke 10: 38-42.

EPILOGUE

What I have given in this work is a general overview of an alchemy of soul that may be interpreted and applied in a variety of ways, depending on individual inclination and development. In the face of turmoil and conflict in international relations, in the face of death and war and violence, this alchemical approach emphasizes peace, non-violence, mutual respect, and cooperation as the highest ideals of an integrated and mature world. As noted many times in the preceding chapters, this goal does not mean the erasure of difference, nor does it mean the end of all creative tension and challenge between existing worldviews. At the heart of the alchemy of soul is the core value of mutual respect for differences due to natural processes of individuation. Such an alchemy does not seek to level collective life to a common ideology, but to promote differences that value a non-violent ethic of cooperation and emergence. In this process, we must all learn to assimilate our aggressiveness and not to project negative tendencies, habits, and attitudes onto others who do not share a particular worldview. From a global perspective, there is no one common worldview that is capable of assimilating all other worldviews.

Cultural hegemony and hierarchical suppression are phenomena of a mentality that favors its own (often class-based) self-interests over diversity and individuation. The assertion that there is a superior culture or a membership whose capacity for leadership may represent an archetypal "regal virility" that sets a standard for such a superior culture is an archaic masculine view no longer tenable in a pluralistic, mutually dependent world.[1] The collapse of the old world order as a culture of dominance, either in the political-military or social-economic sense, is an inevitable necessity for the emergence of more diverse and pluralistic global cultures. No doubt competition, disagreement, and conflict will continue as long as any members of one ideology attempt to dominate, through force or economic coercion, others who choose alternative cultural strategies. This is also true within a culture, and not simply between cultures. In any given cultural context, there exists a diversity of views, and the healthier the culture, the greater the diversity. Such health is based on the capacity to integrate and tolerate a multitude of differences within the context of mutual respect.

The older view, often aligned with masculine centered religious traditions, has functioned through institutional, hierarchical structures of

I

empowered roles for men in a context of traditionalized knowledge. Sociopolitical influence has thus been a function of conformity to role types, each with its own basis in traditional learning and values. I do not mean to imply that all traditional knowledge is coercive or strictly didactic; there are many areas of traditional knowledge which offer highly sophisticated insights into the spiritual goals and values of that tradition. But in the institutional sense, these roles have tended to rely heavily on authority as granted by the institution and not according to the spiritual development or maturity of its members. Furthermore, the male dominant character of those institutions has tended to cultivate a variety of worldviews in which the feminine logos is remarkably absent and often dismissed as superficial or irrelevant. The integration of the feminine into fully human models of maturity will require a complete rewriting of most traditional institutions, and the recasting of traditional teachings will require the full and articulate presence of woman's voice. I say this as a man who has lived with and honored women all my life and seen, again and again, the profound insights that accompany feminine values and spiritual commitments. No doubt, the emergent voice of women as spiritual teachers will move away from the older, male-centered models and seek to articulate spiritual practices and paths that are fully consistent with a more integral, holistic approach to spiritual diversity and differences.

As men pursuing a spiritual life come to recognize the capacities of women now liberated from strictly male, role-assigned relationships, they will be called upon to reevaluate the masculine spiritual role in a less hierarchical and more reciprocal sense. A primary resource for such evaluation in Western cultural history is found in the Hermetic and alchemical traditions, based as they are on a high degree of diversity and a conscious integration of male and female symbolism. This does not mean that such a resource is unbiased or free of all discrimination—by no means! Alchemical and Hermetic texts abound with discriminations and bias, but they also demonstrate a spirit of exploration and symbolic discourse that images its goals in terms of a synthesis of male and female energies. Because alchemy has tended to be marginalized and poeticized, its discourse has a goal of individuation that is quite unique in comparison to the mainstream, more conformist religious institutions of Judaism, Christianity, or Islam. Each of these traditions has esoteric and marginal gnostic-hermetic sub-streams whose members have engaged in an inner practice, an inner alchemy in search of gnostic illumination, as a profound resource for the

II

emergence of a reciprocal, integrated spirituality engendered by its male-female symbolism. But that practice has often been marginal to the collective beliefs and practices of the normative community and thus has required an inner individuation for the secret practitioner.

Much of the conflict that plagues the contemporary world is still a consequence of a violent assertion of power that seeks to impose a hierarchical order over the "uneducated masses". This kind of elitism, which refuses to consider its own inherent flaws and self-interests by espousing a "unification of multiplicity", which it would then enforce by coercion and possible counter-violence, only perpetuates the problem of inequality and injustice.[2] Many so-called traditionalists hold a view that the proper order of human society requires conformity to an esoterically determined formulation of the "vertical degree of reality" (and its underlying essential unity) and places the teaching of such esoteric knowledge in the hands of an elite.[3] While many such practitioners have opted for a policy of non-involvement in "worldly life," they have done so by regarding the world as "illusory," "decadent," or "degraded" in terms of their own elite, romanticized values. Where such individuals have emphasized the intersection of esoteric knowledge and political action, it has usually been conceived of as a function of spiritual dominance based on the intrinsic perfections of the archetypal hero who would lead humanity back to its "golden age" of spiritual harmony and balance. This regressive idealism, coupled with a blunt sense of intrinsic social hierarchy, refers to such balance as a hierarchical norm dominated by men, in a man's world, where aggression is a necessary male action that seeks to defend its normative, "essential" and esoteric hierarchical orders.

But alchemy as a spiritual science need not be hierarchical or male dominant, nor does it need to perpetuate the myths of male esoteric thought. Its intrinsic discourse can be reformulated in a more coequal and mutual language that offers training and direction for personal development and whose success depends on individual effort, application, and a sustained commitment. As a language of soul, alchemy offers a path that is highly individual but not simply "democratic" in the sense that it is only a matter of collective belief or unilateral ideas requiring simple faith and confirmation. There must be practice, and practice will create differences, and these differences will generate diversity in application and realization.[4] The goal of such a practice is not to uncover the "illusion of multiplicity" but to underscore the value and significance of differentiation as a divine, creative process. Some practitioners will advance more quickly than others, and some will have unique gifts and abilities. These practices conjoin in their fundamental ethics of cooperation and mutual respect, and in a commitment to multiplicity as a sacred process of transformation whose goals are attained by individual effort and realizations.

In pursing a peaceful and non-violent way of life, differences emerge that create tension and dialogue around themes of communal life and global integration. The alchemy of soul is a practice based in principles that can apply to all life situations if they are integral to the spiritual commitments of the practitioner. Increase in perceptual awareness will lead to experiences of an underlying unity whose presence is highly significant but is not the goal of the process. Yet this unity is central to the holo-movement of evolving life and knowledge of this unity is crucial in providing a context for the resolution of tensions and disagreement. The intersection of the one and the many is based in a rich diversity that fosters life without the imposition of external norms. To understand this in the genuine sense, it is necessary to experience directly the fullness and complexity of the unveiled invisible worlds. No single order can possibly contain or fully express this rich diversity of spiritual potential; only through the full maturation of each individual can its potential begin to be imagined and actualized. Thus, the unitary ground is not a unilateral "essence" but a profound fullness of possibilities awaiting expression and realization.

The feminine voice in the realization of this potential will provide a connective fabric of ideas and concepts woven around themes of mutual respect for life and an ethic of nurturance. The richness of the symbolism in hermetic alchemies offer unique resources for a reconstruction of spiritual development that is fully aligned with the integration of male and female perspectives.[5] The heart of this alignment is for the practitioner to realize the necessity of acknowledging the value and importance of masculine and feminine insights in living a spiritual life. As we each carry within us masculine and feminine tendencies and attitudes, the alchemy of soul seeks to harmonize those tendencies as symbolized by the alchemical marriage. This will require a greater speaking out on the part of women who find their voices and who articulate an emergent Sophianic wisdom as a new eros-logos of incarnational, world-embracing concern. The politics of spirit in this speaking-out will certainly be an emphasis on greater mutuality, cooperation, non-violence, and intra-species coexistence.

IV

It will be much less hierarchical and much more supportive of diversity and individual gifts and abilities. Such a speaking is compatible with the alchemy of soul and has been part of my own thinking for many years, based on reflective dialogues with many intelligent, spiritually-minded women, foremost among them my beloved wife, Catherine.

Overall, the alchemy of soul is not a system or a method, but an individualized practice that requires study, investigation, analysis, imaginative vision, and a genuine ethic of respect and concern for others. Each person must take up the work in his or her own fashion, and out of the resources of the past and present, undertake the work of inner transformation. To expect any teacher to supply the "answers" for spiritual development is not only naïve, but reflects a lazy way of thinking. You must do the work and make the effort without dependence on others to supply answers and directions for your own growth. Teachers should be honored, and we should always be thankful to those who can share their insights and assist us in our practice. We can learn a great deal from others. But the real work is a direct personal challenge; those who undertake the alchemy of soul in the most authentic sense are those who take full responsibility for an individual realization of the goal. No one can do it for you and one of the greatest illusions that inhibit spiritual development is over-reliance and dependency on others to solve developmental problems. That is not alchemy; it is a loss of center that takes refuge in the authority and insights of others. It is exactly the attitude that fosters the hierarchical model and creates artificial authority figures as "parental guardians" of spiritual truth.

There is no submission in the alchemy of soul, but there is sublimation, distillation, even pulverization, all of which require us to dismantle and deconstruct our illusions and inflated or deflated self views. Authority, in this sense, is an inner authority that guides each of us toward the realization of potential while also teaching us to absorb and shake down our measure in relationship to the good we offer others.[6] Authority is an inner quality of authenticity that stands its own ground respectfully and is free to act in terms of core values that have been fully integrated into our actual, real life interactions with others. On the inner planes of transformation, authority is not projected outward but is internalized in a visionary process by which we discover the value and worth of our own insights. Our measure is not how much others value our teachings, but in how well and how authentically we live according to those teachings, our own inner teachings. Spiritual authority is really a form of integrity; it stems from the root of our ground within Being, and it flourishes in accordance with our ability to reflect that ground in our every action and decision. The illumined heart-mind as a Grail of transformation can be a radiant center of presence if the individual has done the real work of transformation and has fully accepted the responsibility not to falsify, inflate, or magnify that transformation. To live simply with humility can be a profound state of inner attainment.

The formation of a peaceful world is a collective work. The alchemy of soul is only one aspect of that work, but it is a centering aspect that opens onto an inner horizon that moves beyond the present world and its current crisis. The goal is not to be a "world shaker" or "world mover" but to be a calm, centered presence, a source of peace and good will, and a resource for others in terms of assisting them in the processes of their own rebirth and rediscovery. Our alchemies of soul contribute to a process of opening the world to greater mystery and depths, to the visionary evolution of human understanding, and to supporting the development of various kinds of spiritual community. On the emergent front of collective life, it is a resource for creative thought and artistic reflection as well as an inner science of development and perceptual enhancement. Hermetic teachings are complex and I have not fully articulated them, but I have introduced a Hermetic process of soul and self-development. Now, the task is for each individual to take what they find worthwhile in this overview and apply it in the daily round of life, to test its value by actually engaging in the practice. Only through application can the value of these teachings be assessed; without real investigation and inner effort, very little can be gained. The goal is continual inner development, and this requires a different application of will than simple mental reflection. The first step on the path is to start where you are, and from there, apply what you learn by subjecting it to every situation life offers. In that way, you find your own synthesis and through practice, you make your journey and your offering.

1. See Julius Evola (1997) for a more detailed view of "regal virility;" Evola's work, originally published in 1937 and built around themes articulated by Rene Guénon (particularly *Le Roi du Monde,* 1927), gives an interesting but seriously flawed account of the Grail mystery.

2. See René Guénon, 1958: 41-45.

3. See for example: Frithjof Schuon, 1981.

4. For a contemporary theoretical perspective congruent with the alchemy of soul, see Jorge Ferrer's (2002) excellent work on participatory spirituality.

5. For example see Marie-Louise von Franz (1980) for a good overview of new directions in alchemy.

6. Luke 6:38, "Give, and it will be given to you. A good measure, pressed down, shaken together and running over, will be poured into your lap. For with the measure you use, it will be measured to you."

ALCHEMICAL GLOSSARY [1]

Aeons (Archetypes): Aeons refer to the archetypal imagery and spiritually charged manifestations that represent beings more empowered and luminous than ordinary human beings. In classic language, they are the gods and goddesses, the angels and devas, the archetypes of collective mentality, and the storied images of various religious and spiritual traditions. In the language of Hermetic alchemy, the Aeons are those "first beings" whose forms are symbolic of divine qualities such as Silence, Life, Breath, Love, and Wisdom. Aeons, in the language of dreams and visions, are those entities whose psychic presence alters the consciousness of the dreamer and lifts him or her into visionary horizons, new perceptions, and a deeper awareness of the multilayered nature of the cosmos. They are generally, the powers of the deep as manifest in the process of alchemical transformation. As archetypes, the Aeons are the deep patterns of psychic configuration that represent human possibilities in an amplified and dramatized sense; in the alchemical process these archetypes evolve over time, reflecting stages of human development. An archetype is linked to a set of images that represents collective patterns in the form of "family resemblances" without any one image representing the whole of the archetypal complex. The "wise old man" can take many forms, none of which is definitive; all contribute to a synthesis of shared perceptions that can, over time, evolve and develop in relation to human social and cultural change. Aeons are of the same nature, including the more abstract in type, such as the Aeon for Silence or Beauty. In the alchemy of soul, the task is to participate in archetypal perceptions, not to become the archetype, but to seek differentiation through archetypal knowledge (see Gnosis) as a unique, evolving soul.

Aether (Ether): Esoterically, this term refers to the subtle, pervasive quality of psychically perceived life energy immanent in every living form, and in planetary and celestial bodies such as the sun, moon, and stars. It is also known as the "fifth element" that permeates earth, water, air, and fire (see Elements). Aether is an etheric astral vitality, a subtle vibratory radiance of the heavens that is all-permeating and pervasive. The etheric refers to the bio-energetic emanations of living creatures and the radiant field of interconnected energies that surround and penetrate the globe of earth. The Aether is a synonym for solar life-force and the animating capacity of life-giving energies inherent to, and resonant with, the deep molten core of planetary and lunar bodies. As a generic term, it synthesizes an unrecognized number of special energies whose etheric signatures require deeper study and articulation. Overall, the Aether or etheric is a reference to a perceptual power, an ability to "see" subtle energies that are inherent to living bodies of all types (see also, Prana).

Alchemy (see Hermeticism): There is a long and complex history of this term which, generically, refers to the art and science of transformation. The two basic types of alchemy are "inner" and "outer" alchemy. Outer alchemy is visibly transformative, as witnessed in chemical reactions. The goal of such alchemy is the making of subtle substances (see Elixir and Philosopher's Stone) imbued with magical capacities that can induce transformations in other substances. Inner alchemy refers to transformations of soul and psyche and has been used in archetypal psychology to refer to varying stages of growth toward psychological maturity and integration. In the alchemy of soul, the term refers to the process of awakening to depths of Spirit and Being in order to embody, with grace and light, the full potential of our human capacities. It also refers to the processes and stages of refinement and developing self-knowledge that lead to an active, creative life in the world as an agent of transformation for others. Alchemy is an art whose practice is intrinsic to a spiritual path that must be determined by each individual in accordance with his or her true capabilities. There is no one alchemy, only a diverse set of principles that must be applied by each person in a responsible and mature fashion, with discipline, over a lifetime of dedication to shared goals of peace, loving respect, creative intelligence, and world-integration.

Alchemical Marriage (Hieros Gamos, see also Mercury): The "sacred marriage" is an ancient symbol of the fertile union of the female and male through a ritual of deep respect, love, and erotic passion. The symbolism of this marriage is often sexual, referring to the interpenetration of bodies, souls, minds, hearts, and shared, deep emotions as a catalyst of change and personal integration. Symbolically, it refers to the male within the female and the female within the male as natural expressions of the Anima (female soul) and Animus (male soul) integration. This is essential to the Great Work (see below); the male seeks to integrate the feminine, as the female seeks to integrate the masculine, each with a consciousness of his or her own uniqueness as male or female. The symbolism of the marriage in a Christian context is the relationship between the Divine Sophia and the Sacred Christ; their marriage is an alchemical symbol of the processes by which the feminine and the masculine come into harmony and balance, each recognizing and celebrating the worth of the other. The Alchemical Marriage has a "third" partner, which is Spirit as the integrating presence (see Salt) that allows this union and differentiation to fully express the value of each individual and the importance of their enduring relationship. Spirit is present in the relationship insofar as Spirit is acknowledged and revered as a true partner in the Alchemical Marriage. There is no deep marriage without the Third whose energy and depth holds the dynamics of conflict, disagreement, and denial in the regenerative field of possible reconciliation and love. The symbolism of this marriage is found in the creative union of the Lunar-Solar and Salt-Sulphur-Mercury (see below).

Aqua Vitae (Water of Life): This is one of the many metaphors of the alchemy of soul referring to the vital life force or fluid depth of emotion and feeling that supports loving relationships with others. It is the distilled essence or "dew of life" that washes and whitens the dark shadows of doubt, fear, and confusion. The water of life, as a blessed cleansing, is seen in the baptismal fluids of tears and sweat, sustaining and preceding the birth of new life identity. These Waters mix sweetness with joy and gratitude. The metaphor also refers to healing water, the water that was once wine but has now become a source of purity, clarity, and health-giving, liquid vitality. The waters of life bless, transform, uphold, and vivify each person as a drink from the pure springs of Spirit. The flowing energies of life in all bodily fluids reflect this spiritual quality of water because humans are composed of that permeating liquid presence in the flesh (see also Blood).

Aura: This refers to the field of energies surrounding the body that reflects the physical, emotional, mental, and spiritual condition of each person. The baseline for these energies is an integrated field that holds a variety of shifting patterns that surround and express the state of the person. This field is grounded in the physical and reflects the etheric (see Aether) energies of a more global nature. It is not an isolated or strictly self-generated field but an interactive field whose form and patterns reflect the environment physically, psychically, and spirituality. Auras intersect, can infuse or impact others on a subtle plane, and have a dynamic, changing state that reflects mood, emotional and mental conditioning, and habitual attitudes and beliefs. They can be very expansive or very contracted, depending upon circumstances. In the alchemy of soul, the aura is a sign or signifier of noetic and psychic states reflecting stages of development in relationship to states of individual being.

Being: This refers to the Great Mystery, to God, to the Infinite, Limitless, Unbound Totality. Its primary symbol in this work is the Sign of Infinity. The metaphor of Being refers to the ultimate ground of all existence, the primal source of consciousness and joy in the creative processes of infinite manifestation. In the alchemy of soul, Being is the presence that sustains the transformation of each individual, each collective, each world, in all their various physical, subtle, and noetic manifestations. Being is the basis of all soul life, the ontological reality through which, and within which, all beings become incarnate. In the more subtle worlds, where psychonoetic forms abound, Being is the life-giving source that sustains those worlds. I call it "sacred beingness" — the holy ground which gives, sustains, and absorbs all life energies. The manifestations of Being are beyond measuring and the "divine forms" of its most recognized appearances are seen as gods, goddesses, devas, or sacred spirits (see Aeons). These manifestations reflect only the particular, ideal forms valued in various religious traditions, sacred narratives, and creative arts. Being is not limited to religion, nor is it contained or best known in the religious or philosophical context. Being is beyond containment and definition. Yet, Being continually manifests in the life of each person; the alchemical task is to know it as such, to be a "temple of light," and to stand in presence as a living, particular embodiment of Being.

Blood: Often used as a symbol for Mother Mercury (as solvent and coagulator), Blood is the Red Tincture or Elixir, the Water of the Dragon. It is a frequent symbol of death and rebirth, as revealed in the feminine cycle, a washing away and a renewal, a life gift and a cleansing, an expansion, opening, flowing quietude, and a solitary period of reflection. Also, Blood is the medium representing the sacrifice of Christ, death, healing and the cleansing of wounds; sun and moon are bathed and renewed in the blood red sunset, the red moonrise. The Mercurial Blood dissolves the hard, resistant matter of the Stone in order to make it smoother, rounder, and more reflective of light. Blood color is the Dragon color of the rising soul as it becomes increasingly self aware, able to bring light into the world as a bearer of the living Serpent Power, the rising energies of the awakened psychonoetic body. The alchemy of blood is a deep mystery; it is a sacramental blessing, representing sorrows and pain. It has been shed for others, and a luminous drop of it can heal the world.

Body: This refers to the holy ground of transformation and Spirit manifestations, the basis of the creative change, the Prima Materia (see below) of the psycho-spiritual development required in all incarnational alchemies of soul. Body is also earth and water, fire and wind, aether-filled with energies of noetic light and erotic passion. Body is the temple of Spirit, the grounding medium of cosmogenic evolution, and the sacred basis of gender differences. The sexual aspects of body reflect the primary processes of biological life, infused with Spirit, and are an ecstatic means for union, joy, and love. Body is holy and complex, sustaining life energies for the purpose of co-evolutionary relationships in a multitude of expressive forms — dance, gymnastics, sports, martial arts, many sculptural forms, and most importantly, wise living in relationship to nature. The body is neither a static medium, nor a prison; body is the very basis of soul's alchemy, the medium that is transformed into the Philosopher's Stone, like a radiant jewel illumined by presence.

Christ (Logos): This is the masculine symbol of the awakened soul, a unique manifestation of Spirit and, in the tradition of esoteric Christianity, the fully joyful spiritual man. It is masculine love as expressed in a caring father, brother, son, friend, and husband. Christ symbolizes the integrated power of the Animus, the male predisposition that offers guidance, practical advice, skillful abilities, and a knowledge of the world that is not bound by the conventions of collective behavior. Christ is a healing presence and "Son of God" insofar as we are each sons and daughters of God and he is the symbol of the illumined soul as a master, teacher, guide, and spirit being transfigured through the gifts of the Holy Spirit. Christ is the "Word of God" as embodied in sacred teachings, wise sayings, spiritual guidance, and an articulate expression of the mysteries of incarnation, soul relations, death, and rebirth. A sacred symbol of the higher Self, the Christ manifests in loving presence, deep integration of body, soul, mind, and spirit. A sign of willing sacrifice for the good of others, not as a victim of ignorance, but as a creative partner who is willing to share the burdens of those less able to free themselves from sorrow, pain, and trauma. This Archetype combines lion and a lamb, dove and olive branch, and reflects as the light of the jewel in the Golden White Lotus.

Dreams (Visions): One of the most important sources for the alchemy of soul is dreams and visions; either may occur in a waking state as in "day" dreaming or visions seen in waking imagination. The dream is a form of soul activity; it communicates through imagery, feelings, stories, myth, psychic manifestations, and a wide variety of possible perceptions that reveal many subtle worlds of experience. The participation in dreaming is not always ego derived, nor is it based on a simple replay of daily experiences. Dreaming is much more than epiphenomenal and its bio-chemical basis is only a minor aspect of its ontological significance. Dreams reveal Being and Spirit; they are an opening to larger and more complex realms of perception in which extra-mental abilities can unfold and develop. They provide a template for waking perceptions that instigate the metaphor of "life as dream" by which the dreamer seeks to integrate both waking and dreaming awareness. Many dreams are revelatory, charged with sacred contents, illuminative, mystical, and a guiding source of presence on the spiritual path. Remembering, interpreting, and applying dream knowledge are crucial aspects of the alchemical task. I recommend recording dreams in detail in order to study dream symbols and patterns over the years, and as a way to index self-development.

Elements: This refers to the basic processes of nature as reflected in the archetypes of Earth, Water, Air, and Fire (with the "fifth" or quintessence as Aether). In the alchemy of soul, the elements are interpreted as symbolic of internal processes, not in any fixed system, but as interpreted by each individual. For example, Earth, symbolized by the Stone, is the body, groundedness, stability, firmness, physical sensations, the ripe fruits of the garden, the flowers of the field, the joy of sexuality, the pleasure of good food, the touch and taste of sensory awareness. Water, symbolized by the Cup, is fluid, flowing motion, feeling and emotional depths, deep empathy, love, the Eros of connection, the expansive ocean of all conscious life, the rain, the dew, the mountain stream. Water fills our bodies with precious life source, blesses and baptizes us, quenching our thirst and satisfying our need for slippery, fluid fecundity (see Aqua Vitae). Air, symbolized by the flowering Staff, is the breath of life, source of expansive, light, openness to the infinite, the vastness of pure, open skies. The wind and the turbulent storm, hurricane or tornado, are its great expressions in human life, when upheaval, shock, a sudden gust, blows us off our beaten path and into the wilderness of new discovery, blows away the cobwebs of old thinking and reveals a higher, vaster expanse. Fire, symbolized by the Sword, is the creative flame of inspiration, brilliant ideas, thoughts, intuitions, mental flexibility, burning up old patterns, transforming solid matters into smoke and ash, the burning flash of lightning, the purity of the sun, the softness of the moon, the starry heavens. Fire gives warmth, and warmth is necessary in the alchemy of soul to heat the depths slowly, bring them to a boil, in order to absorb the distilled essence of the changes. All Elements interpenetrate, their relationship to warmth, coolness, dryness, and the moist must not be underestimated; the quintessence is the Fifth Element (Aether). Other systems offer additional Elements, such as metal, wood, mineral, gem stone, bone, and more.

Elixir (or Tincture): The primary symbol of the universal essence or "miraculous medicine" of the Philosopher's Stone, the Elixir will transmute ordinary base metal into gold, cure diseases, heal wounds, grant immortality, and even bring the dead back to life. Transformed from the original white rose color to the soft brilliance of the red-gold fire rose, the Elixir of Life, the divine Tincture, is the distillation of Spirit within the human heart and mind. Distilled and refined through life experience, clarified with the heat of love, strained with the net of life-enhancing values, the Elixir is slowly purified. There is an art to this distillation. In the alchemy of soul, the work of purification requires a continual willingness to reflect upon personal values and the continuity of thoughts, words, and deeds until these come into perfect resonance. This Elixir manifests in a touch, a smile, a true word, and in acts of kindness; the essence requires enduring commitment and determination. Faith also is necessary. The essence is in the stone; it can be drawn out through life experience if the alchemist is wise enough, deeply practiced, and constant in faithful application of the alchemical principles. The world is filled with Elixir; it is neither precious nor rare, but those caught in the work often lose sight of its abundance. Rain is an Elixir, if rightly understood.

Gold: The precious metal that is often symbolized as a red-gold, representing vibrant wealth of soul; the pure molten fluid refined and purified from the dross. A father substance of brilliance, burnished metal, a solar aspect of the Great Work, said to be conjoined Mercury and White Sulphur. Other metals may be transformed into gold, as all share a common nature; the ripening of any metal into gold is the heart of the alchemical task. Hardness of heart, mental fixation, the granular density of iron, must all be subtlized, animated, purified, and transformed in order for the Gold of pure radiance to show its luster. Gold withstands the test of fire, will not transmute its essence, but only transform its brilliance into polished purity. Gold is flowing, malleable, easily shaped into a multitude of forms. Is the gold lion the gold? Or is the gold, a lion? Form and essence melt and dissolve. Gold adapts, it is an artistic, visionary medium of expression. A precious golden ring inscribed with the mantic teachings symbolizes the marriage of the alchemist and the work. It is a magical substance that must always be refined to perfect purity and formed with creative freedom that reveres and respects the gold of others. All gold is not dross, but gold without value is the gold hidden away and unspent.

Gnosis: The ancient Greek word for "knowledge" that is usually associated with many diverse groups of the early Christian era. These groups taught theosophical creation stories and initiatic rituals that were passed on in written and oral traditions. These teachings may be traced back to the Isiatic Mysteries (Isis and Osiris) or the Rites of Eleusis (Demeter and Kore) in which the Goddess was unveiled and a revelatory knowledge was given to the initiate. Assimilated into Arabic thought, and thus into Islamic mysticism, Gnosis became a technical term used by Sufi teachers to indicate the soul's extinction (*fana*) in God, complete union of the soul with the Beloved. In Greek Orthodox Christian mysticism, Gnosis also refers to a special state of grace by which the soul was united with God. In the West, in Catholic and later Protestant writings, "knowledge" became the province of rational theological speculation tied to Biblical texts; conventional theologians tended to disapprove of mystical Gnosis, as did the rational philosophers of the Enlightenment. Nevertheless, some Christian mystics did experience and extol special forms of mystical insight or illumination which could be called Gnosis. In esoteric circles, Gnosis as "secret or initiatic knowledge" was reconstituted in the 15th century Renaissance during which "primal theology" (*prisca theologos*) was believed to be based in direct revelation given to the seeker, cultivated through magical means. Underground currents in Western Esotericism developed mystical theosophies based in Gnosis and mystical insights. In this work, Gnosis refers to knowledge attained through illuminative perceptions—in dreams, visions, insights, and the expansion of consciousness into higher orders of awareness.

Gnosticism (see also Hemeticism): A generic term that is used to describe the general mythic theophanies of diverse groups in the early era of Christianity, centered in Alexandria, Antioch, and other urban centers of the Mediterranean. The term is largely a modern construct, created by scholars in the mid-20th century to designate an indistinct set of beliefs and practices found in non-Christian texts of that era. No group or sect of that era called itself "gnostic", though the use of the term Gnosis (see above) was common to those texts. Scholars seeking a unifying term to designate the spiritual philosophy of these texts, created "gnosticism" as a generic reference, which other scholars have challenged as misleading. There are many classical gnostic schemes but the general goal is to attain a revelatory vision of the Higher Aeons (see above), including divine feminine figures such as the Sophia or Barbelo, as guiding deities of the religious and mythical worlds of these groups. In a later, more constructed sense, Gnosticism has been characterized as "world renouncing" because the world is thought to be a place of entrapment, imprisonment, and a lower state of being which must be escaped through Gnosis. The classic expression of Gnosticism, in a generic sense, requires ascetic renunciation, denial of the body as the instrument of physical passion, waking to the immorality of the "unknowing masses" that create war and conflict based in greed, ignorance, and pride. Gnosticism teaches liberation from the illusions of the world and material entrapment. Thus Buddhism, Hinduism, and Christian Gnostic teachings are "gnostic" insofar as they are world renouncing and world denying; they affirm the value of Gnosis as liberation from suffering, pain, confusion, and ignorance. Gnosticism can also refer to secular attitudes toward any knowledge that claims to be ultimate and world transcending.

Grail (Cup): A symbol that refers to the mysterious object of a spiritual quest, the Grail legend initially developed in the twelfth century in France and later in Germany and England. The original author of the Grail quest was Chrétien de Troyes, a French poet who wrote *Perceval* (or *The Story of the Grail*) in 1190 CE. Following this text were many "continuations" as Chrétien left his original tale unfinished. Subsequently, other authors grafted onto the story the quest adventures of Arthurian heroes and maidens, such as Lancelot, Guinevere, Galahad, Blancheflor, Perceval and other Knights of the Round Table. By 1250, the major texts of the Grail legend had established the motif of the Grail as a holy object, often associated with Christ, cared for by a beautiful Grail princess or priestess, and found only by the pure in heart whose motives were unquestionably dedicated to the highest ideals. Many different objects are described as Grail objects, the most conventional being the Cup (though all the Hallows are named as Grail objects, see below). The Grail as Cup has strong associations with the Eucharist and the Cup of the blood of Christ, believed to be present at the crucifixion. The challenge of the Grail, when it is finally seen by the seeker, is to ask the right questions and to answer the question: "Whom does the Grail serve?" Failure to answer the question will extend the search far beyond the initial encounter; asking no questions causes the Grail to disappear. The right question is neither a formula nor a stock question, but must be formulated in the immediate presence of the Grail. In this work, the Grail is the symbol of the quest for illumination and a version of the Vas Hermeticum. It has many forms.[2]

Great Work: This refers to the work of alchemical transformation and the creation of the Philosopher's Stone and the Elixir of Life whose application is transformative for the alchemist and for others when used correctly. Classically, the Work has three stages: *nigredo* (darkness), *albedo* (whiteness), and *rubedo* (redness)—the shadow seen and made volatile, followed by purification through increasing whiteness, resulting in the red gold, pure quintessence of the Elixir. The Great Work is a work of a lifetime, not a technique or a practice, but a philosophy of spiritual transformation that must be internalized and made manifest in the day-to-day life of the alchemist. Gold is a symbol of the work, as is Silver. The Alchemical Marriage is an essential aspect of the Work; the integration of polarity and duality, and their eventual transcendence, is a crucial feature of creating the Stone (see below). The emblem of the Great Work is the life of the individual and the perfection of the practice in a visible but subtle form that acts for the good of others and magically induces positive growth without effort in others. The work is cyclical and must be applied to all aspects of life, including the most mundane and circumstantial.

Hallows (Stone, Staff, Cup, Sword): A traditional name for the sacred objects of the Grail Quest, the Hallows are usually the four named above but may also refer to a spear, a platter, a variety of candles, and other objects as cited in the various Grail texts. Hallows are sacred in the sense that they carry special symbolic meanings connected to the transformational process leading to the illumination of soul. The Stone represents the Philosopher's Stone (see below), the goal of the alchemical work, the magical properties of which can heal, awaken, induce visions, and give understanding. Stone contains the word "one" which is part of its secret nature, as knowing the Stone leads, indeed, to Oneness. The Staff is the symbol of the messenger (see Hermes) or of sacred pilgrimage, as a journey to the Land of the Midnight Sun (see below) where the staff becomes a torch, lighting the way through the visionary landscape. It is that upon which we depend and lean, and which we use as support and protection against the hounds of darkness. The Cup is the traditional Hallow of the Grail quest (see Grail) and also holds the ambrosia that awakens mind and soul to the visionary landscape that the alchemist must enter. The Cup is a symbol of protection, guardianship, love, and inspiration. The Sword is the weapon of defense against the falsehoods of self love and arrogant pride; it cuts through illusions, penetrates the Stone and stirs, in its depths, the Elixir of Life. Sword contains "word," and this Word is the means by which truth is communicated and passed onto the generations. Those who use the Sword rightly will understand that it must not be gripped too tightly; those who use it wrongly will learn that it must not be wielded too strongly.[3]

Heliocosm (Microcosm, Mesocosm, Macrocosm): The term "Helio" is Greek and refers to the Sun that is our star, thus, the great solar light that holds the planetary bodies in orbit. A Heliocosm is any star system and its planets—in particular, our ten planets (including Quaoar) as a living structure animated by the Prana of the Sun. A Heliocosm is the self-sustaining system linked with planets, moons, comets, and other bodies including the Kuiper Belt and the Oort Cloud that extends three light years from the Sun to the limits of its gravitational field. The Heliocosm also includes all the psychic constituents of UrSpace (see below) associated with these same worlds; a Heliocosm is a metafield of consciousness united with the energetic properties active in solar and planetary physics. What we imagine, see, know, and comprehend in that total space must completely incorporate all consciousness inherent to the field. However, this metafield is itself an index of a higher metafield, which I call the Mesocosm, identical with the Galactic structure, our Milky Way, about 100,000 light years in diameter, disk-shaped within a sphere of "dark matter," containing roughly 200 billion other stars. Life in that structure is rare but present and creatively active; all conscious life within that structure contributes to the metafield of the Mesocosm. We are a relatively immature species in the Mesocosm. Crossing the horizon into communion with the greater Continuum of consciousness within the Mesocosm is one of the greatest experiences of human existence. A collective crossing into that field will change humanity forever. The Macrocosm refers to the universe at large, including our local supercluster, uncounted numbers of other galaxies, dark energies and dark matter, and many other theoretical anomalies. The Macrocosm as an expression of consciousness is yet an unknown dimension of psychic exploration, but the theory of consciousness as universal and omnipresent suggests that all space-time is integral to a metafield of supraconscious Being throughout the universe (or multiverses). The Microcosm is the visionary reality held by humanity, individually or collectively, integral to all the above structures of Being.

Hermes (see Psychopomos): This is the "guide of soul" (*psychopomos*), in the figure of a god-man, whose original Greek form was as the "God of Boundaries" or the "Messenger of the Gods." Hermes (or Mercury in Latin) is the winged messenger, a trickster who has magical powers, carries the Caduceus, or Winged Staff, with two intertwined serpents whose heads at the top of the Staff symbolize the Twin Wisdoms of compassion and insight. A story relates that Hermes placed his staff between two fighting serpents who were calmed by his presence. These twin forces reflect the duality of thought and feeling on the alchemical path that must be integrated with soul. Hermes is the guide to dreams and visions, but stands at the border of the Infinite to bring back those who cross into the Unknowable, so that they may return safely. Hermes has a trickster nature that can lead the seeker into challenging situations that require the utmost care to avoid dangers that can lead to negative consequences. Crossing boundaries requires great skill and patience, and as a patron of alchemy, Hermes Trismegistus is the wise teacher, mage, and master who knows all arcane arts, mysteries, and occult sciences—a guide to souls seeking alchemical wisdom.

Hermeticism: A spiritual philosophy of the early Christian era, Hermeticism was articulated in a corpus of seventeen short texts known as the Corpus Hermeticum. These texts were thought to be written by Hermes Trismegistus (see above) as the great philosopher of arcane and mystical knowledge; the actual authors are unknown. The texts were collected in Byzantium in about 1100 CE and later translated into Latin (then Italian) in the 1470s by Marsilio Ficino, the great Italian scholar, doctor, and Hermeticist. Hermeticism, based in these texts and later assimilated with other alchemical texts, is best symbolized in the descent of the soul of humanity in the first text of the collection called the *Poimandres* (the Shepherd or more esoterically, U*nderstanding of Re*). As the Adamic soul descends from the highest realm, he acquires power from each planetary level until he reaches the world where he can embrace the beauty, wonder, and sensuality of earthly Nature, to unite with her sexually, and to incarnate the soul of humanity into the world of material creation. Hermeticism celebrates nature, beauty, love, sexuality, poetry, science, and all the arts as vital expressions of incarnate soul life. There is no rejection of the body; sensory life and incarnation are the basis of soul development. The alchemy of soul is a Hermetic art and science—primal matter is nature formed as the body in which we are challenged to develop our utmost capacities as spiritual beings. It is not by world rejection (see Gnosticism) but by world affirmation, the celebration of life and beauty, that we are led to the Gnosis of incarnational spirituality. The world is a place of greatest reverence and opportunity for soul development, not a place of ignorance or lower consciousness. The goal of Hermeticism is to know Being and Spirit, to celebrate life as a spiritual seeker, and to actualize the creative, imaginative, and visionary powers of soul for the benefit of others and not just for self alone. Alchemy is the great Hermetic art of soul awakening.[4]

Incarnation (Reincarnation): An act of embodiment that results in the profound union of soul, mind, feeling, imagination, and memory with organic, biological existence. There is no one purpose to incarnation, only a field of possible meanings whose purpose is to know, explore, and actualize the potentials of incarnational life. The division of soul tendencies into sensory, emotional, artistic, intellectual, and spiritual aspects reflects various areas of emphasis in soul life. These five tendencies should be balanced and developed through the practice of the alchemy of soul. We each bring with us into incarnation the knowledge and tendencies or habits of other lives; we have lived before as incarnate beings and reincarnation is a natural process of species development. Without such multiple lives there would be no such development, because we would not carry the inherent wisdom necessary to truly comprehend the complexity and subtle, profound nature of the Creation. Thus, every incarnation is an opportunity to draw upon past incarnational wisdom, not through memory, but through intuitive knowing, through a spontaneous wisdom that is a distillation of the past into present mind, heart, and soul life. There is no need to "remember past lives" because the distilled learning of those lives shapes and characterizes the present life of each person. Learning capacities reflect past life knowledge, as does the ease with which skills of all types are acquired. Incarnation is a gift and opportunity for growth and development of the deep learning we each carry within us. Remembering past lives is simply an enhancement of that knowledge, not a necessity.

Light and Dark: Light is the operative metaphor of the alchemy of soul, symbolizing illumination, enlightenment, mystical wisdom, and divine presence. The metaphysics of Light are inseparable from consciousness by which all and any Light is seen or known. Light is a phenomenal quality inherent to certain mystical states, and Light can be a manifestation of Spirit, as in a luminous aura or a healing energy. Purity of Spirit leads to Light, and Light leads beyond itself into the Infinite. However, in the alchemy of soul, Light is not opposed to Dark because the Dark symbolizes rest, peace, stillness, quiet, and mysterious depths. The body is a grounding medium of the interplay of light and dark in the most positive sense, similar to the theory of Yin-Yang in Chinese philosophies. Dawn and Twilight are equally part of the 360 degrees of the circle of day and night; thus, Light is the synthesis of all colors, a uniting media of energies that make us more keenly aware, even in the Dark (see Lotus).

Lotus: A flower whose symbolic meaning is reflected in an ancient symbolism, the Lotus is a plant which rises from the dark waters toward light. Reaching the surface, the new horizon, the Lotus bud opens to the light while its roots are still sunk deep into the rich, dark mud of the earth. When the light fades, the bud closes; the seeds of the Lotus, if carefully preserved, are said to last for hundreds if not thousands of years. They can be replanted and still grow a vital, living plant, opening again to new light, water, earth, and air. In the alchemy of soul, the Lotus is the symbol of the illumined heart, the petals must open to reveal the seed pearls that are in the pod of the flower, one of which burns brightly as a sign of the divine spark (see Pearl).

Lunar: The Lunar side is the feminine side, the softer light of dancing maidens and wise women who know the cycles of the day and night. The lunar is the water sign of creative, flowing juices, the ambient mist, the Lady of the Lake whose arcane wisdom teaches how to live in harmony with the natural cycles. Lunar light and shadows reflect deep feeling, a landscape of creative dreaming and visionary potential transferable into artistic forms and expressions. The Lunar represents the soft, subtle, expansive, ancient Beingness of Mother Moon, whose deep memory includes the birth and death of entire worlds. It symbolizes the Bride and Healer, the moist, wet, womb of soul, the receptive silver egg, damp field of procreative life, nurturing strength, agility, and adaptive quicksilver intelligence. In the alchemy of soul, the Lunar is the empathic, intuitive power to blend and harmonize with others without friction, harm, or contest. The art of the Moon is magical, mysterious, and miraculous — few are those who comprehend her deepest mysteries. Too much lunar essence can lead to dreamy, ungrounded fantasy no longer connected to genuine alchemy and integration; Lunar energy must be united with the Solar without losing its purity or depth.

Magic: In the alchemy of soul, Magic is the capacity to see and know the world with imagination, creative artistry, and openness to the unknown and unexpected. The Magical aspect of soul work is the unexpected consequence of actions that link synchronistically with other events and persons in a larger field of correspondences often ignored or unseen. Magical relationships are ones that develop spontaneously with great ease and freedom of mutual expression. The core of Magic is cosmological harmony, the subtle and occult relationships between persons, objects, natural phenomena, and invisible presences frequently linked through ritual and ceremony. In a more formal sense, I define magic as "a harmony of sympathetic relationships actualized by intent for the purpose of transformation." A magical intent is one directed by the Law of Resonance, like to like, but tempered through the practice of natural correspondences, for example, of being in the right place at the right time. In the alchemy of soul, Magic is a natural aspect of the work, not a particular set of ritual or symbolic practices.

Mercury (see Hermes): Also known as Mecurius-Hermes, Mercury is a central symbol of alchemy, symbolizing the agent of transformation, usually distinct from the substance "mercury" (Hg), often called "quicksilver", as a vital symbol of a fluid and cohesive nature. Mercury (cool, moist, receptive, feminine) is usually created by combining Sulphur (hot, dry, active, masculine) with Argent Vive (vital spirit, often symbolized by wine and its distilled essence, brandy) to produce, with the agency of Salt, the Alchemical Marriage (see above), transformed Mercury, essence of the Philosopher's Stone. In the alchemy of soul, Mercury is regarded as the fluid, feminine presence of the Alchemical Marriage. It has the power to dissolve all fixed matter, metals, hardness, and stubborn resistances. The mother of all metals, Mercury is a manifestation of feminine divine Spirit hidden in the depths of matter. She must be balanced with Sulphur (see below), the heat of form, structure, and order. Symbolizing a capacity to combine water and fire, through interior alchemical art; present in the Prima Materia (see below) as well as in the finished work, Mecurius is said to be fluid matter, the process, and the agent by which the goal is attained. One alchemical saying on Mecurius is, "It devours itself, spits itself out, and then regenerates itself." This refers to the cycles of inner alchemy, the processes of refinement which eventually produce the true, shining quintessence (see Stages). Mercury is the agent of the well known alchemical epigram, "*solve et coagula*" (see below) describing the construction, deconstruction, and reconstruction of the alchemy of soul. Too much Mercury without Sulphur produces dreamy illusion, ungroundedness, detached indifference, and fantasy disconnected from pragmatic needs. Failure to integrate Sulphur means an overpowering presence of the feminine without practical survival skills necessary to meet, with equality, the full strength of the externalized, extroverted masculine.

Midnight Sun (Luminous Night): A symbol of crossing the boundary into the mysterious realms of the inner landscape, the Midnight Sun is illumined by Spirit in the midst of the creative dark. It can symbolize the *nigredo* ("dark") stage of the work and the death of matter, reflecting its transformation by the arising of inner light. A well-known symbol in Persian Sufism, the "Land of the Midnight Sun" refers to the invisible realms (see Mundus Imaginalis) visited by the soul in dreams, visions, and in out-of-body experiences. The luminous orb of the Midnight Sun in deep darkness is a sign of the perfect union of light and dark, day and night, yin and yang, and all opposites reconciled beyond the veils of human reason and thought. The Midnight Sun is a star burning brightly in the Infinite dark of all space-time, known through visionary intuition; also an ecstatic symbol of inner realization uniting perfect calm with infinite expanse.

Mundus Imaginalis (Arabic, *Alam al-mithal*): This is a traditional esoteric term for the higher perceptions of the imagination and visionary power of the human soul. Mundus refers to the "world" in the non-physical sense of the psychic world of human thought, art, imagination, science, history, and cultural creations. This is the "world" of human mentality, of the noetic and poetic aspects of intelligence harmonized with imaginative, creative insight. Imaginalis refers to the "imaginal" capacity of human beings to envision, to creatively "see" through creative visions, all the possibilities of life and alternate existences. The Imaginal Realms are many, including all heavens, hells, in-between worlds, psychic planes, subtle dimensions, astral levels, and so on, as reflected imaginal psychomental creations. The autonomy of these various realms is a direct function of collective visualization, a power great enough to actually create a subtle realm inhabitable by soul when separated from the body (in dreams, visions, or in death). The *alam al-mithal* is a Sufi designation of the "Imaginal Worlds" often separated into three worlds: the physical world of soul incarnation; the psychic worlds of imaginative projection and subtle beings such as deva, jinn, or angels on increasingly more powerful levels; and the higher noetic worlds of pure mind and soul beyond all images and forms. The creative powers of Spirit and Being sustain these worlds, giving birth to all beings within them, and absorbing the energies of change and reconstruction as part of the process of world transformation. In the alchemy of soul, the Mundus Imaginalis is a designation for all possible visionary worlds, contiguous with UrSpace (see below), and dynamically animate in every soul, accessible through visionary knowledge.

Nature: The positive ground of human spiritual life, Nature symbolizes the beauty and power of the fecund world, the source of art and inspiration. The relationship between art and Nature is best expressed in the human body, a miracle of sensitive systems combined to support the rich emotional, intellective, and aesthetic perceptions of the soul. Nature is the great world of all ecological niches, all the diverse habitats of human, animal, plant, insect, bird, and sea life. The ecologies of nature also include the ecologies of the Heliocosm (see above) that extend to the moon and all the planets, comets, and other celestial bodies of our system. Nature is not "red in tooth and claw" nor is it a "place of imprisonment." Nature is the basis of human spiritual development as encoded into the biological processes of evolutionary change; it is also the basis of enrichment for our erotic, emotional, and mental lives, and the healing powers of nature are abundant. Nature is the mother of soul life, the supportive matrix that provides, with our efforts and wise decisions, a fruitful multitude of diverse habitats for human growth. Nature is a holy ground whose alchemical symbolism abounds in the "occult virtues" found in a vast multitude of plants, animals, minerals, metals, and organic substances of all kinds.

Numinous: This term refers to the human capacity to encounter, know, and directly perceive the presence of the sacred, however defined by the individual. The Numinous refers to the affirmation of a luminous presence in the form of various energies, entities, divinities or sacred qualities, including the aura accompanying certain objects, places, and persons. The Numinous manifests as a sense of the strange, uncanny, occult, or mysterious, creating a fascinating attraction to the sacred or to a spiritual power or to manifestations of a visionary kind. Also it manifests in dreams as very powerful, luminous figures or events or objects which communicate a sense of the holy to the dreamer or visionary.

Pearl: A symbol of the quest for wisdom, it symbolizes the "pearl of great price" referred to by Jesus when telling the parable of the merchant who sold all he had in order to gain this treasure. Also referred to in a Gnostic text called the *Hymn of the Pearl*, related by the disciple Thomas "in the country of the Indians (India)" after the resurrection of Christ. In this tale, the pearl is guarded by a dragon who puts to sleep all those who would claim it. Only those who are most determined, who resist the slumber of consensual life, will be able to gain that pearl whose luster reflects the open flower. The pearl is the symbol of luster in the heart of the Lotus (see Lotus) of the truly awakened soul; a meditative symbol of the heart center, a bright, healing gem of great power and transformative effects. The Pearl is made around the grit of sand that irritates the subtle, sensitive tissue of the oyster; in just this manner, the alchemy of soul seeks to transform the irritants of human life into the luster of the pearl, purified by alchemical transformations into light and presence.

Philosopher's Stone (see Hallows): A primary symbol of the Great Work, the Stone is a magical object capable of inducing positive spiritual change in other persons, places, and things. The Jewel in the Lotus, the Pearl, it is the Medicine that heals all illness and provides insight and illumination. It symbolizes the unification of the psyche, the integration of conscious and unconscious soul aspects resulting in the illumined Heart-Mind. The most precious treasure, it is the touchstone of alchemical metamorphosis, often hidden, invisible, and known only to the advanced practitioner. Often compared to the ruby, sapphire, and diamond, as in the Diamond Mind of Perfect Insight, the Stone has two forms: the White Stone (Pearl) representing the Lunar phase, and the Red Stone (ruby) representing the Solar phase. When these two aspects are united, the Stone is capable of transforming base metal into Silver or Gold. Said to be born "like a child" from the perfect union of opposites and to grow into maturity through the internalization of the teachings of the wise. The secret of the Stone is found by "plunging into meditation", where its secret and source are ever active and vital; imagination is an important aspect of this process. The Stone personifies unity-in-difference and oneness-in-the-many. The Stone does not create images, but fosters the hidden image within each thing, person, and situation.

Prana: From Sanskrit, *prana* is a Hindu term for the life-force energies of the Sun, the planets, the moon, and stars. It is inherent in every living thing, and circulates throughout Nature to sustain and enhance life (see Aether). The Pranic energies are embodied energies and part of the coalescent fields that sustain each living being. The primal animate source is the Sun and, more distantly, other stars; planetary bodies also have Prana and it manifests through diverse ecologies producing subtle differences in the living beings of those ecologies. Prana is equated symbolically with "breath" or "life force" representing the vitality of the body-mind-soul complex and inseparable from the natural processes of life in the Heliocosm. A "pure energy" of Spirit flowing through and within all matter, Prana is held within form by the archetypes of species life. Prana can be directed by thought as exemplified in healing techniques of many types; it can be imaged in the aura of the human body and enhanced by receptivity to its subtle effects as manifest in every living creature. Certain sounds (mantras, prayers, chants) and types of music (sacred) are capable of enhancing the effects of Prana.

Prima Materia: This is the "primal matter" of all alchemical work; in the alchemy of soul, the body, the earth, nature. The Prima Materia is said to be the "first substance" or "first energy" from which came the universe and all its life forms. In the Great Work (see above), form and consciousness must be dissolved into the Prima Materia as a necessary aspect of full transformation. This immersion is the union of Mind and Spirit, Soul and Being, One with the All. Once dissolved into the Prima Materia, the soul can be imprinted with the images and forms of the living quintessence which must then be regenerated in the warmth of collective world awareness. Each individual is a Vas Hermeticum (see below) for the creation of spiritual forms born out of the dissolving of soul in Sacred Beingness; each form must be incubated in the vessel like a flame whose sparks will be as abundant as the bounty of the Light allows. The Lunar and Solar must be reduced to the Prima Materia and then reconstituted according to the inclinations of soul-awakened perception.

Psychopomos (see Hermes): The "guide to souls" which, in classical alchemy, is Hermes-Mecurius. In the alchemy of soul, Psychopomos may be any luminous figure who acts as a guide to the visionary or dreamer. it may be another human being (or animal, spirit, guide) who appears as a teacher and mentor, one who heightens soul awareness, stimulates growth, and acts to lead the individual to a realization of deep potential. This figure can have a shadow side that leads the soul into its own fears, appetites, excesses, or unintegrated tendencies. Symbolizes a figure who stands on the border, in the shadow land between awakened and unawakened heart-mind, calling the soul to greater awareness.

Salt: The active agent that brings the Solar-Sulphur and the Lunar-Mercury into creative relationship, like yeast in bread that makes the dough rise—that which gives taste and texture, overcomes blandness, and brings out the unique flavors of each individual. Salt is the symbol of Spirit as the active agent drawing souls together and bringing forward differences. Too much Salt leads to unreconciled conflict, too little salt leads to dullness and complacency. Salt holds the fluid form (Mercury, see above) and gives it firmness and some degree of fixity, but Salt also breaks down the rigidity and resistance of Sulphur (see below). Salt challenges and heightens awareness of difference; it also blends and harmonizes as an agent of change. The "spiritual Salt" is the crystalline essence or "white ash" residual in the soul and body, like karmic seeds, whose energies are released through the Alchemical Marriage and must be refined through alchemical work to produce the harmonious effects of uniting the Lunar and Solar powers. This salt is particularly active on the full moon, on the dark of the moon, at dawn, and at twilight. The Woman in White, the Aged Hermit, and the Serpent are symbols of its activity; it is also known as *sal sapientiae*, "lucid wisdom".

Silver: (Argent Vive or "living silver") Often symbolized as the serpent, Silver is the sinuous, fluid moon glow serpent of the deep earth, the mother substance of transformation in the Lunar sense. Silver refers to the *albedo* ("pure, clear, white") stage of development as an element of purification, brought to perfection through Argent Vive, living, animate quicksilver, called "milk of the virgin bride." Silver must be united with the male principle to fully realize its inherent beauty and purity; symbolized by Venus-Aphrodite as the Morning Star and by the Roman goddess of dawn, Aurora, which after union, becomes Aurea Hora, "the hour of gold." The power to transmute base metal into pure lunar Silver is symbolized in the halo of the full moon, but also inherent to the deep earth. It can be symbolized by the White Dove as the descent of Holy Mother Spirit.

Solar: The masculine side, the bright light of the conscious masculine, the Solar is outwardly represented by thought, intellect, analysis, and science. Internally, the golden Sun represents hidden virtues or mysterious power brought forth through deliberate efforts, discipline, and determination. Symbolized by the Bridegroom and the Red King, also by hot, dry Sulphur, the Solar is the active seed, the aroused male energy, phallic strength, sperm as seeds of gold sown in the fields of Luna. Burning water, heat of passion, fire and war, wrath, the Red Lion aroused, the Solar leads to madness if not tempered by the healing coolness of the Lunar and the soothing waters of the Argent Vive (see Silver). The Red Elixir, the Red Stone, the rubedo, "Redness" of the golden scepter, represents Re on the Throne of Isis. The Sun is called the Father of the Stone in the Emerald Tablet, and the Source of Life in the Hermetic texts. Coagulation and heat working to combine the dissolving and unbound energies of the feminine; the ripening power that quickens the hidden potential. In the alchemy of soul, the Solar expresses the life-giving energies of Spirit as manifest in work, creative inspiration, and the required analysis of layered, inner life. Its manifestation requires clear goals, purposes, and objectives. Too much Sun burns and overwhelms, dries up moisture, parches, and dehydrates the juice of life; too little Sun produces shadows, uncertainty, indecision, melancholy, sadness, and sorrow. Solar and Lunar must be balanced for perfect health.

Solve et Coagula: A well-known alchemical axiom, it summarizes the Great Work. Meaning to "dissolve and to coagulate," it reflects the dynamic cycles of the Lunar and Solar integration. The work extends over a lifetime of cycles, of drawing the strands of the weaving into a pattern and then, courageously letting go of that pattern, allowing the threads to separate, dissolve and be recreated with new insights as more patterns emerge and consolidate. Too much dissolution leads to confusion, vagueness, and a lack of actualization; too much coagulation leads to stubborn patterns, fixated habits, inflexibility, and creative loss. The "old seeds" must be dissolved and liquefied; the "fluid streams" must be channeled and their energies directed to specific tasks. The seeds must grow; the water must flow. Only through continual cycles of this practice can the Elixir be created with vital purity that leads through refinement after refinement to the magical quintessence. This saying is also associated with the axiom *separatio et coniunctio*, "to separate and to conjoin", which reflects similar cycles of construction and deconstruction, of making and unmaking, of creating and uncreating as a necessary art in the process of exploring and understanding a multitude of spiritual worlds.

Sophia (Wisdom): Also known as Mary-Sophia, the Sophia is distinguished in Christianity as the three Mary images of the Virgin, Mother, and Teacher (Mary Magdalene), united by the Sophia as the transcendent, unifying Wisdom inherent to all three roles. A primary symbol of the Divine Feminine, Sophia unifies the roles of innocent maid, nurturing co-worker, and wise elder guided by mystical insight and illumination. Sophia is manifest in the woman who knows her own limits and yet still reveres the Limitless Depths of Creation. When the Sophia descended into the world of Creation, she gifted each creature with a divine spark as the seed of true Gnosis. But her grief and sadness over the embroiled suffering of humanity, over the violence and wars of men who elevated male gods over her, caused her to withdraw to the subtle realm of the Aeons. Now is the time of Her return, in the works of woman and in the teachings of the Wise. The Sophia is purity of insight uniting the manifest and unmanifest, the visible and the invisible, the sacred and the mundane. She is All creatures and is present to all suffering and sorrow; She is the healing source, the touch of grace, the blessing in all true love. The transpersonal nature of Her capacity cannot be described but is known to the true initiate. Her Mysteries are many and her gifts are few, but those who hold them, hold the most precious of all offerings. Use them wisely and flourish; use them poorly, and lose them. As the Teacher, she combines all teachings; as Partner and Mother, she blesses all children and heals all wounds; as Virgin Maid she offer the inspirations of Beauty, Innocence, and a perfect image of Creation.

Spirit: The dynamic essence that enlivens all creatures, Spirit is woven of a multitude of energies subtle and great; this is a name of the Most Holy in its dynamic form. Spirit is the ever present, ever active, ever inspiring source of love, understanding, intelligence, compassion, and humility. The deeper we embrace Spirit, the deeper we descend into our own soul depths, until, transparent to the Infinite, we see into the Depthless Ocean of All Being and behold the awesome work of All Creation. Spirit is the source of creative life through the activation of multiple energetic manifestations, beings, intelligences, and worlds. A perfect synthesis of creative forces and energies aligned with the intentional desires of each living creature, Spirit is the Mother of All Life, the Holy Mother Spirit that imbues Creation with soul. The ground of Sacred Beingness is the vast resource from which Spirit draws an unending plurality of possible life forms and creatures through the alchemical work of creating inhabited worlds, through endless cycles of evolution, rising and falling in rhythms of the Dance. Sophia is the source of all wisdom and insight, the Giver of Gifts, and the Weaver of Destines on uncounted worlds through all space and time. The nurturing breath of life, Sophia gives the soft touch of new thought and perception, the sustaining means for soul awakening and is the blessed Source of soul's illumination.

Stages: There is no agreement on the exact nature or number of Stages in the Great Work; each alchemist organized the Stages in accord with his or her understanding and refinement. The seven classic stages are: *calcinatio* (purified through fire), *solutio* (dissolved into pure water), *coagulatio* (solidified into earth), *sublimatio* (refined into air), *mortificatio* (death and darkening), *separatio* (distinctiveness, individuated creation), and *coniunctio* (unity-in-diversity). These stages do not occur in a lineal order, one after the other, but reflect key aspects of the alchemical path. Life circumstances present various conditions in which we can practice any of these stages. The Great Work is a constant challenge to adapt the teachings to the needs of the moment without leaving the path or losing the center. This includes the synthesis of dreams and intuitions of the heart with pragmatic needs and rational actions required by external circumstances. The intermediary stages require careful attention to each stage as it applies to the present. The last stage of *coniunctio* has two classic stages: the lesser and greater conjunction. The lesser conjunction is the "union of opposites" without tension or polarity, a creative harmony that adapts with balance and poise in every situation, dissolving conflict and offering alternatives; the greater conjunction is the illumination (Gnosis) of the heart-mind-soul immersed in Being, inspired by Spirit, and actualized in a Hermetic way of life, Spirit led and Spirit guided.

Sulphur: The dry, hot, masculine Logos aspect, Sulphur balances the quicksilver of the wet, cool, feminine Eros aspect; these two must be conjoined (see Alchemical Marriage). Sulphur is the heat that gives form and structure; it symbolizes the architectural capacity that can logistically construct plans and organize actions with great accuracy and precision. Sign of the designer and builder, as well as the analytic deconstructor, Sulphur gives rise to the mentality of theoretical and abstract thought as applied to the development of principles and theories that elucidate the workings of nature and the energies of creation. Sulphur is the dry heat from which the metallic order, the technological, and the industrial are engendered. It symbolizes the power to coagulate and fixate, to hold a steady form, to sustain long-term, formal, didactic teachings. When conjoined with the Argent Vive, the Lunar Mercury, Sulphur-Mercury results in a profound wisdom that is both mystical and pragmatic; when separated from the Lunar Mercury, Sulphur alone produces dogmatism, inflexible law, closure, aggression, war, and violence. The integration of Sulphur is crucial in the Great Work; failure to attain the correct balance will lead to instability, blindness based on authority, and willful assertion without heart.

Tincture (see Elixir and the Philosopher's Stone)

UrSpace: In the alchemy of soul, UrSpace is the "mental space" which incorporates all human imagination and visionary perceptions, all mythic worlds, into the space that is also all "physical space." In UrSpace, the space-time continuum includes all mental, psychic, subtle, and occult levels, all worlds, heavens, hells, in-between, after-death, higher and lower planes of all possible psycho-noetic perceptions. UrSpace includes the Heliocosm (see above), Mesocosm, Macrocosm, Microcosm, and World Soul as the "all inclusive" space of the Big Bang; UrSpace includes all possible space, all possible time, all possible worlds and beings, all physical dimensions, structures, molecules, particles, and superstrings. The alchemical aspect of UrSpace is a vastness that leads to a direct perception of its multidimensionality, into the bubble-worlds that interpenetrate as co-creative dimensions through which beings may communicate, including all past and future worlds. UrSpace is the psycho-mental-physical-energetic space of on-going creation sustained and upheld by Sacred Beingness, the Ground of All Life, the Holy Mother Spirit for the good of manifesting life and plurality. UrSpace is the ground of all-containment in God, Ultimate Being, Sat-Chit-Ananda, and it sustains the utmost transcendental essences of illumined soul awareness. It is the Space that dissolves all space into its own Infinite Boundlessness and yet it preserves even a single thought in all its relativity within a vast depth of Memory. All that Is and Is-Not is contained by UrSpace.

Vas Hermeticum: The "Hermetic Vessel" symbolized by the female womb, as the place of sustenance, nurturance, and growth; the vessel of the heart, the symbol of the Grail (see above). It is often imaged as a glass globe (alembic) with an extended, narrow neck above, sometimes curved, within which the alchemist gently cooks the substances of the Great Work.

Frequently sealed and very carefully heated to produce slow stages of change and refinement (see Stages), it is the single most important vessel of the Work. Also called the Egg, Castle, Coffin, Bed, Garden, Temple, Treasure House, and Ark (and many other terms); as the Garden, it is the place in which blooms the Black, White, and Red Roses (see the Great Work). The Vas Hermeticum as a transparent vessel (glass), refers to the inner processes of change that are observed by the alchemist in order to guage the Work and its development; a dirty glass will not allow for observation and turbulence in the vessel will inhibit the subtle transformations required for soul expansion. Sometimes, however, contraction is a necessary stage of birth, and obscurity is a requirement for work that must be done in secret.

World Soul (Anima Mundi): The evolving consciousness of a collective planetary awareness now in the process of awakening, but not yet fully self-aware. The World Soul is an evolving awareness based on the psychic currents of humanity and our treatment of the earth and all its creatures. The World Soul includes all life forms, all beings, visible and invisible, of this world. It will be known when the appropriate degree of self-awareness has evolved for the majority of humanity in concert with all species life. As an evolutionary stage of planetary awareness, the World Soul is the animate collective life whose currents are sustained by the Prana (see above) that nurtures life on this world, the psychic currents of connectivity between beings striving for greater illumination. The psycho-cybernetic networks of communication are an electronic means for symbolizing this consciousness, still nascent but growing through the physical, electromagnetic, gravitational fields of influence that conjoin with human and animal mentalities to form the coherent hyperfield of the World Soul. In the alchemy of soul, the World Soul is the medium of the under-currents and over-currents of collective life known through visionary perceptions or intuitions, including the mentality of all the living, the dead, the devas, angels, and spirits, as well as the vast and uncountable multidimensionalities of UrSpace. The unique collective field of all living creatures associated with this world, sustained and nurtured by Spirit.[5]

1. For a more traditional introduction to traditional alchemical symbolism, see Lyndy Abraham, 1998.

2. For a good over-view of the Grail, see Richard Barber (2004) and my review of that work in Irwin, 2005.

3. For a more thorough overview of the Hallows and their relationship to the Tarot, see Irwin, 1998.

4. An accessible translation of the classic *Hermetica* texts is found in Clement Salaman et al (2000); for the more esoteric meaning of Poimandres, see Peter Kingsley (2000).

5. See also Lee Irwin, 2006, for a more emergent view of World Soul.

BIBLIOGRAPHY

Abraham, Lyndy.
    1998   *A Dictionary of Alchemical Imagery*. UK: Cambridge University Press.
Barbar, Richard.
    2004   *The Holy Grail: Imagination and Belief*. MA: Harvard University Press.
Beck, Guy.
    1993   *Sonic Theology: Hinduism and Sacred Sound*. SC: University of South Carolina Press.
Blake, William.
    1968   *The Portable Blake*. NY: Viking Press.
Bruce, Robert.
    1999   *Astral Dynamics*. Charlottesville, VA: Hampton Roads Publishing Company.
Bulgakov, Sergius.
    1997   *The Holy Grail and the Eucharist*. Translated by Boris Jakim. NY: Lindisfarne Books.
Burkert, Walter.
    1985   *Greek Religion*. MA: Harvard University Press.
Chown, Marcus.
    2001   *The Magic Furnace: The Search for the Origins of Atoms*. NY: Oxford University Press.
Croswell, Ken.
    1997   *The Alchemy of the Heavens: Searching for Meaning in the Milky Way*. NY: State University of New York Press.
Cutsinger, James.
    1997   *Advice to Serious Seekers*. NY: State University of New York Press.
Dancy, Jonathan and Ernest Sosa (Editors.)
    1994   *A Companion to Epistemology*. MA: Blackwell Publishers.
Deutsch, Sid.
    1999   *Return of the Ether: When Theory and Reality Collide*. NJ: Scitech Publishing.
Dong, Paul and Aristes Esser.
    1990   *Chi Gong, The Ancient Chinese Way to Health*. NY: Marlowe and Company.

Edinger, Edward.

    1996 *Anatomy of the Psyche: Alchemical Symbolism in Psychotherapy*. IL: Open Court.

Evola, Julius.

    1997 *The Mysteries of the Grail*. VT: Inner Traditions.

Ferrer, Jorge N.

    2002 *Revisioning Transpersonal Theory: A Participatory Vision of Human Spirituality*. NY: State University of New York Press.

Ficino, Marsilo.

    1980 *Book of Life*. Translated by Charles Boer. TX: Spring Publications.

Guénon, René.

    1958 *Symbolism of the Cross*. Translated by Angus Macnab. London: Luzac & Company.

Hart, Tobin, Peter Nelson, and Kaisa Puhakka (Editors).

    2000 *Transpersonal Knowing: Exploring the Horizon of Consciousness*. NY: State University of New York Press.

Hillman, James.

    1991 *A Blue Fire*. Edited by Thomas Moore. NY: HarperCollins Publishers.

Hume, Robert.

    1971 *The Thirteen Principle Upanishads*. NY: Oxford University Press.

Irwin, Lee.

    1994 *The Dream Seekers: Native American Visionary Traditions of the Great Plains*. OK: University of Oklahoma Press.

    1996 *Visionary Worlds: The Making and Unmaking of Reality*. NY: State University of New York Press.

    1999 *Awakening to Spirit: On Life, Illumination and Being*. NY: State University of New York Press.

    2001 "Review Essay on Robert Sardello," *Esoterica* Vol. III (2001) at http://www.esoteric.msu.edu/: pp. 265-276 (Accessed May 2006).

    2005 "The Exoteric Grail" *Elixir*: Consciousness, Conscience, and Culture Issue 1: 99-111.

    2005 *The Gnostic Tarot: Mandalas for Spiritual Transformation*. NY: U.S. Games System.

    2006 "World and Soul: An Alchemy of Conjoined Loves," *Elixir*: Consciousness, Conscience, and Culture Issue 2: 17-22, 117.

Kaku, Michio.

    1994 *Hyperspace: A Scientific Odyssey Through Parallel Universes, Time Warps, and The Tenth Dimension.* NY: Oxford University Press.

King, John Robert.

    1996 *The Celtic Druids' Year: Seasonal Cycles of the Ancient Celts.* Blandford Press.

Kingsley, Peter.

    1996 *Ancient Philosophy, Mystery, and Magic: Empedocles and the Pythagorean Tradition.* Oxford: Claredon Press.

    2000 "Poimandres: The Etymology of the name and the Origins of Hermetica." In Roelof van den Broek and Cis van Heertum (eds), *From Poimandres to Jacob Bohme: Gnosis, Hermetism, and the Christian Tradition.* Amsterdam: Bibioteca Philosophica Hermetica.

Kopas, Jane.

    1994 *Sacred Identity: Exploring a Theology of the Person.* NY: Paulist Press.

Loomis, Roger.

    1991 *The Grail: From Celtic Myth to Christian Symbol.* Princeton, NJ: Princeton University Press.

Luibheid, Colm (Translator).

    1987 *Pseudo-Dionysius: The Complete Works.* NY: Paulist Press.

Monroe, Robert.

    1994 *The Ultimate Journey.* NY: Doubleday.

Radhakrishnan, S.

    1973 *The Bhagavadgita.* NY: Harper & Row.

Salaman, Clement, Dorine van Oven, William D. Wharton, and Jean-Pierre Mahé.

    2000 *The Way of Hermes: New Translations of the Corpus Hermticum and The Definitions of Hermes Trismegistus to Asclepius.* VT: Inner Traditions.

Sardello, Robert.

    1992 *Facing the World with Soul: The Reimagination of Modern Life.* NY: HarperPerennial.

    1996 *Love and the Soul: Creating a Future for Earth.* NY: HarperPerennial.

    1999 *Freeing the Soul from Fear.* NY: Riverhead Books.

    2001 *Love and the World: A Guide to Conscious Soul Practice.* MA: Lindisfarne Books.

Schuon, Frithjof.

    1981 *Esotericism as Principle and as Way.* Translated by William Stoddart. London: Perennial Books.

Sheng-yen, Master and Dan Stevenson.

    2001 *Hoofprint of the Ox : Principles of the Chan Buddhist Path as Taught by a Modern Chinese Master*. NY: Oxford University.

Shou-Yu, Liang and Wu Wei-Ching.

    1993 *A Guide to Taijiquan*. Boston, MA: YMAA Publication Center.

Smith, Huston.

    1977 *Forgotten Truth: The Primordial Tradition*. NY: Harper & Row.

Spangler, David.

    2001 *Blessing: The Art and the Practice*. NY: Putnam Publishing Group.

Vieira, Waldo.

    1995 *Projections of the Consciousness*. Rio De Janeiro: International Institute of Projectology.

von Franz, Marie-Louise.

    1980 *Alchemy: An Introduction to the Symbolism and the Psychology*. Toronto, Canada: Inner City Books.

Walker, D. P.

    2000 *Spiritual and Demonic Magic from Ficino to Campanella*. PA: Pennsylvania State University Press.

Ware, James.

    1963 *The Sayings of Chuang Chou*. NY: New American Library of World Literature.

Wax, Murray.

    1999 *Western Rationality and the Angel of Dreams: Self, Psyche, Dreaming*. MD: Rowman & Littlefield.

Wolf, Fred.

    1999 *The Spiritual Universe: One Physicist's Vision of Spirit, Soul, Matter, and Self*. NH: Moment Point Press.

Lee Irwin

Lee Irwin, Ph.D., is Chair of the Religious Studies Department at the College of Charleston, SC. His areas of expertise are Native American religions and western esotericism, particularly in Hermetic spirituality and its relationship to eastern religious traditions. He also teaches in the areas of the transpersonal religious experience, incarnational spirituality, and on the importance of the divine feminine - particularly around themes connected to dreams and visions. He is Vice President of the International Association for the Study of Esotericism, and gives frequent presentations at the Sophia Institute, the Institute for Dream Studies, and other esoteric groups in North America. He can be reached at: IrwinL@cofc.edu.

LaVergne, TN USA
21 June 2010
186944LV00004B/36/A